LED ZEPPELIN

FROM A WHISPER TO A SCREAM

LED ZEPPELIN
FROM A WHISPER
TO A SCREAM

DAVE LEWIS

OMNIBUS PRESS

LONDON / NEW YORK / PARIS / SYDNEY / COPENHAGEN / BERLIN / MADRID / TOKYO

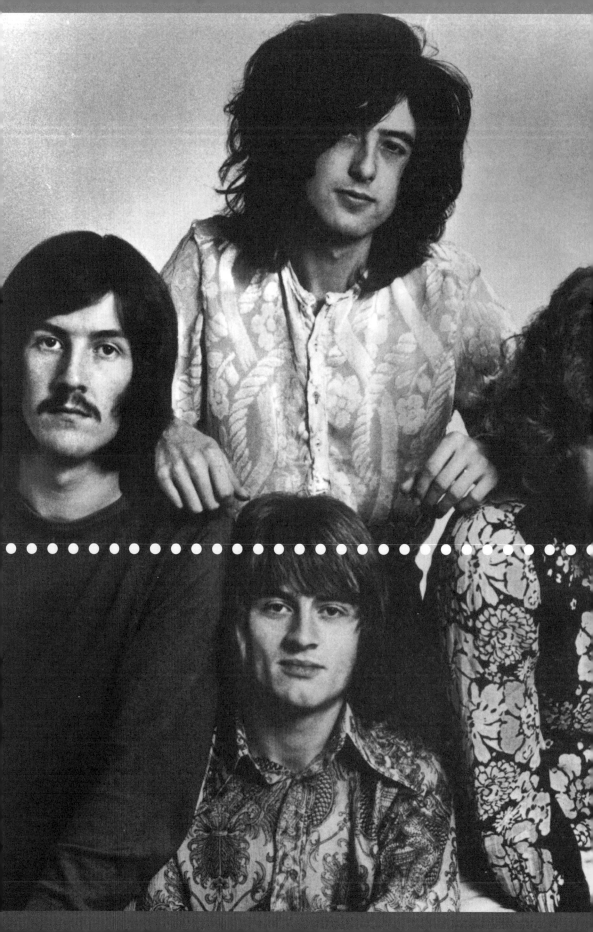

1944

January 9 - James Patrick Page born in Heston, Middlesex.

1964

April - John Paul Jones releases a solo single - 'Baja'/'A Foggy Day In Vietnam'. Jones establishes his name as one of London's top session arrangers and Jimmy Page similarly makes a name for himself as one of the top UK session guitarists, playing on countless hit records of the era.

Robert Plant performs in his first groups - Andy Long & The Original Jaymen, The Black Snake Moan and The Crawling King Snakes.

John Bonham played in his first groups - Terry Webb & The Spiders and The Senators.

1963

January - Jimmy Page's first appearance on record, a session for Jet Harris & Tony Meehan's 'Diamonds'.

1965

February - Jimmy Page releases a solo single - 'She Just Satisfies'/'Keep Moving'.

John Bonham joins A Way Of Life.

1946

January 3 - John Paul Jones (Baldwin) born in Sidcup, Kent.

1948

May 31 - John Henry Bonham born in Redditch, Worcestershire.
August 20 - Robert Anthony Plant born in West Bromwich, Staffordshire.

1962

Jimmy Page joins Neil Christian & The Crusaders.

1966

Robert Plant joins Listen
May - Jimmy Page records Beck's Bolero with Jeff Beck, John Paul Jones, Nicky Hopkins and Keith Moon - talk of forming a band has Moon stating they would go down like a 'lead zeppelin'. The track is released as the B-side to Beck's 'Hi Ho Silver Lining' hit the following May.
June - Jimmy Page joins The Yardbirds, initially on bass but soon switched to dual lead guitar with Jeff Beck. His first performance with the group is on June 21 at London's Marquee Club.
October - Listen's single 'You Better Run'/'Everybody's Gonna Say' is released on CBS with Robert Plant on lead vocals.
October 31 - Page takes over as The Yardbirds' lead guitarist following Jeff Beck's departure.

1968

April - Band Of Joy split. Robert records with Alexis Korner.
June - John Bonham tours with Tim Rose.
June - It is announced that Keith Relf and Jim McCarty are leaving The Yardbirds.
June 5 - Last Yardbirds US gig at the Montgomery Speedway in Alabama.
July - Jimmy Page, Chris Dreja and Yardbirds manager Peter Grant see Robert Plant play with Obs-Tweedle in Walsall. Plant is offered the vocalist job in the new Yardbirds line-up. Chris Dreja decides not to carry on as bassist and Page calls in John Paul Jones. John Bonham completes the new Yardbirds line-up on Plant's recommendation.
August - First Page, Plant, Jones and Bonham rehearsals in Chinatown, London.
September 7 - The new Yardbirds line up commences a series of Scandinavian dates at the Teen Club in Gladsaxe, Denmark.
September/October - Led Zeppelin's debut album recorded at Olympic studios.
October - Page and manager Peter Grant decides to change the group name to Led Zeppelin, a phrase coined by Keith Moon during the Page 'Becks Bolero' sessions.
October 25 - The debut 'Led Zeppelin' gig at Surrey University in Battersea Park Road, London.
December 26 - Led Zeppelin commence their first American tour at the Denver Auditorium Arena in Denver, Colorado supporting Vanilla Fudge & Spirit.

1970

January 7 - UK tour commences in Birmingham.
January 9 - Royal Albert Hall gig filmed and recorded for an intended Zeppelin TV documentary.
January - 'Whole Lotta Love' reaches number four on the *Billboard* chart.
March 21 - Fifth US tour opens in Vancouver, Canada.
May - Plant and Page write and prepare material for their third album at a remote cottage in Machynlleth, Gwynedd in Wales called Bron-Yr-Aur.
June 28 - Bill-topping appearance at the Bath Festival.
September 19 - Sixth US tour ends with two shows at Madison Square Garden, New York.
Led Zeppelin end The Beatles' reign as Top Group in *Melody Maker*'s annual readers' poll.
October 23 - *Led Zeppelin III* released.

1969

January 12 - Led Zeppelin debut album issued in America.
February - Led Zeppelin's debut album enters the *Billboard* Top 40.
March 23 - First BBC radio session airs on John Peel's *Top Gear* show.
March 28 - Led Zeppelin debut album issued in UK.
April 18 - Second US tour commences at the Fillmore West San Francisco
June 13 - First proper UK tour commences in Birmingham Town Hall.
June 28 - Appearance at the Bath Festival.
July 5 - Third US tour commences with an appearance at the Atlanta International Pop Festival.
October 17 - Led Zeppelin become first rock act to play New York's Carnegie Hall when they open their fourth US tour with two performances at the prestigous hall.
October 22 - *Led Zeppelin II* released.

1967

April - Robert Plant joins The Band Of Joy - later to be followed by John Bonham.

1971

March 5 - British tour commences at Belfast Ulster Hall. 'Stairway To Heaven' is played live for the first time.
July 5 - A crowd riot curtails a show at Milan's Vigorelli Stadium.
August 19 - Seventh US tour commences in Vancouver.
September 23 - Five date tour of Japan commences at Budokan, Tokyo.
November 11 - UK tour commences in Newcastle.
November 12 - *Led Zeppelin IV* album released.
November 20/21 - Two appearances at Wembley Empire Pool billed as 'Electric Magic'.

1975

January 18 - The band open their tenth US tour to support *Physical Graffiti* with a gig in Bloomington, Minnesota - their first concert in almost 18 months.
February 24 - *Physical Graffiti* released.
May 17/18/23/24/25 - 85,000 people attend Led Zeppelin's five shows at the Earls Court Arena in London.
August 4 - Robert and Maureen Plant seriously injured when their rented car goes off the road in Rhodes. Both are air lifted back to the UK. Plant is forced to recuperate in Jersey due to his tax situation. The band are forced to cancel their planned 10-date US summer tour.
December 10 - Surprise appearance at the Behan's West Park night club in St. Helier, Jersey.

1974

May 7 - The group's own record label Swan Song Records launched with all members in attendance at two receptions in New York and Los Angeles. During these celebrations the group attend Elvis Presley's LA Forum concert and gain an audience with him after the show.

1973

March 28 - *Houses Of The Holy* released.
May 5 - 56,800 attend Led Zeppelin's second show of their ninth US tour at Tampa Stadium. This sets a record for the largest attendance for a one-act performance, previously held by The Beatles for their Shea Stadium show in 1965.
July 27/28/29 - Final concerts of the ninth US tour at Madison Square Garden - recorded and filmed for their movie project.

1972

February 16 - Australian tour commences in Perth. On the route back in March, Page and Plant made some experimental recordings of 'Friends' and Four Sticks' in Bombay with the Bombay Symphony Orchestra.
June 6 - Eighth US tour commences in Detroit.
October 2 - Second Japanese tour commences at the Budokan Hall Tokyo.
November - Fifth album mixed and completed. Announcement of their longest ever UK tour of 25 dates prompts 100,000 ticket sales in one day.
November 30 - UK tour commences at the City Hall, Newcastle-upon-Tyne.

1977

April 1 - The band commence their eleventh US tour with a gig at the Dallas Convention Center - their first concert in over 22 months.
April 30 - A show at the Pontiac Silverdome in Michigan attracts 76,229, breaking their own record set in Tampa 1973 for the largest audience attending a single-act show.
June 7-8-10-11-13-14 - Six nights at Madison Square Garden, New York.
June 21-22-23-25-26-27 - Six nights at The Forum in Inglewood, California.
July 23 - After a show at the Oakland Coliseum, Peter Grant, John Bonham, tour manager Richard Cole and security man John Bindon are involved in violent clashes backstage with a member of promoter Bill Graham's staff.
July 24 - The second Oakland Coliseum date - their last ever US show.
July 26 - Robert learns of the sudden death of his five-year-old-son Karac due to a stomach infection. The remaining seven US dates are cancelled.

1979

July 23/24 - Led Zeppelin play two warm-up shows at the Falkoner Theatre in Copenhagen.
August 4 - First Knebworth show.
August 11 - Second Knebworth show.
August 20 - *In Through The Out Door* released.

1980

June 17 - Led Zeppelin open their European tour at the Westfalenhalle in Dortmund.
July 7 - Final show of the tour (and final ever gig with John Bonham) at the Berlin Eissporthalle.
September 25 - John Bonham found dead at Jimmy Page's Windsor home after a drinking bout, following rehearsals for the impending US tour.

1976

April 5 - *Presence* released.
October 19 - The Led Zeppelin film *The Song Remains The Same* receives its world première at Manhattan's Cinema One in New York.
October 22 - *The Song Remains The Same* soundtrack double album released worldwide.

1978

May - Led Zeppelin reunite at Clearwell Castle in the Forest of Dean to rehearse and plan their future.
November 6 - Recording sessions begin at Abba's Polar Music studios in Stockholm.

1980

December 4 - Led Zeppelin issue the following press statement: "We wish it to be known that the loss of our dear friend, and the deep respect we have for his family, together with the sense of undivided harmony felt by ourselves and our manager, have led us to decide that we could not continue as we were."

1982
November 22 - *Coda* released.

1995
November 21 - Led Zeppelin manager Peter Grant dies of a heart attack.

1995
January 12 - Page, Plant and Jones attend the Hall of Fame ceremony at the Waldorf Astoria in New York for Led Zeppelin's induction and perform with Jason Bonham, Neil Young, Steven Tyler, and Joe Perry.

1985
July 13 - Jimmy Page, Robert Plant and John Paul Jones reunite for an appearance at the Live Aid concert at JFK Stadium in Philadelphia.

1997
November 24 - Led Zeppelin *BBC Sessions* released.

1990
October 29 - The *Remasters* box set and compilation released.

1995
February 26 - Page and Plant commence world tour in Pensacola, Florida.

1988
May 14 - Page, Plant and Jones reunite for appearance at the Atlantic 40th Anniversary show at Madison Square Garden, New York.

1998

February 21 - Page And Plant
commence a planned world
tour in Croatia in support of
the release of their *Walking
Into Clarksdale* album.

2007

June 10 - Page, Plant, Jones and Jason
Bonham commence rehearsals in
London for a planned reunion show.
September 12 - Promotor Harvey
Goldsmith announces that Led Zeppelin
will reunite for the Ahmet Ertegun tribute
show - One million apply for tickets.
November - *Mothership* compilation and
The Song Remains The Same revamped
album and DVD released.
November - Led Zeppelin catalogue
made available on iTunes.
December 10 - Led Zeppelin reunite for a
concert in honour of Ahmet Ertegun at
the 02 Arena London.

1998

December 10 - Final Page & Plant
appearance concert at the Amnesty
International benefit show in the Palais
Omnisports Bercy Paris - future
planned shows in Japan are cancelled
after Plant decides to end the
association.

2008

September - Robert Plant states
that he has no plans to work with
Page and Jones on a reunion.

1998

April 21 - Jimmy Page
and Robert Plant's
Walking Into Clarksdale
album released.

2005

February 13 - Page and Jones attend the
Grammys in Los Angeles to receive Led
Zeppelin's Lifetime Achievement award.

2009

January - Jimmy Page's manager Peter
Mensch ends Zeppelin reunion speculation
by stating "It's over - if you didn't see them
in 2007 you missed them. It's done."

2003

May 26 - Led Zeppelin *DVD* and
How The West Was Won live set
released.

In September 2007, it was announced that Led Zeppelin would reunite for one night only to honour the life of the legendary Atlantic Records founder Ahmet Ertegun. The demand to be at this event, to be staged at the 02 Arena in London, was nothing less than staggering.

Over a million people worldwide applied to the ballot for the 17,000 tickets available. It was testament to the enduring legacy this remarkable group of musicians had established over the last five decades.

Come the celebrated night of December 10 2007 when Jimmy Page, Robert Plant, John Paul Jones and Jason Bonham (the son of the late John Bonham) took to the stage once again, the results were electrifying as they defied the advancing years with a performance that exceeded all expectations.

Central to the success of that night were the 16 songs drawn from every stage of their catalogue that made up the set list. From the appropriate opening number 'Good Times Bad Times' (the first track on their debut album from 1969) through to the celebratory encore ending of 'Rock And Roll', every facet of the Zeppelin spectrum was touched upon.

RODUCTION

It's that catalogue of music, recorded in the space of a mere ten year period from 1968 to 1978, that comes under scrutiny in this book.

Linked by an album by album summary that unfolds the Led Zeppelin saga, every recorded song is dissected. Masses of little known facts about the tracks emerge to create the most accurate account of when, where, and how Led Zeppelin created their enduring recorded legacy.

Alongside the original ten albums, it offers full analysis of the *Remasters* box set, *BBC Sessions* album, *How The West Was Won* live set, *Mothership* compilation, *The Song Remains The Same* revamped edition and the official Led Zeppelin *DVD*. There's also an enlightening guide to bootleg records and outtakes plus an overview of their historic reunion at the Ahmet Ertegun tribute concert at the 02 Arena in December 2007.

Over the past few years, interest in Led Zeppelin has continued to increase. Aside from that remarkable night at the O2, the individual members have extended their own reputations. John Paul Jones has applied his vast musicianship to a variety of projects, not least the involvement with Dave Grohl and Josh Homme in Them Crooked Vultures which exposed his bass and keyboard prowess to a new generation of fans.

Robert Plant has extended his journey through Americana, country, folk, rock and roots which brought such massive success with Alison Krauss on the *Raising Sand* album into The Band of Joy, an eclectic outfit that has taken his music to an even wider audience and much acclaim.

Jimmy Page remains the keeper of the flame, documenting his 50 year career in the lavish *Jimmy Page By Jimmy Page* book. He continues to reveal anecdotes on his daily 'on this day' entries on his official website, as well as putting in the odd cameo performance with the likes of The Black Crowes, Donovan and Roy Harper.

Jason Bonham also flies the flag for his father's legacy in the Black Country Communion collaboration with Glenn Hughes and Joe Bonamassa and his JBLZ Experience tours.

All of these projects pay homage to the spirit of Led Zeppelin in one way or another. With tribute bands treading the boards nightly, internet message boards analysing their every move and musicians young and old continuing to pay their dues – witness Jack White's wry comment "I don't trust anyone who doesn't like Led Zeppelin" – Page, Plant, Jones and Bonham's influence casts a mighty shadow over the contemporary music world.

This book's objective is to take you deep inside the core of their music and investigate the creative process that made this music stand out from the competition.

However familiar you may be with their albums, this guide to all aspects of their output is designed to take you back to the music with renewed perspective. This is Led Zeppelin - from blues to rock, light to shade, loud to soft and from a whisper to a scream.

Consider this as your one stop, easy access companion to their timeless catalogue of work.

Dave Lewis, March 2012

Acknowledgements:
Very special thanks to Mike Tremaglio.

Thanks also to:
Gary Foy, Gerard Sparaco, Nick Anderson, Graeme Hutchinson, Gary Davies, Cliff Hilliard, Michaela Firth, Dan Firth, Mark Harrison, Andrew Ricci, Jerry Bloom, Terry Boud, Chris Charlesworth, Ross Halfin, Bill McCue, Julian Walker, Dave Linwood, Mike Warry, Phil Tattershall, Terry Stephenson, Larry M. Bergmann Jnr, Brian Knapp, Steve Sauer, Steve Jones, Lou Anne & Frank Reddon, Jeff Strawman, Eddie Edwards, Donna Hamilton, Kathy Urich, Pete Gozzard, Krys Jantzen, Mark McFall, Jose Manuel Parada, John Parkin, Richard Grubb, Stephen Humphries, Lorraine Robertson, Billy & Alison Fletcher, Steve Way, Ian Avey, Tom Locke, Dec Hickey, Phil Harris, Max Harris, Barry Farnsworth, Mick Lowe, Janet Lewis, Samantha Lewis and Adam Lewis.

Dedicated to Howard Mylett 1947-2011 and Alan Johnston 1961-2012.

PART I
THE TEN ALBUM LEGACY

PREFACE

The origins of the group that became Led Zeppelin can be traced back to the early months of 1968 and the demise of The Yardbirds. By that time, the erstwhile R&B outfit, which had spawned the talents of Eric Clapton, Jeff Beck and Jimmy Page, had reached a crossroads. Their UK hits had long since dried up, but they had created a significant niche in the American market. Under the shrewd management of Peter Grant, they had built up a decent following on the US college circuit and also established a strong reputation at Bill Graham's East and West Coast Fillmore venues.

After Jeff Beck's departure in late 1966, Page led the group through a difficult period. A US-only album, *Little Games*, had made little impression, suffering from a hurried production by Mickie Most and uneven content that combined pop covers such as 'Ha Ha Said The Clown' and 'Ten Little Indians' with the more experimental edge of Page's 'White Summer' and 'Glimpses'. Page clearly felt there was scope to move their music forward but vocalist Keith Relf and drummer Jim McCarty's interest was waning. After a final US tour in June 1968, Relf and McCarty quit The Yardbirds to form the short-lived duo Together.

Page, bassist Chris Dreja and manager Peter Grant were left with the rights to the group name and a handful of unfulfilled dates in Scandinavia. "I knew Jimmy wanted to carry on," remembered Peter Grant years later. "He told me he wanted to produce the group himself, so we set about getting a new line-up and a deal." In the summer of 1968, Page began the task of replacing Relf and McCarty. He had long admired Steve Marriott and Steve Winwood, but both were still tied to their own groups, the Small Faces and Traffic, respectively. It's also worth mentioning that before he auditioned for Mott The Hoople, Ian Hunter had considered offering his services to Page's new unit. A firm approach was made to Terry Reid, then enjoying critical acclaim. But Reid had

just signed a solo deal to Mickie Most's RAK stable and was unwilling to risk linking up with Page – a decision that would leave him forever labelled as 'The Man Who Turned Down Led Zeppelin'. "I had just got a settled deal with Mickie Most and it was just a case of not being available," he reflects now. But Reid did suggest that Page check out a young blues singer from the Midlands who had built up a reputation with a group called The Band of Joy and more recently worked with Alexis Korner. Page travelled to Birmingham to see Robert Plant, who was then performing with a group called Obs-Tweedle.

In mid-July Page, Dreja and Grant saw for themselves the potential of this 19-year-old Midlands blueswailer. The venue was a teachers' training college in Walsall and, allegedly, on that night Obs–Tweedle were billed as Robert Plant and The Band Of Joy because Plant had built a bit of a reputation with his previous band at this venue.

"I was appearing at a Teachers College when Jimmy and Peter Grant turned up," Plant recalled, "And they asked me if I'd be interested in joining The Yardbirds. I think they nearly mistook me for the roadie! I knew that The Yardbirds had done a lot of work in America which to me meant audiences who did want to know what I might have to offer. I was very much into the West Coast scene and acts such as Moby Grape. So, naturally, I was very interested."

Page was well impressed with Plant and the next logical step was for Page to find out if they would be musically compatible. He invited Plant to his Pangbourne home where they discussed their influences and the kind of direction the new look Yardbirds might take. Page recalled: "When Robert came down to my place, we found we had a lot of musical tastes in common, which was very important. I played him the Joan Baez version of 'Babe I'm Gonna Leave You' and said I wanted to do an arrangement of it." By late July, Plant was confirmed as the replacement singer for Keith Relf, though he

THE TEN ALBUM LEGACY

had already continued to finish off some commitments with Obs-Tweedle. By this time, Chris Dreja had also decided to quit the group and take up a career in photography. Page already had another bassist in mind - well respected session man John Paul Jones, with whom he'd worked on many recordings over the years. Jones had already declared an interest in joining up with Page in a permanent group. With his past pedigree and ability to play both bass and keyboards, he was the ideal choice.

The drum stool proved more difficult to fill. Initially Page had searched out Procol Harum's drummer, B.J. Wilson, and there was talk of auditioning another session drummer, Clem Cattini. When these ideas came to nothing, Plant suggested to Page that he check out John Bonham – whom he had known for years. "Bonzo", as he was known, was another ex-member of The Band of Joy and before that had gained a reputation for being the loudest drummer for miles around in a Midlands band called A Way of Life. At the time, Bonham was touring with Tim Rose and considering offers from Joe Cocker and Chris Farlowe. Page went to see him perform with Rose at the Hampstead Country Club on July 31 and was immediately impressed. But Bonham was reluctant to give up a steady £40-a-week income, and took some time to accept. "When I was asked to join The Yardbirds, I thought they'd been forgotten in England," he said. "I knew that Jimmy was a highly respected guitarist, and Robert I'd known for years, so even if it didn't take off, it was a chance to play in a really good group. When I met Jimmy and he told me his musical ideas, I decided that his were preferable to Cocker or Farlowe anyway."

With Bonzo stalling, Plant did think of putting a couple of other Midlands names in the frame - Mac Poole who had replaced Bonham in A Way Of Life and was currently in a band called Hush, and Phil Brittle of the local Birmingham outfit Sissy Stone. In any event, neither were required because after some cajoling, Bonham accepted the job

and, in mid August 1968, the new line-up of Page, Plant, Jones and Bonham undertook their first rehearsals in a basement rehearsal room in the Lisle/Gerrard Street area of London's Chinatown.

Jones remembers being wary of how the younger, more inexperienced Plant and Bonham might perceive him. "They had heard about this session man bassist, and I think they expected me to be smoking a pipe and wearing slippers," he says. "So we all got together in this room and someone said, 'What shall we play?' Jimmy suggested 'Train Kept A-Rollin', and away we went. The whole room exploded, and it was pretty obvious that this was going to work very well indeed."

On September 7, the group – still billed as The Yardbirds - kicked off a handful of Scandinavian dates with a debut gig at the Teen Club at Egegård Skole in Gladsaxe, Denmark. Their last dates under The Yardbirds name occurred on the weekend of October 18 & 19, 1968 at London's Marquee and Liverpool University respectively. On October 25, they played their very first gig under their new name, Led Zeppelin, at London's Surrey University, then situated on Battersea Park Road.

After rejecting names such as Mad Dogs and the Whoopie Cushion, Page recalled a phrase Who drummer Keith Moon had used a couple of years earlier, when there had been a vague plan to form a new group out of the sessions with Jeff Beck for 'Beck's Bolero'. Moon had joked about the group going down like a 'lead balloon' or even a 'lead zeppelin'. Grant too remembered the phrase and, given the circumstances, the name seemed perfect: "I got rid of the A – it just looked better. I also didn't want any confusion over the pronunciation in America."

Page and Grant had booked time at Olympic Studios in Barnes to record their debut album. "We had begun developing the arrangements on the Scandinavian tour and I knew what sound I was looking for. It just came together very quickly," remembers Page.

Sessions for Zeppelin's debut album began immediately after the group returned from a tour of Scandinavia in late September 1968. It was recorded at Olympic Studios in Barnes, where Page had played on numerous sessions, and it enjoyed a very good reputation not least for hosting The Rolling Stones. Page enlisted the assistance of Glyn Johns, then an up-an-coming studio engineer who had been a tape operator on Page's first session recordings for Decca in the early sixties (and who went on to work with both The Beatles and the Stones).

"That was one of the best albums I ever worked on," Johns recalled. "I'd never heard arrangements of that ilk before, nor had I ever heard a band play in that way before. It was unbelievable, and when you're in a studio with something as creative as that, you can't help but feed off it. I think it's one of the best-sounding records I've ever done.

"We're talking about 1968, so the actual recording process was a live mike set-up. Back then, you didn't record any other way. There were two or three guitars on most tracks, so obviously two of them were overdubbed and one was live. The heavy sound of the record was very much to their credit but I'm sure I contributed to it overall." Johns received a 'Director of Engineering' credit on the album sleeve.

Page remembered being well prepared to make the record: "I had a lot of ideas left over from the days of The Yardbirds. They allowed me to improvise a lot in live performances and I started building a textbook of ideas that I eventually used in Zeppelin. Ultimately, I wanted the group to be a marriage of blues, hard rock and acoustic music with heavy choruses – a combination that hadn't been explored before, lots of light and shade in the music. As for the sound, I'd learnt a lot during the session days about distance miking. I also had developed techniques like the use of backwards echo and reverb."

Plant recalled being somewhat nervous on those first sessions: "I was a little bit intimidated by it all. Looking back I could have sung a little less nervously. It was like, 'Do I really belong here?', but as a collection of tunes and a way to play and expand, it was great."

LED ZEPPELIN

*Atlantic Records - Original issue 588
171, March 28, 1969 reissue K40031
UK Album Chart: No 6; US: No 10
Sales figures approx. and counting:
UK 600,000 - 2x Platinum;
US 8,000,000 - 8x Platinum*

The debut Led Zeppelin album is the
recorded statement of their first few weeks
together. It's also a fair representation of
their initial blues/rock stage act that had
been tested on Scandinavian audiences. The
material selected for the album had been
well rehearsed and pre-arranged by the four,
one of the primary reasons it took so little
time to complete. It took a mere 36 hours to
record *Led Zeppelin* in Olympic Studios, just
south of the River Thames in Barnes in West
London. Allegedly Page still has the bill to
prove it.

The album was recorded in just nine days
with a total use of 36 studio hours. The
whole project cost a mere £1,782. Not bad
for a record that went on to clock up sales of
two million within its first year of release.
With the possible exception of the 12 hours
that The Beatles took to record their first
album at Abbey Road, rarely has studio time
been used so economically.

The artistic control of their output would
extend to their sleeve designs, and on the
first album Jimmy chose a simple black on
white illustration of the Hindenburg airship
going down, as Keith Moon had put it, like a

'Lead' Zeppelin. It was later claimed by The
Who's John Entwistle that this sleeve design
had been earmarked for the group he, Moon
and Page had talked about forming a couple
of years earlier.

The distinctive black-and-white sleeve
designed by artist George Hardie for the first
Zeppelin album has became one of the most
enduring and iconic Zeppelin images. The
basis of the cover, a photograph of the
famous Zeppelin Hindenburg crashing in
Lakehurst, New Jersey in 1937 – was
chosen by Jimmy Page. "I remember
meeting the group at their RAK offices," said
Hardie. "The rough I showed them was a
multiple sequential image of a Zeppelin with
clouds and waves, based on an old club sign
in San Francisco, which I'd visited. That
image became the back cover logo, and was
also used on *Led Zeppelin II*. Jimmy showed
me the Hindenberg image, and I set to work
with my finest rapidograph dot, and stripped
a facsimile of the photograph, some seven
inches square, onto a sheet of tracing paper.
I think I was paid around £60 for the job.
The drawing made a good and memorable
cover, but it was more down to Jimmy's
choice of image than to my skill as a dotter."
The back cover of the album was a group
shot taken by outgoing Yardbirds bassist
Chris Dreja in his new role as professional
photographer.

When it came to securing a new record deal
for the group, manager Peter Grant
negotiated a massive five-album $200,000
package with Jerry Wexler of Atlantic Records
in New York. This ended speculation that
they would extend The Yardbirds' previous
association with Epic in America and EMI in
the UK. Part of the Atlantic deal allowed
Grant and Zeppelin to retain virtually
complete control of artistic matters. They
also formed their own company, Superhype,
to handle all publishing rights. It was agreed
that all Led Zeppelin records would appear
on the famous red Atlantic label, as opposed
to its less distinguished Atco subsidiary
which had been used for Atlantic's non-soul
or R&B acts in the past. This gave them the

distinction of being the first white UK act on the prestigious Atlantic label.

The *Led Zeppelin* album was initially released in America on January 12, 1969, to capitalise on their first US tour. Prior to their arrival, Atlantic distributed a few hundred advance white label copies to key radio stations and reviewers. A positive reaction to its contents, coupled with extremely positive reaction to their opening gigs, resulted in the album generating 50,000 advance orders. It entered the *Billboard* chart at number 99. From there it rose to number 40, then 28, reaching the Top 20 and rising as high as number 10. In all, it enjoyed 73 weeks on the chart, returning for further spells in 1975 and 1979.

In the UK, it was issued on March 28. Originally it appeared as Atlantic 588 171 via Polydor's distribution. It was one of a new breed of stereo-only releases, as up until 1969 most albums were available as stereo or mono versions. When the Warner group took over the Atlantic catalogue in 1972, the number switched to K40031. On April 12, 1969, the Led Zeppelin debut album began a 79-week run on the British chart, peaking at number six.

The album was advertised in selected music papers under the slogan 'Led Zeppelin - the only way to fly'. And fly it certainly did. Time has done nothing to diminish the quality of one of the finest debut albums ever recorded.

The album's content presents a concoction of high energy performances taking in unique interpretations of blues and folk standards – all expertly produced by Jimmy Page. Led Zeppelin's practice of using the influence, and sometimes almost entire songs, from outside sources and dressing them up as their own is well-known. The fact that some of these sources did not receive the appropriate credit (and royalties) got the band into trouble on more than one occasion. The redeeming factor in this often blatant 'borrowing' of ideas is that while the

content of *Led Zeppelin*, and indeed many of their subsequent releases, was very derivative in both style and material, it was always performed in a way which made it totally distinctive.

The unique combination of Page's unimpeachable riff writing and producing skills, John Paul Jones's immense musicianship, Bonham's ferocious and incisive backbeat and Plant's quintessential howl set a new benchmark and changed the face of rock almost overnight. It's worth mentioning that Robert Plant did not receive any writing credits for the lyrics as he was still contracted to CBS.

GOOD TIMES BAD TIMES
Page, Jones & Bonham
Studio: Olympic Studios, London
At two minutes, 43 seconds, this is a perfectly compact overture to set the scene. Bonham and Jones hold down a powerful and inventive rhythm section, and when the time comes, Jimmy flexes the Telecaster (played through a Leslie speaker to create that soaring effect) in a late Yardbirds-era fashion. From the onset though, it's the Plant vocal that strikes home instantly. He executes all manner of vocal somersaults with the lyric but never loses control.

Bonham's intricate bass drum patterns, the rolling bass lines from Jones and Page's fluttering guitar solo were all applied with a gusto that completely overwhelmed the listener. The song's commercial edge made it an ideal choice of US single from the album, and it was also lined up as the flip to the planned but subsequently withdrawn UK 45, "Communication Breakdown". Surprisingly, this *Zep 1* opener was never a regular live number. Fittingly, however, they did select this number as the set opener to their historic reunion at the Ahmet Ertegun tribute show at the O2 Arena in December 2007.

Live performances: Never an integral part of their set, 'Good Times Bad Times' was featured on their debut tour of Scandinavia and resurfaced on their late 1969 set as an opening instrumental riff link for 'Communication Breakdown'. On the sixth US tour in the late summer of 1970, it returned as a vocal version inserted in the 'Communication Breakdown' medley and it made a brief return to the set during the 'Whole Lotta Love' medley in Japan at the Budokan on September 23, 1971 and again in Osaka on September 29, 1971. It was revived for one night only on the Page & Plant *Unledded* tour in New Orleans on March 11, 1995.

On September 14, 2006, Plant performed a rare version of the song at a Sunflower Jam benefit show at London's Porchester Hall in a line up that included Paul Weller and Deep Purple's Jon Lord and Ian Paice.

For their 02 reunion concert, it was selected as the opening number, bringing it full circle.

BABE I'M GONNA LEAVE YOU

Traditional - arranged by Page (Remasters credits - Anne Bredon/Page)
Studio: Olympic Studios, London
This was a number Page had played to Plant during their initial meeting at Jimmy's riverside home at Pangbourne in August 1968. It was then that he first suggested covering the song with his new-found singing partner.

When it came to recording, Jimmy rearranged this traditional folk tune to fit both acoustic and electric modes. Thus, it emerges as an early example of their musical diversity, combining the energy of a forceful Plant vocal, and a strident crash-cymbal driven chorus, with some superbly picked Spanish guitar. Vocally, this track is an early flowering of Robert's much repeated 'Baby, baby, baby' vocal mannerism.

Early outtake versions reveal that Plant originally approached the song with a very forceful vocal. Page, however, opted for light and shade dynamics and this required Plant to apply his softer approach on the released version as well as the more strident tones.

'Babe I'm Gonna Leave You' was a song Page knew as a folk club favourite, as performed by Joan Baez and Marianne Faithful (with Page himself on guitar). Page had first heard the song on the Joan Baez album *Joan Baez In Concert* released in 1962. Another key version was recorded by The Association in 1965, in an arrangement similar to Page's. It may not be a coincidence that The Association was on the same bill as The Yardbirds at the University of Massachusetts on April 6, 1968.

On the original album, the song was credited as "traditional, arranged by Page". By the time of the *Remasters* box set in 1990, the credits had changed to a joint composing credit of Anne Bredon and Page & Plant. Bredon had actually written the song back in the late fifties and had only been alerted to the Zeppelin song in the eighties by her son. It was by no means the only counterclaim to songwriting credits that Zeppelin would face.

In 2008, a three-minute 46 second black and white film of the band miming to 'Babe I'm Gonna Leave You' surfaced from the archive of the German Radio Bremen network. It was recorded for the *Beat Club* TV show on March 27, 1969.

Live performances: Used on the initial 1968/69 tours and then discarded after the second US tour. A particularly vibrant version exists from their Danish TV special filmed in March 1969. A much loved Plant song, he performed it with Fairport Convention at their Cropredy Festival in 1992 and returned to it on his 1993 tour and with Strange Sensation in 2001/2. It was also revived by Page & Plant on their 1995/96 and 1998 world tours.

YOU SHOOK ME

Willie Dixon
Studio: Olympic Studios, London
JB Lenoir has also been cited as a co-writer of this track. It's often forgotten just how heavily the early Led Zeppelin relied on the blues for inspiration. Their launch coincided with the British blues boom of 1968, and as

can be seen from this showcase, they felt very at home in the company of standards like 'You Shook Me'. Robert, in particular, reveled in the song, extending the style he had perfected in The Band Of Joy to great effect. Instrumentally, the track certainly packs some punch. From Jones' swirling organ through Plant's harmonica wailing to the point where Jimmy's solo cascades around Bonzo's stereo panned tom-tom attack, this is prime vintage Zeppelin. And the final incessant by-play between Page and Plant that leads out of the track is a masterful production technique, and one that would be further emphasised on stage.

'You Shook Me' also appeared on The Jeff Beck Group's album *Truth*. Released a few months before the debut Led Zeppelin album with coincidentally, a guest appearance by John Paul Jones on organ. Beck has gone on record as stating that Jimmy copied their arrangement for his own devices and was well upset when the Zeppelin album stormed the charts – a claim Page vehemently denies.

'You Shook Me' was given a robust delivery – more aggressive and free-flowing than on Jeff Beck's *Truth* album. Page's affinity for this blues style could be traced back to his session days, when he backed the likes of Sonny Boy Williamson. His solo on the Zep version is very similar to the track 'Jim's Blues' which he cut in his session days for an album issued by the London All Stars on the French Barclay label in 1965. Plant derived the "I've got a bird that whistles" lyric from Robert Johnson's 'Stones In My Passway'.

'You Shook Me' also featured the organ work of John Paul Jones, whose improvisations greatly extended this piece on stage (as demonstrated on the *One Night Stand BBC In Concert* version on *BBC Sessions*). The climactic finale of this "Zep 1" performance was a good example of the call-and-response vocal-guitar battles Page and Plant perfected on stage.

For Jones the blues was a previously unchartered territory: "I wasn't used to playing this style of urban blues and it did seem to be in a very slow-moving mould. However, Bonzo and I quickly developed a way of playing the blues that allowed us all sorts of improvisational freedom. You can hear it here clearly on the organ part in 'You Shook Me'." In 2011, a previously thought lost March 1969 clip of the band miming to the studio version of 'You Shook Me' surfaced from the archive of the German *Radio Bremen* network.

Live performances: Featured on all the early 1968/69 tours, and then deleted for the late 1969 US tour. It was revived for the US, Japan, UK and Australian dates in 1971/72, when it was part of the 'Whole Lotta Love' medley. A brief reprise of the song was tagged on to the end of 'In My Time Of Dying' at Earls Court, and on the 1977 US tour. Post-Zep it was performed by Plant on his 1993 world tour and by Page with The Black Crowes on their US dates in 1999.

DAZED AND CONFUSED
Page
Studio: Olympic Studios, London
This composition had already been performed extensively by The Yardbirds in 1968 when it was know as 'I'm Confused'. Despite its "Page" composing credit, the song was based on an original recording by sixties US singer-songwriter Jake Holmes, originally appearing as a slow acoustic piece on his album, *The Above Ground Sound Of Jake Holmes*. Page allegedly heard him performing the song at the Village Theatre in New York City on August 25, 1967 when Holmes supported The Yardbirds.

Page adopted 'Dazed And Confused' and turned it into a dramatic extended number, featuring his legendary guitar/violin bow technique. This was a gimmick Page adopted during his session days, recommended to him by the session violinist father of actor David McCallum. The technique was also pioneered by Eddie Phillips, guitarist with the Creation, notably on The Creation's June

1966 single 'Making Time'. For the *Zep I* version, Page also incorporated a solo from 'Think About It', one of the last Yardbirds tracks to be recorded.

Despite its derivative origins, 'Dazed And Confused' emerged as a key *Zep I* performance, its compelling air of menace and drama led by Jones's walking-bass style and Page's mid-song guitar effects.

'Dazed' was selected as the number they showcased for the *Supershow* movie shot in late March 1969 in Staines.

In June 2010, Jake Holmes sued Jimmy Page for copyright infringement, claiming to have written and recorded 'Dazed and Confused' two years before it appeared on Led Zeppelin's debut album. In court documents, Holmes cited a 1967 copyright registration for 'Dazed and Confused' and a further renewed copyright in 1995. The matter was allegedly settled out of court in November 2011.

Live performances: A cornerstone of virtually every Led Zeppelin live show until 1975, it became one of the band's most durable pieces, a vehicle for improvisation that often extended to over 30 minutes in length, usually encompassing snippets of other songs. These included Plant vocal ad libs of Scott McKenzie's 'San Francisco', 'Woodstock', 'Spanish Eyes', The Eagles' 'Take It Easy', plus Page riffing out on 'The Crunge', 'Walter's Walk' and Bernstein's *West Side Story*. On the 1975 US tour, the number had to be dropped for the first two weeks after Jimmy injured his finger just before the tour. It made its reappearance during a stunning show at Madison Square Garden in New York on February 3. For the 1977 tour dates and Copenhagen/Knebworth in 1979, the violin bow section was extracted from 'Dazed And Confused' to form the visual centrepiece of the set. This section was also used with The Firm and on Page's solo *Outrider* tour. It was also performed by Plant in a rare encore version at the NEC Birmingham July 14,

1993. Page & Plant included the song as part of the 'Calling To You'/'Whole Lotta Love' medleys on their 1995/96 world tour. Page also performed an instrumental version of the track at his Net Aid performance in 1999 and at his Teenage Charity concert appearance at the Royal Albert Hall in 2002. Finally, it was recalled in a compact delivery for the 02 reunion show in December 2007. As Plant explained before performing the song on that night: "There are certain songs that have to be here and this is one of them."

YOUR TIME IS GONNA COME

Page, Jones
Studio: Olympic Studios, London
This showcases John Paul Jones as a keyboardist and arranger. The hypnotic fade out featured effective backing vocals and Page embellished the track with some tasteful pedal steel guitar lines. "It's got that church sounding organ introduction that I used the Olympic Hammond for," recalled Jones. "This was another of my main ideas. I also arranged the backing vocal parts. I was always OK at arranging vocals: the problem was singing them, because neither Jimmy nor I would consider ourselves singers." 'Your Time Is Gonna Come' holds the distinction of being the first ever Zep song to be covered by another artist, appearing on Sandie Shaw's 1969 album *Reviewing The Situation*.

Live performances: This may have been performed on their early tour dates though no recorded evidence has emerged. It did make a one-off appearance in a medley of 'Whole Lotta Love' at the Budokan in Tokyo on September 24, 1971. The song was performed by Plant on a few occasions during his 1993 US tour. It was also performed by Page with The Black Crowes on their 1999 and 2000 US tour dates and on a TV slot in July 2000 with the Crowes on the Conan O'Brien US TV show.

BLACK MOUNTAIN SIDE
Page
Studio: Olympic Studios, London
The melody on this Page virtuoso acoustic guitar instrumental owes more than a passing nod to a traditional folk song sung in the folk clubs by Anne Briggs. It was recorded by both John Renbourn, and Bert Jansch, notably in a vocal arrangement on the latter's 1966 *Jack Orion* album under the title 'Black Waterside'. In an interview with *Guitar Player* in 1977, Page did confess: "I wasn't totally original on that. It had been done in the folk cubs a lot. Anne Briggs was the first one that I heard do the riff. I was playing it as well and then there was Bert Janch's version." Jansch passed away in 2011.

Whatever its origin, Page played it superbly, using a borrowed Gibson J200 acoustic and incorporating his "DADGAD CIA" (Celtic Indian Arabic) tuning, later employed on 'Kashmir'. The piece also featured a rare cameo appearance from tabla player Viram Jasani.

For their live act, Page merged 'Black Mountain Side' with 'White Summer', another instrumental opus that had first seen the light of day on The Yardbirds' *Little Games* album.

Live Performances: Incorporated into the Page/Yardbirds solo number 'White Summer' on all gigs up to the fifth US jaunt in 1970. Page restored to the set for the 1977 US tour, the Copenhagen and Knebworth shows in 1979, and the 'Over Europe' tour in 1980. It later emerged in the Firm era composition 'Midnight Moonlight' and part of this number was revived by Page on his Outrider tour of 1988. Page again revived the piece on his tour of Japan with David Coverdale in 1993.

COMMUNICATION BREAKDOWN
Page, Jones, Bonham
Studio: Olympic Studios, London
Communication Breakdown was something of an early anthem – and another compact burst of energy, typifying their urgent chemistry. It's also a vivid example of Page's deft ability to build a song around a repeated guitar riff. The track became one of their most durable live numbers, dating back to their first tour of Scandinavia in September.As Jones explained: "This is Page's riff – you can tell instantly because there's few notes. He was a master at developing riffs like those. This was an instant thing that came out of the first rehearsals. It was always great fun to play live."

It has survived the test of time to become one of the true all-time greats of the Zeppelin catalogue. The song was used as an early promo film by the band recorded at Thee Image Club in Miami in Feb. 1969. It was also mimed for an appearance on Swedish TV. It was the track they performed on their one and only UK TV appearance on BBC's *How Late It Is* on March 21, 1969 - and was also the very last live track they performed on their final UK appearance at Knebworth on August 11, 1979.

Live performances: Developing during their first tour in September 1968, it went on to be a lasting part of their show. It was used on all dates in 1969 and in 1970 it was elevated to encore status. On the sixth US tour it was used as an encore medley. It subsequently appeared as an encore on each successive tour, including the last night at Earls Court, and the second Knebworth date. It was again an encore special for their Over Europe tour 1980, and was part of Plant's 1988 and 1990 solo set. John Paul Jones also performed the song with Diamanda Galas on their 1994 tour.

I CAN'T QUIT YOU BABY
Willie Dixon
Studio: Olympic Studios, London
Another slow Willie Dixon blues, this is notable for its ambient production quality that brings to the fore John Bonham's wonderfully laid-back drumming, and Jimmy's deceptively mellow guitar sparring. There's a great 'just having a blow' atmosphere about this track that makes for a very relaxed outing. The arrangement is similar to the Otis Rush version of the song.

Live performances: Included in their set from 1968 up to the fifth US tour in 1970. It was revived as part of the 'Whole Lotta Love' medley on the Japan, UK and Europe tours 1972/3. This track was also rehearsed for the Atlantic 40th Anniversary reunion in May 1988, but was not included on the night. Page and Plant performed a short version of this song at the Hammersmith show a month earlier. They also performed it on their first reunion prior to the *Unledded* filming at the Alexis Korner benefit show staged at the Buxton Opera House on April 17, 1994.

The song was occasionally used as an insert within 'Babe I'm Gonna Leave You' by Page & Plant on their 1995/96 shows and also on their 1998 world tour within 'How Many More Times'. At their 02 reunion show, Jason Bonham sang the opening lines of this song prior to their performance of 'Misty Mountain Hop'.

HOW MANY MORE TIMES
Page, Jones, Bonham
Studio: Olympic Studios, London

The closing number of their early stage act and appropriately enough the parting shot of their debut album, 'How Many More Times' is a lengthy, high energy exit. It's a marriage of Howlin' Wolf's 'How Many More Years' and The Yardbirds arrangement of 'Smokestack Lightning'. There are also elements in the instrumental rhythm of the track 'Beck's Bolero' cut by Page and Beck in 1966. From the Jazzy Bonham/Jones intro and stinging Page wah-wah, the track develops into a medley of its own – an early studio example of how such performances would be improvised in their stage set. The appearance of extracts of 'Rosie' and Albert Lee's 'The Hunter' came spontaneously on the night of the session itself. Note also here Page's bowing technique. Alongside 'Dazed And Confused', this track had its origins in the old Yardbirds repertoire.

'How Many More Times' was the closing number to many of their early shows and the parting shot on this debut album; curiously, this was incorrectly timed on the back cover at 3'30", but actually clocked in at over eight minutes. This is Plant's stand-out performance on this album, displaying a confidence which belied his 20 years.

Musically, the piece owes more than a passing nod to a mid-sixties track of the same name by The T. Bones whose line up included Keith Emerson, which came out as part of the *Rock Generation* series of French albums produced by early Yardbirds manager Giorgio Gomelsky. Given Gomelsky's involvement with Page and The Yardbirds around that period, it's likely that Page would have been aware of Farr's version. Lyrically, the Zeppelin song was based on Howlin' Wolf's 'How Many More Years'.

After the trademark bowing episode, the drama really unfolds as the band speeds through a spontaneous medley that encompassed 'Oh Rosie' and Albert Lee's 'The Hunter'. The 'Steal Away' phrase Plant included was a direct influence of the track 'Steal Away' Plant recorded with the father of British blues, Alexis Korner, just prior to him joining Zeppelin in 1968. One of the outstanding performances of the song is the January 9, 1970 Royal Albert Hall performance as captured on the official DVD.

Live performances: 'How Many More Times' held down the closing slot in the Zeppelin set up to and including their 1970 Bath Festival appearance. It reappeared briefly on the Japan 1971 dates, and at a date at Southampton University in January 1973. It came back into the set for the 1975 US tour, when it replaced 'Dazed And Confused' for the first two weeks due to Jimmy's injured finger. Its live appearance on the 1997 *BBC Sessions* album prompted Page & Plant to revive it very successfully on their 1998 world tour.

LED ZEPPELIN II

Atlantic Records - original issue 588 198,
October 22, 1969 reissue K40087
UK Album Chart: No 1; US: No 1
Sales figures approx. and counting:
UK 1,200,000 - 4x Platinum;
US 12,000,000 - 12x Platinum

With the debut riding high on the charts, Page and co. soon began focusing on recording a follow-up. Their hectic on the road schedule dictated that much of the studio time had to be grabbed between months of intense touring, principally in the US. It all began with rehearsals at Page's Pangbourne home and initial sessions for 'Whole Lotta Love' and 'What Is And Should Never Be' at Olympic in spring 1969.

So keen were Atlantic for a second album, they informed Grant that the band should continue recording during their second US tour as the label was aiming at a July release. While Grant was happy for the sessions to re-commence, he did not buckle to Atlantic's scheduling demands - the first of many occasions when he, rather than the record company, dictated how Zeppelin would conduct their business.

While on the second US tour they did begin road testing some of their newly recorded material. 'Whole Lotta Love' made its full stage debut at a date at the Winterland Ballroom in San Francisco on April 26. They were also regularly featuring a version of Howlin' Wolf's 'Killing Floor' which would be

retitled 'The Lemon Song' when they took it into the studio as Plant also threw in lines from Robert Johnson's 'Travellin' Riverside Blues'. This live arrangement of the song was similar in structure to the version recorded by US rock act The Electric Flag. John Bonham had been showcasing an extended drum solo piece dubbed 'Pat's Delight' - a reference to his wife - which he would then take into the studio and rename 'Moby Dick'.

Stopping off in Los Angeles, Page called up engineer Chris Huston to book in some sessions at Huston's Mystic Sound studio. This was a low ceilinged 16x16 room with four-track facilities. Page had previously used the studio on a session with Screaming Lord Sutch. "The sessions came out great," recalled Huston. "He was very easy to get on with - we did the tracks live with Plant standing in the middle of the room with a hand held mic. You can hear that at the end of 'The Lemon Song' where Plant sings 'floor floor floor' - well that echo was recorded in real time." 'Lemon Song' and Bonham's drum solo piece were initially laid down at Mystic.

It's worth noting at this point that for the *Led Zeppelin II* sessions Page switched to using a Gibson Les Paul guitar as opposed to a Telecaster which had dominated his late Yardbirds and early Zeppelin work. Page was already in possession of a vintage 1958 Les Paul but added another model during the early US tours. "I had been mainly using the Telecaster both on stage and in the studio," remembered Page. "We were at the Fillmore at the time and Joe Walsh, who was then playing with the James Gang, said he had a Les Paul for sale, a 1959 model. He wanted to sell it for $500, a right price at the time. Once I started playing it that was it."

Back in the UK in June they did further recording. At Morgan Studios in Willesdon, North London they added another batch of tracks, notably 'Thank You', and 'Livin' Lovin' Maid (She's A Woman)'. The Morgan sessions also saw them work on a track titled 'Sugar Mama', an uptempo, riff led piece that was discarded.

The growing confidence for the new in progress *Led Zeppelin II* material led them to preview two of the tracks during sessions for BBC Radio One in June. A version of 'What Is And What Should Never Be' was cut on June 16 at the Aeolian Studios for broadcast on the June 22 edition of Chris Grant's *Tasty Pop Sundae*. At the BBC's Maida Vale studios just over week later, they recorded another version of the same track, alongside a superb version of 'Whole Lotta Love'. This was part of a session broadcast on John Peel's *Top Gear* on June 29.

Their hectic schedule continued into the summer of 1969. Grant had them undertake their third US tour running through July and August. This included a variety of high profile outdoor festivals including Atlanta Pop Festival, the Newport Jazz Festival and the Texas International Pop Festival. Grant actually passed on Woodstock, opting instead for dates in Texas, New Jersey and Connecticut. "I said no to Woodstock because I knew we'd just be another band on the bill," he reflected years later.

During the tour, Page hooked up with engineer Eddie Kramer - noted for his work with Jimi Hendrix on Electric Ladyland. Kramer had also worked at Olympic Studios when Page and Jones were session musicians in the mid-sixties.

Kramer later noted: "John Paul was the first to make me aware of them when he told me he was joining a group with Jimmy - this was before I left England to work in the US. The first time I saw them was at the Fillmore East. They were sensational. I'd known both Jimmy and John from working with them at Olympic and had followed their careers over the years. I periodically bumped into them and then I was asked to work on their second album."

Further tracks were developed at this point. 'Heartbreaker' was recorded in two parts - initially at A & R Studios and then the famous Page virtuoso guitar solo was added at an entirely different studio across town -

Atlantic Studios. 'Bring It On Home' was also perfected there.

Other studios deployed around this period included New York's small, independent set up, Juggy Sound, which was used to lay down the Tolkien inspired 'Ramble On'. They also attempted to record in run down R&D Studios in Vancouver which had no proper working headphones, plus A&M Studios in Los Angeles, and the Mayfair again in New York.

It was around the end of the tour that Page met up with engineer Eddie Kramer to complete the final mixing of the album. This was done over a marathon session at New York's A&R Studios, gaining Kramer a 'Director Of Engineering' credit.

"Something like 'Thank You' with the long fade was down to Mr John Paul Jones. He was something of an unsung hero of the band," recalls Kramer. "For me 'Heartbreaker' is a stand out. I think we did some of that at Juggy Sound. That was a very dense studio with a very tight room. The solo was genius Page. That track goes straight into 'Living Loving Maid'. I know it's been said that's a bit of a throwaway song, but that's because it's not a heavy duty track. It was a fun thing and it was always good to include one of those. 'Ramble On' for me, well that's all about the bass line. It's Jonesy again. Such a talented musician. You can pinpoint certain things on the tracks, it's the whole band looking into each other eyes. Getting the result. Sometimes they went head to head and argued it out. If you don't have that one on one method then it's not a band. I mean Lennon and McCartney certainly had that. As for 'Moby Dick', that was a bit of a job piecing and editing performances from two different studios. Whenever I hear it I think of the job that took but it's Bonzo and he was the best."

Page asked Kramer to bring cohesion to the sound of the tracks as they had been recorded in various locations. "I wound up cutting a few new tracks, overdubbing some of the tracks they already had and then I mixed the whole album with Jimmy."

The fragmented nature of the sessions did give rise to a rare lack of confidence from Page at the time. "It took a long time on and off," he said in late 1969. "Having to write numbers in hotel rooms. It was insane really. We'd put down a rhythm track in London, add the vocals in New York, put in a harmonica say in Vancouver and then go back to New York to do the mixing. By the time the album came out I'd lost confidence with it." He need not have worried.

In between the harder-edged material, however, there were some examples of the ever widening scope of the group's intentions. This album also marked the emergence of Robert Plant as a serious songwriter. His name had been notably absent from the debut album credits due to previous contractual commitments. Now, his influence on tracks such as 'What Is And What Should Never Be' and 'Ramble On' were definite pointers to the musical future of Led Zeppelin.

Page also experimented with the art of distance miking, a trick he had picked up from his session man days. This technique considerably enhanced the sound of John Bonham's straight from the wrist drumming and Plant's wailing vocal. "I discovered that if you move the mic away from the drums the sound would have room to breathe. I kept exploring and expanding that approach." The combination of Page's deft ear for sound and Bonham's percussive force created a totally fresh approach to how drums could be captured on record. There's no finer example of that than the catalytic opening to 'Whole Lotta Love' - the moment when Bonham comes roaring in is as startling now as it was when it was first issued back in 1969.

The album sleeve for Led Zeppelin II artwork was designed by David Juniper and features the four faces of the group superimposed on an old World War I photo of the German Jasta II squadron – the famous Flying Circus led by Manfred von Richthofen, the Red Baron. Juniper edited the picture and added the faces of the four members of Zeppelin

taken from a 1969 publicity photo. He also superimposed other figures onto to the original photo. Some sources state that the blonde-haired image is English actress Glynis Johns who played the mother in the film version of Mary Poppins; it's feasible the inclusion of Johns was an inside joke reference to noted producer Glyn Johns who had worked with Page on the debut Zeppelin album. Johns often claimed he had produced the record and it may have been a retort by Page and co. to include the Glynis Johns photo. Another theory is that it depicts Andy Warhol's so called 'superstar' artist Ultra Violet. The design was wrapped in an elaborate gatefold sleeve that opened up to show the shadow of a Zeppelin airship. Its distinctive outer colouring earned the album the nickname 'The Brown Bomber' in America.

Led Zeppelin II was issued in the US on October 22, 1969. With advance orders for half a million, it was an instant success and by the years end had significantly dislodged The Beatles Abbey Road from the top spot where it remained for seven weeks. It was clear indication that Zep were set to rule the US charts in the seventies as The Beatles had in the sixties.

In the UK it was a similar story. It quickly established a top five placing and by the time the group were completing an eight-date UK tour early in 1970 (including the memorable show at London's Royal Albert Hall as captured on the official DVD), it had moved to the number one position. It went on to enjoy a remarkable 138 week unbroken run on the UK chart and was still riding high on the album chart when the third Zep album was issued a year later.

During 1970, they added three more tracks from their second album – 'Thank You', 'Bring It On Home' and 'Whole Lotta Love' to their live shows. It was their dynamic interpretations of these staple tracks from the new album that elevated them into the world's top live attraction - a status they would retain for the rest of the decade. Led

Zeppelin II marks the beginning of a very creative period for the group, and it remains an authentic reflection of the sheer exuberance inspired by the band's intensive touring schedule aimed (successfully) at conquering America.

WHOLE LOTTA LOVE
Page, Bonham, Plant, Jones
Studios: Olympic, London; Sunset Sound, Los Angeles; A&R, New York
The catalyst. A masterful Page/Kramer production. From Plant's off-mic cough through to the 'Keepa coolin' baby' squeals, this is five minutes and 33 seconds of aural and sexual delight. The song originally took shape around Page's killer three-note riff with its octave E conclusion, and a descending chord structure which employed backwards echo effects first used by Jimmy on a Mickie Most session.

Plant borrowed wholesale from Willie Dixon's 'You Need Love'. Surprisingly, it took some 15 years for the Chicago blues man to claim that his composition 'You Need Love', as recorded by Muddy Waters in 1962, was used without credit as the basis for the lyrics of the *Zep II* opening track. He successfully won a court case in 1985 for royalties. It's worth noting that the Zep version also bears a strong resemblance to a Marriot/ Lane composition titled 'You Need Loving' recorded by The Small Faces.

Whilst 'Whole Lotta Love' may have been highly derivative, the end result was very much seeped in Zeppelin histrionics. This was most apparent during the apocalyptic central section in which Page mixed all manner of crazy sound effects - full tilt whoops, screams, sirens and demolition noises interspersed with what sounded remarkably like Robert squealing in orgasmic bliss from the depths of a coal mine - into a truly mind-blowing sequence which careened wildly from speaker to speaker and suggested total mayhem.

In America, where singles extracted from albums gained valuable airplay and in turn led on to album sales, Peter Grant had no real problem with Atlantic Records issuing an edited version of Whole Lotta Love. It's ascent to the top five of the *Billboard* chart by January 1970 confirmed their appeal as the hottest act of the new decade.

However, Grant had no plans to allow such a release in the UK. Atlantic presumed wrongly that Grant would sanction a release and went ahead and pressed an initial quantity of the 3.12 edit of the song backed with 'Livin' Lovin' Maid (She's A Woman)'. Allegedly, around 500 copies were distributed to press and radio stations and around 500 ended up in a warehouse in Manchester ready for release.

Grant immediately requested their recall, pointing to a clause in their contract that stated he and he alone would have control of any single releases. At the time, of course, Zep were an integral part of the underground scene and had no desire to make the obligatory appearance on *Top Of The Pops* that a hit single might demand. As *Led Zeppelin II* was selling more than most 45's anyway, Grant promptly pulled the plug on the planned UK release, issuing a curt statement that Zeppelin intended to issue a special track as a single in the future. That plan never came to fruition.

The catalogue allocated to the UK edit of 'Whole Lotta Love' (584 309) was subsequently given to Clarence Carter's UK single on Atlantic 'Take It Off Him And Put It On Me'. Surviving copies of that withdrawn run of UK 'Whole Lotta Love' singles now command over £600, making it one of the rarest UK singles of all time.

'Whole Lotta Love' did go on to become a huge European smash, most notably in Germany where it reached number one. This was aided by a promo film cut together by the German *Beat Club* TV show.

In November 1970, CCS, the big band rock outfit formed by bluesman Alexis Korner, scored a top twenty UK hit with their version of the song. It was this big band arrangement that was subsequently adapted as the theme tune for the UK weekly TV chart show *Top Of The Pops*, thus ensuring that it would seep into the consciousness of every pop fan in the land, whether or not they were fans of Led Zeppelin. The programme revived the song as its theme in 2000, adapting elements of the Zep original with a drum and bass makeover. In 1996, dance act Goldbug took 'Whole Lotta Love' into the UK top five with an arrangement that merged the Pearl And Dean cinema ad theme.

A year later, in September 1997, the surviving band members finally relented and sanctioned a belated UK release for a new edit of 'Whole Lotta Love' which was issued as a CD single to promote the re-issuing of the Zeppelin catalogue to mid-price. It reached number 21 on the chart.

To accompany the single, the band commissioned a superb accompanying video with the track cut to a montage of archive live footage including their Earls Court '75 and Knebworth '79 shows - a preview of the visual delights that would follow on the 2003 official DVD. Jimmy can be seen performing the riff of the song on a soundstage in 2008 in front of Jack White and The Edge for the *It Might Get Loud* documentary film.

Live performances: 'Whole Lotta Love' made its live debut on the second US tour at a show at the Winterland Ballroom in San Francisco on April 26, 1969. They also played the song on their support gig for The Who in Columbia, Maryland on May 25, 1969. In June 1969, they previewed it on a BBC session, but they didn't play it again until 1970. For the early 1970 dates it was an encore number. From the sixth US tour in 1970 up to the 1973 US tour it was the closing finale of virtually every Zeppelin performance, extending in length to include a rock'n'roll medley. On their 1975 dates, it was an encore medley with 'Black Dog' and in 1977 it was used as a medley encore with 'Rock And Roll' and, on one occasion at

the LA Forum, with 'Communication Breakdown'. It was given a new revamped arrangement for the 1979 Copenhagen/Knebworth encores (the same version was revived for the Atlantic 40th Anniversary reunion in May 1988), and returned to the 'Let That Boy Boogie' medley workout for the 1980 European dates. It holds the distinction of being the last track Led Zeppelin performed live with John Bonham, when it received a 17-minute workout at the final gig in Berlin on July 7, 1980. It was also played at the Live Aid gig on July 13, 1985. Post Zep: Plant performed the song on his 1993 and 2000/2002 tours. Page & Plant revived it for their 1995/96 and 1998 world tours. Page played it with David Coverdale in a 1993 Nagoya, Japan show and with The Black Crowes on their 1999/2000 US tour dates. Finally, it was performed at the 02 reunion show in December 2007 as an encore.

WHAT IS AND WHAT SHOULD NEVER BE
Page, Plant
Studios: Olympic, London; Groove, New York; A&R, New York
The genesis of Robert Plant's career as a songwriter, this dreamy affair is a marked departure from the dizzy atmosphere of 'Whole Lotta Love'. It's also another superb Page production with its flanging vocal effects and powerful stereo separation on the fade out. Jimmy had now switched to the Gibson Les Paul for recording, and the sustained solo here is really quite beautiful. The song is allegedly about an on tour romance Plant had experienced. The semi-whispered verses are reminiscent of Julie Driscoll's version of Donovan's 'Season of The Witch'.

The song gained renewed attention when Plant revived it on his 1993 *Fate Of Nations* tour and subsequently when it was played live by Page & Plant on their world tours. Page also selected it as the radio airplay cut from his *Excess All Areas-Live At The Greek* album drawn from his appearances with The Black Crowes in 1999.

Live performances: Previewed in June 1969 on a BBC radio session, premièred live at the Carousel Theatre in Framingham, Massachusetts on August 21 and then inserted on the late 1969 US tour and played at every gig through 1970/71 up to the US tour in June 1972 (it was discarded thereafter). Plant performed it on his 1993 world tour, and it was revived by Page & Plant at their MTV Unledded London filming in 1994 and on their 1995/96 and 1998 world tours. Page with The Black Crowes also included the track on their 1999 and 2000 US tour dates.

THE LEMON SONG
Chester Burnett
Studios: Mystic Sound, Los Angeles; A&R, New York

This track was originally credited to Page, Plant, Jones and Bonham but claims by ARC Music, the copyright holders of 'Killing Floor', a track written and recorded by Howlin' Wolf, were quick to reclaim the song. They argued that on *Led Zeppelin II* Wolf's composition, written under his real name Chester Burnett, appeared under the title 'The Lemon Song' and was credited as a group composition. An out of court settlement was agreed, and for a period UK copies listed the track as being titled 'Killing Floor' on the insistence of publishers Jewel Music.

This arrangement also takes from Albert King's 'Cross-Cut Saw', a staple of the gigs Plant would perform with The Honeydrippers in 1981. Recorded virtually live in LA's Mystic studios, the track combined 'Killing Floor', which they had been performing at their early gigs, with the Robert Johnson inspired 'squeeze my lemon' sequence with its intense erotic overtones.

Live performances: 'Killing Floor' was used on the debut American tour (Jimi Hendrix had also been performing a live version at the time) and was to evolve into 'The Lemon Song' for the second and third tours. Dropped in late 1969, though the 'squeeze my lemon' sequence was often inserted into the 'Whole Lotta Love' medley and ad-libbed

elsewhere. Lines from the song were also occasionally used within 'How Many More Times' on Page & Plant's 1998 world tour. The track was revived by Page in the original *Led Zeppelin II* arrangement for his 1999/2000 dates with The Black Crowes.

THANK YOU
Page, Plant
Studios: Morgan, London; A&R, New York

This emotional love song to his wife brings out the best in Robert Plant, as he commits to tape one of his finest vocal performances. Elsewhere in the arrangement, John Paul Jones excels on Hammond organ, and Jimmy complements it all with some delicate Rickenbacker 12-string picking. It has also been noted that the chord structure of 'Thank You' bears a resemblance to the Traffic song 'Dear Mr Fantasy' issued in 1968. Lyrically, some of the lines draw from the Jimi Hendrix track 'If Six Was Nine'. A long standing favourite of the composers, it was the number Page and Plant selected to open their 1994 historic *MTV Unledded* filming sessions at the London Studios on August 25, 1994. It was covered in the nineties by both Tori Amos and Duran Duran. In February 2011, it was also played at the funeral of John Bonham's mother, Joan.

Live performances: Made its debut in the set on the January 1970 UK tour. It stayed in the show throughout 1970/71, acting as a spotlight for Jones' keyboard solo. On the 1972/3 tours it was used as a marathon encore and then deleted from the act. At the Freddie Mercury Tribute Concert at Wembley Stadium in April 1992, Plant sang a few lines from the song as a bridge intro to his version of Queen's 'Crazy Little Thing Called Love'. Plant performed it on his 1993 world tour and it was revived by Page & Plant at the *MTV Unledded*, London filming in 1994, and on their 1995/6 and 1998 world tours. Plant resurrected the track for his *Band Of Joy* tour in 2010/11.

HEARTBREAKER
Page, Plant, Jones, Bonham
Studio: A & R, New York

Another integral part of the recorded Zeppelin canon 'Heartbreaker' became a perfect platform for Page to display his guitar virtuosity. On this studio cut, he offers up a breathtaking exercise in string-bending guitar technique, while on the road he extended the track to include snippets of Bach's Bourée in E minor and Simon & Garfunkel's '59th Street Bridge Song (Feelin' Groovy)'. Page has revealed that the middle solo section was recorded in an entirely different studio to the main structure of the piece. One of the great all time Zeppelin riffs as acknowledged in the nineties by the US TV cartoon satire *Beavis And Butthead*.

Live performances: A long-standing live favourite, it joined the set during their European dates in the autumn of 1969 premiering at Scheveningen, Holland on October 3, 1969. From the Bath Festival onwards and throughout the rest of their dates in 1970/71, it provided a dual thrust set opener with 'Immigrant Song'. For the US, Japan, UK and Europe tours of 1972/73, it became part of the encore. It was back in the main set as a medley preceding 'Whole Lotta Love' for the 1973 US dates (see *The Song Remains The Same* movie). It became an encore again on the 1975 US tour, the last night at Earls Court, selected dates during the 1977 US tour, the first Knebworth show, and the Europe 1980 tour. It was also performed at the Atlantic 40th Anniversary reunion in 1988. Additional live elements that Page brought to this track included a few chords from 'Greensleeves' and a regular instrumental passage based on Bach's 'Bourée in E minor'. When employed as an encore during the 1975 US tour, versions of 'That's Alright' and 'I'm A Man' were inserted into the song at Madison Square Garden (February 12) and Long Beach (March 12) respectively. Page & Plant revived the song on their 1995/96 and 1998 world tours and Page with The Black Crowes played it on their 1999 and 2000 US tour dates. A snippet of the song was deployed by John Paul Jones within his solo track Bass 'N' Drums on his 1999 tour dates.

LIVIN' LOVIN' MAID (SHE'S JUST A WOMAN)
Page, Plant
Studios: Morgan, London; A&R, New York

Jimmy returned to the Telecaster to knock out what the band always considered to be something of a production line filler; however, this tight, hook-laden ditty, found much favour on the radio, and when 'Whole Lotta Love' finished its chart run in America, 'Livin' Lovin' Maid' was flipped over to become an A-side in its own right. It then climbed to Number 65 on the *Billboard* chart. The song is rumoured to be about one of their early, persistent West Coast groupies. On US FM radio stations it became a playlist favourite being frequently sequenced after Heartbreaker as on the album.

Live performance: Such was their distaste for this track that it never received a full public airing. On a date in Hamburg in March 1970, Plant slipped the first line of the song into 'Heartbreaker' and he sang the opening line in jest at Earls Court on May 24, 1975. Explaining the intention of this show he said, "We don't just mean we're gonna groove around on anything that could be groovy like 'With a purple umbrella and a 50 cent hat' no… none of that!" In a surprise move, Plant brought the song into his 'Manic Nirvana' US/UK solo tour set in 1990, turning it into a rousing encore with a mock Beach Boys arrangement.

RAMBLE ON
Page, Plant
Studios: Juggy Sound, New York; A&R, New York

Enter the ethereal Page and Plant. 'Ramble On', with its Tolkien-inspired *Lord Of The Rings* lyrical content was for Plant, in particular, the highlight of *Led Zeppelin II*. It remains a splendid illustration of the light and shade dynamism that would characterise so much of their future work. It slips effortlessly from quiet mournful passages into an uplifting chorus, and Page's overdubbed interweaving Gibson run is an early attempt at the guitar army assault that would become his trademark. Bonham meanwhile plays a straightforward top tom rhythm. This is one of the tracks that has gained in prominence in recent years via the many post Zep performances it has enjoyed. Jimmy can be seen performing an instrumental version of the song in a London studio in 2008 for the *It Might Get Loud* documentary film.

Live performances: Surprisingly, 'Ramble On' was never performed live in a full version during the Zep era. On the spring 1970 US tour, Plant did throw in lines from the song during 'Communication Breakdown' (as heard on the famous *'Mudslide'* bootleg) and 'Whole Lotta Love'. It was performed by Plant on his 1993/2002 tours and was a set list standard on Page & Plant's 1995/6 and 1998 world tours. It was also performed at the 02 reunion show in December 2007 and it was given a fresh arrangement by Plant on his *Band Of Joy* tour in 2011.

MOBY DICK
Bonham, Jones, Page
Studios: Mirror Sound, L.A.;
Mayfair, New York; A&R, New York
John Bonham's percussive showcase took shape on the second US tour when it was known as 'Pat's Delight' (a reference to his wife). Built between a killer Page riff, which was used as the theme to BBC 2's *Disco 2* rock show, Bonzo does his thing with sticks and bare hands.

Outtakes from the *Zeppelin II* sessions reveal the 'Moby Dick' drum solo to have been edited down from a much longer version. The opening and closing riff part of the track can be traced back to the BBC session track 'The Girl I Love She Got Long Black Wavy Hair' which was laid down in June of 1969. It also echoes traces of the 1961 Bobby Parker track 'Watch Your Step' which the band had rehearsed early on but never performed live. In 1990, Jimmy Page merged this studio performance with 'Bonzo's Montreux' to create an amalgamated Bonham drum presentation.

Live performances: Came in on the October 1969 US tour at a date in Buffalo on October 30 and stayed in the set on every tour up to 1977 (although it was not played at every single show). It developed into an excessive 20-minute showcase which provided the others with a break in the show. By 1975, Bonzo was incorporating a 'Whole Lotta Love' riff segment played on electronically treated kettle drums. On the 1977 US tour, the track was aptly renamed 'Over The Top', and employed the intro riff of 'Out On The Tiles' instead of the 'Moby Dick' theme.

BRING IT ON HOME
Page, Plant
Studios: Mystic, Los Angeles; R & D, Vancouver; A&R, New York
Another Willie Dixon tune, 'Bring It On Home' was plagiarized for the closing track of *Zep II*. Though credited to Page/Plant, this was a blatant cover of Sonny Boy Williamson's 1963 arrangement of the track issued on the Chess album *Real Folk Blues*. 'Bring it On Home' was named in the same legal action as 'Killing Floor', but did not include the changing of songwriting credits. Opening with a straight lift from Sonny Boy Williamson's 'Bring It On Home' with Plant on harmonica, it soon snaps into electric action via a riveting Page riff and Bonham/Jones rhythm beef up. Plant's harmonica solo was over-dubbed at a session in Vancounver.

Live performances: Used on stage from the November 1969 US tour and retained for their 1970 itinerary. Live, it developed into a lengthy piece with a great Page/ Bonham guitar-drum battle. It was revived briefly for the 1972 US tour as an encore (as can be heard on the *How The West Was Won* live set) and re-employed on the 1973 US tour as an opening sequence riff link to merge 'Celebration Days' with 'Black Dog'. 'Bring It On Home' was played at the reunion staged at Jason Bonham's wedding reception in May 1990. It was played extensively on

Page & Plant's 1995/96 and 1998 world tours and was also in the set list for the Jimmy Page and the Black Crowes' 1999 and 2000 US tours. It was also performed with Steve Tyler, Joe Perry, and Jason Bonham at the 1995 Led Zeppelin Hall of Fame induction in New York.

LED ZEPPELIN III

Atlantic - original issue 2401 002
October 23, 1970, reissued as K50002
UK Album Chart: No 1; US: No 1
Sales figures approx. and counting:
UK 600,000 - 2x Platinum;
US 6,000,000 - 6x Platinum

At around 9pm on the evening of Saturday June 28, 1970, a pivotal moment occurred that would shape the whole future of Led Zeppelin. Following a performance of 'Thank You' from their second album, 40 minutes into their bill topping set at the Bath Festival, Jimmy Page exchanged his Gibson Les Paul for a Martin D28 acoustic guitar and John Paul Jones switched to mandolin. After a few minutes of tuning up, Robert Plant joked with the audience that "This is a medley of Lonnie Donegan tunes" before announcing, "This is one of the really good ones, especially for John Bonham!"

As Page strummed the first chords, Plant revealed "This is called 'The Boy Next Door', for want of a better title," and Led Zeppelin played acoustically on stage for the first time in the UK. The better title would subsequently emerge as 'That's The Way', one of the centrepiece recordings on their landmark third album.

The significance of their Bath Festival acoustic performance could not be understated. This was a band that had often bludgeoned their listeners into submission with the full on rock assault of the likes of

'Whole Lotta Love', 'Dazed And Confused' and 'How Many More Times'. Indeed performances of those songs at the Bath Festival did much to cement their growing reputation as the most popular band in the world. Clearly though, as indicated by that acoustic rendering of 'That's The Way', Led Zeppelin were going to be much more than just purveyors of tuned-to-ten Marshall amplifiers.

"We are not a rabble rousing group," Page informed journalist Chris Welsh earlier that year. "We are trying to play some music."

Unsurprisingly, there was a mixed reaction to the album when *Led Zeppelin III* was released in October of 1970. Many critics and fans could not quite believe their ears; however, the clues had long since been there. The acoustic overtones of 'Babe I'm Gonna Leave You', the folk instrumental 'Black Mountain Side' and the subtly of 'Thank You' and 'Ramble On' all displayed evidence of Page's intention to bring what he would often describe as a "light and shade" to the proceedings.

Misleadingly, the overall bombastic thrust of *Led Zeppelin II* clouded the musical diversity that lay ahead. Despite the successful formula applied to their second album, for their next recorded statement they were determined to extend their musically boundaries.

Initially, sessions for their third album carried on from where *Zep II* had left off. When they gathered in Olympic Studios in late 1969, contrary to popular belief, there was a plan to try and record something for single release. Announcing the withdrawal of the planned release of 'Whole Lotta Love' in the UK in December of that year, Peter Grant issued a statement that read: "The group had no intention of issuing this as a single as they felt it was written as part of the concept of the album. They've written a special number intended as their first British single which they are recording this week." It's possible one of the numbers under consideration for this planned single was the semi-acoustic 'Hey Hey What Can I Do', which eventually emerged as a future American single B-side to 'Immigrant Song'.

In the end, the plan to record a single came to nothing; however, the late 1969 session did see the beginnings of what would emerge on Led Zeppelin III a year hence. Page experimented with a chord progression that overlaid a series of Hendrix-like runs. This was dubbed 'Jennings Farm Blues', a reference to Plant's then farmhouse in Blakeshall. This track would remain voiceless and unreleased, but the melody of this electric piece would later emerge in an acoustic arrangement titled 'Bron-Y-Aur Stomp'.

After a hectic 18-month period of touring, in May 1970 they finally took a break. Page and Plant decided to head for the hills and stay at a run down cottage Robert had remembered holidaying at when he was a child. The cottage known as Bron–Yr-Aur which is Welsh for "golden hill", "breast of the gold" or "hill of the gold", was an 18th century building located in South Snowdonia situated near the market town of Machynlleth. It should be noted that all credits for Bron–Yr-Aur on the Led Zeppelin III album incorrectly named the cottage as Bron–Yr-Aur. It was restored to Bron-Yr-Aur for all future album credits, notably the 1970 Bron-Yr-Aur acoustic track that eventually surfaced on Physical Graffiti. This trip to the serenity of the Welsh countryside would emerge as a working holiday. Together, with roadies Clive Coulson and Sandy McGregor, Jimmy and Robert spent the month at the cottage, entertaining their significant others, Maureen and Charlotte, and working on songs. Given the lack of domestic electricity, the arrangements for the new songs that emerged were entirely acoustic, thus setting the flavour for much of their third album.

These compositions were influenced by a variety of sources. America was already feeling the soft rock influence of Crosby Stills Nash & Young – in fact, Page and Plant were in attendance at the band's London show earlier in the year. Joni Mitchell was another key influence on Plant at the time. There was a definite Neil Young lilt about 'I Wanna Be Your Man', an acoustic skit that they left unfinished, and 'Down By The Seaside' which would eventually surface on Physical Graffiti. Plant's reflective 'That's The Way' (aka 'The Boy Next Door') was another number borne under the influence of the cottage. 'The Rover', 'Hey Hey What Can I Do', 'Poor Tom' and 'Friends' were other songs that were first developed there.

When the group reconvened for studio sessions at Olympic in late May, they had a good ten numbers at the ready-to-record stage. "We'll be recording for the next two weeks and we are doing a lot of acoustic stuff as well as the heavier side," John Bonham told Melody Maker's Chris Welch from the studio. "There will be better quality songs than on the first two albums."

On the recommendation of their office secretary Carole Browne, they next decamped to Headley Grange in East Hampshire. Originally built in 1795, Headley Grange was formerly a workhouse known as Headley Workhouse for the poor, infirmed and orphaned. In 1870, the building was bought for £420 by builder Thomas Kemp, who converted it into a private residence and named it Headley Grange. In keeping with the then trend of bands 'getting it together in the country', Fleetwood Mac had recently rehearsed there as Page commented: "Headley Grange was somewhat rundown, the heating didn't work. But it had one major advantage. Other bands had rehearsed there and hadn't had any complaints. That's a major issue, because you don't want to go somewhere and start locking into the work process and then have to pull out." Zeppelin would use this location more extensively on the recording of Led Zeppelin IV and Physical Graffiti.

For the Zep III recordings, they employed the Rolling Stones mobile studio and tackled the wealth of song ideas at their disposal. Aside from the softer numbers, they also had a series of full on rock numbers to work on. Material such as 'Immigrant Song', 'Celebration Day' and 'Out On The Tiles' would showcase the more familiar side of the band.

They supplemented the Headley Grange sessions with continued work at their regular studio haunt, Olympic Studios, and in mid-July they also took advantage of the newly built Island Studios in Basing Street, London. The Studio Two facilities had opened there the previous March – Zeppelin had the distinction of being the first band to use the Studio One facility when it opened, allegedly beating Country Joe in booking album sessions. There was a rumour at the time that Page, alongside Keith Richards, assisted Country Joe in the recording of his album at De Lane Lea Studios.

During the 1970 US summer tour Page took time out in Memphis to add a final mix to the record, employing the talents of Terry Manning, an engineer at Ardent Studios. Terry had befriended Page in 1966 when he supported The Yardbirds while in a band called Lawson & Four More on a Dick Clark Caravan of Stars tour. He saw Zeppelin perform many times in the US and went on to get involved in studio production. Jimmy had asked him to be involved in the recording of the album and there was talk of him coming to England to engineer. "Jimmy asked me if I could finish the mixing, editing and mastering in Memphis," he told journalist Phil Sutcliffe.

This mixing period would lead to the delay of the record – a worrying situation for Atlantic Records, anxious to cash in on the band's touring popularity. It led to a curious news story that appeared in the UK trade press stating that distributors Polydor had been forced to postpone the release to October due to "Non-availability of tapes from America." Page and Manning certainly knew where the tapes were, and by the end of August they completed the banding, sequencing and mixing of the album. It would feature ten songs from the pool of 17 recorded.

For their third album sleeve release, Page searched out the eccentric Zacron, a former student of Kings College of Art whom he had first met in the early sixties. Zacron had produced a variety of artwork including *A Window On London*, a painting with multi-layered collaged panels. Graduating to the Royal Academy, one of his designs experimented in a "volvelle" wheel rotation – the idea he would later develop for the *Led Zeppelin III* sleeve. In early 1970, Page commissioned Zacron to come up with a sleeve for their third album. Then a fine arts lecturer at Leeds University, on January 24 Zacron met with the band at their gig at the venue. In the early spring he spent time at each of the four member's respective homes. He took a series of photos of each of them, eventually selecting four individual images that would make up the back cover black and white group image. "I was careful to get all the images of the band members right," Zacron said years later. "'It was important to set up images which showed them as the giant force they were in music."

The elaborate gatefold design employed a rotating wheel, enabling the purchaser to circle through the various images of the group as they appeared in the relevant holes in the sleeves. This was based on his previous rotating wheel design. Other random images, ranging from off beat photos of Page, Plant, Jones and Bonham to airships, butterflies, and planes, with a predominant connecting theme of flight, adorned the white background of the sleeve. A meeting with Atlantic Records execs to determine the positioning of the then all important Atlantic logo led him to gain freedom for it to be placed where he deemed it most appropriate within the design.

Page and Plant also made sure a statement regarding their trip to the Welsh mountains was added to the sleeve. It said "Credit must be given to Bron-Y-Aur a small derelict cottage in South Snowdonia for painting a somewhat forgotten picture of true completeness which acted as an incentive to some of these musical statements - August 1970."

Page was initially unsure about the finished work. "The sleeve was intended to be something like one of those garden calendars or zoo wheel things that tell you when to plant cauliflowers or how long whales are pregnant," he said at the time. "We ended up on top of a deadline and I think it was a compromise." Deadline or not, the *Led Zeppelin III* cover has gone on to become one of the most iconic album sleeve designs of all time.

Led Zeppelin III was finally released in the US on October 5. It entered the *Billboard* chart at number three and by the end of the month had toppled Santana's *Abraxas* album to take the top spot. In the UK it was released on October 23 - the distinctive circle wheel sleeve qualified it for Atlantic's Deluxe series with an expensive price tag of £4 7/6d. This did little to deter the record buying public of the day and it entered the UK chart at number one.

Atlantic again made provisions for a UK single and 'Immigrant Song' made it onto a UK acetate, but a full release was once again shelved.

In the US and many other territories, 'Immigrant Song' was released as a single, coupled with a leftover from the *Led Zeppelin III* sessions – a semi-acoustic number titled 'Hey Hey What Can I Do'. The track was later featured on the 1972 *New Age Of Atlantic* sampler.

The press reaction to the album was decidedly mixed. *Disc & Music Echo's* headline of "I,II,III - Zep weaken" was typical of the stance taken by many journalists who could not get their head around the fact that Zep had avoided the trap of recreating *Zep II*. An indigent Robert Plant went on record in the following week's *Record Mirror* and under the headline "Plant Slams Zep III Critics" he vehemently defended the album.

"You can just see the headlines, can't you," Robert remarked. "Led Zeppelin go soft on their fans or some crap like that. The point is that when you begin a new album you don't know."

Mixed critical reaction or not, *Led Zeppelin III* was a very strong seller throughout the next six months, but perhaps a combination of its eclectic content and the lack of a massive US hit single prevented it from repeating the sales longevity of their second album either in the UK or US. Not that it bothered the principal players too much. As a creative exercise the album had been a unanimous success.

"There is another side to us" Page said soon after the album's release. "Everyone in the band is going through changes. There are changes in the playing and the lyrics. Robert is really getting involved in his lyric writing. This album was to get across more versatility and use combinations of instruments. I haven't read any reviews yet but people have got to give the LP a reasonable hearing."

In 2011, Plant drew a parallel between his eclectic *Band Of Joy* album and the mood captured on *Led Zeppelin III*. "I think of the *Led Zeppelin III* era. There was a dynamic about the *Zeppelin III* period where we could go from reflective acoustic stuff to some heavy shit... 'Hats Off To Harper', 'Gallows Pole'... I'm not interested in doing late-middle-age cabaret. I want it heavy and spooky. There should be some mystery, big and deep, that makes people's skin tingle."

The affinity for the third Led Zeppelin record is undoubtedly a lasting one. It's an album that has had a massive impact on both artist and listeners alike. It was a crucial turning point that would lead them to even greater success. Four decades on, *Led Zeppelin III* can rightly take its place as one of the landmark albums of the era.

While never attaining the sales success of *Led Zeppelin II* or the critical acclaim of *Led Zeppelin IV*, it remains one of their most important works. It was the album that proved that Led Zeppelin could encompass many different styles within their rock mode foundations.

IMMIGRANT SONG

Page, Plant
Studios: Headley Grange,
Hampshire; Island and Olympic, London;
Ardent, Memphis

Built around an incessant Page/Jones/Bonham battering riff, this Plant tale of Viking lust is a compulsive attack on the senses as well as a call to arms. In addition to containing some of Plant's most memorable lines, it also boasts a wailing war-cry destined to delight rabid audiences across the world. Plant's war cry refrain is reminiscent of 'Bali Hai' from the Rodgers & Hammerstein musical *South Pacific*.

The basis of this track was already recorded before their trip to play in Iceland on June 22, 1970. It was this vacation that inspired Robert to construct a new set of lyrics full of Icelandic imagery. As he put it in a 1970 radio interview: "We went to Iceland, and it made you think of Vikings and big ships... and John Bonham's stomach... and bang, there it was - 'Immigrant Song'!"
The count in at the start, by the way, is coupled with echo tape feedback - hence the hiss. In America, 'Immigrant Song' was lifted as a single and after a 13-week chart run peaked at 16.

In 2003, the Led Zeppelin official DVD featured a stunning visual and aural combination of this track sourced from the 1972 Sydney Showground cine film and the audio track from their 1972 Long Beach show. A stark reminder of the sheer power of this composition.

In 2011, a cover version of the track by Nine Inch Nails' Trent Reznor and Yeah Yeah Yeahs singer Karen O was used on the soundtrack of the film *Girl With the Dragon Tattoo*.

Live performances: 'Immigrant Song' was premièred to UK audiences at the opening of Led Zeppelin's 1970 Bath Festival appearance. This version features varying verses and alternate lyrics to the later studio issue. The live arrangement included an extended guitar solo. It was the set opener of every show played from Bath 1970 up to the 1972 US tour. For the Japan, UK and Europe 1972 dates it emerged as part of the encore though it was only performed once post 1972 at their Bradford show on January 18, 1973. It was then deleted from the set. One odd live improvisation occurred on August 22, 1971, at the LA Forum when 'Immigrant Song' opened the set and Page prefaced the intro with a few bars of The Ventures' 'Walk Don't Run'. Robert Plant was to revive the song in an amended arrangement on his solo tours of 1988/1990. It was also used as a riff intro to 'Wanton Song' by Page & Plant on their 1995/96 world tour. This was a number allegedly rehearsed for their 02 performance but did not make the final set list.

FRIENDS

Page, Plant
Studios: Olympic, London; Ardent,
Memphis

A few seconds of studio chat precedes this hypnotic, swirling mass of sound.
Careful analysis of this has revealed that the dialogue includes several four letter words and a conversation between Plant, Page and engineer Richard Digby Smith in which reference is made to the wiping of the intro of 'Celebration Day' (see next track info).

It's surprising that John Paul Jones has no composing credit here, as he is wholly responsible for the track's compelling string arrangement. There's a Moog synthesiser added on the outro which provides a link to the next track. With its repeated acoustic guitar motifs and bongo percussion, this bizarre outing was unlike anything else they attempted. In his photographic autobiography published in 2010, Jimmy Page revealed that he wrote this number on the balcony of his Pangbourne boathouse home. He used a Harmony Sovereign H-1260 acoustic on the track in an open C-tuning.

Page used an Altair Tube Limiter to enhance the acoustic quality of his Harmony guitar, a device recommended by Dick Rosemenie, an acoustic guitarist who recorded an album entitled *Six String, Twelve String and*

Vanguard. The same device was used on 'All My Love' on the *In Through The Out Door* album.

'Friends' employed another odd tuning. Jimmy revealed how it was tuned as follows: "Top E is E, B is a C, G is a G, D is a C, A remains the same, and the low E goes down to C. We also did that on 'Bron-Yr-Aur' and 'Poor Tom'."

Live performances: The only documented live performance of 'Friends' is a version played at the September 29 appearance in Osaka on the 1971 Japanese tour. This was also, along with 'Four Sticks', one of the experimental songs Jimmy and Robert recorded with the Bombay Orchestra in March 1972. It was, however, extensively performed by Page & Plant on their 1995/6 world tour and performed at the *MTV Unledded* London filming in 1994.

CELEBRATION DAY
Page, Plant, Jones
Studios: Headley Grange,
Hampshire; Island and Olympic, London;
Ardent, Memphis
A track that nearly didn't appear at all. Due to a studio oversight, the intro of this track was crinkled on the master tape, making it impossible to thread, but by segueing the swirling link from 'Friends' into the guitar riff and Plant's opening lyrics, the song was salvaged. As Page explained: "I was very good at salvaging things that went wrong; for example, the rhythm track in the beginning of 'Celebration Day' was completely wiped by an engineer. I forget what we were recording, but I was listening through the headphones and nothing was coming through. I started yelling 'What the hell is going on!' Then I noticed that the red recording light was on what used to be the drums. The engineer had accidentally recorded over Bonzo! And that is why you have that synthesizer drone from the end of 'Friends' going into 'Celebration Day', until the rhythm track catches up. We put that on to compensate for the missing drum track. That's called salvaging."

'Celebration Day' is an excellent vehicle for a succession of Page's guitar effects, while lyrically Plant takes the listener on an inspiring tour of New York.

Live performances: 'Celebration Day' came into the set as part of a medley with 'Communication Breakdown' at the KB Hallen date in Copenhagen in the spring of 1971, was then used on the late summer tour of America in 1971, and stayed for the Japanese, UK and Australian tours of late 1971 and early 1972. It was revived for the 1973 US dates and then again for the Copenhagen and Knebworth gigs in 1979. Page & Plant revived it for their 1995/6 and 1998 world tours, and Jimmy performed it with The Black Crowes on their 1999 and 2000 US tour dates. Plant also performed the song with the Strange Sensation on his 2002 tour.

SINCE I'VE BEEN LOVING YOU
Page, Plant
Studios: Island & Olympic, London; Ardent, Memphis
One of the first songs prepared for *Led Zeppelin III*, this was previewed as early as the January tour of the UK in 1970. A self-styled custom blues, though Robert Plant clearly derived some of the lyrics from the Moby Grape track 'Never' which appeared on the *Grape Jam* bonus disc that came with their 1968 *Wow* album. It contains one of Page's best ever solos – listen carefully and you can hear John Bonham's drum pedal squeaking throughout. There is also a subliminal piece of audio – at around one minute 15 just as Robert sings "Working from seven" there is a sound that appears to be a slight groan and it hides Robert singing the next line "I've gone".

Live performances: Entered the set in early 1970 and retained throughout their 1970/71 dates. From the Japan tour in 1972 up to the 1973 American dates, it formed the second half of a medley with 'Misty Mountain Hop'. It came back into the set in its own right for the latter part of the

1975 US tour, and reappeared for the 1977 US tour, Copenhagen/Knebworth 1979, and the European 1980 tour. On Plant's solo tours part of the track was performed during 'Slow Dancer'. It was also performed in a version at the Hammersmith Odeon in 1988 with Page guesting. Page & Plant revived it at their *MTV Unledded* London filming in 1994 and for their 1995/96 world tour. Finally, it was performed at the 02 reunion concert in December 2007.

OUT ON THE TILES
Page, Plant, Bonham
Studios: Headley Grange, Hampshire; Olympic, London; Ardent, Memphis
After Page's domination of the first two albums, the more leisurely paced recording of *Led Zeppelin III* allowed for a more democratic pool of ideas. This track came out of a Bonham-inspired riff and is a much underrated part of their output. With an infectious chorus and enthusiastic Plant vocal, it bubbles along with an unnerving energy. The title relates to a previously written set of lyrics that were revamped for this version. The spacey sound mix evident here is another example of distance miking in the studio by Page. An early master tape box of the album lists it under the title 'Bathroom Song'.

Live performances: This track was only ever played live on the sixth US tour of September 1970, notably at shows at the Inglewood Forum, Los Angeles, and Madison Square Garden in New York. However, the opening riff was later applied to the live arrangement of 'Black Dog'. Then on the 1977 US tour the riff structure of 'Out On The Tiles' replaced 'Moby Dick' as the lead intro to Bonham's drum solo which was retitled by Plant as 'Over The Top'. The riff was also used to open Black Dog on Page & Plant's 1995/96 and 1998 world tours. It was performed by Page with the Black Crowes on their 1999 and 2000 US tour dates.

GALLOWS POLE
Traditional: arranged by Page and Plant
Studios: Headley Grange, Hampshire; Olympic, London; Ardent, Memphis
The traditional blues tale 'Gallows Pole', which opened side two was discovered by Page on an album titled *12 String Guitar* released in 1962 by American acoustic performer Fred Gerlach. The track was originally recorded as 'Gallis Pole' in 1939 by iconic bluesman Leadbelly. Other recordings include a version by mid-sixties jazz and blues singer Odetta who recorded it under the title 'Gallows Tree'. It can be found on her album *At The Gate Of Horn*. It was also covered under the title 'Hangman' by African American singer Dorris Henderson who performed on the UK folk circuit in the mid-sixties. Henderson collaborated with another acclaimed folk guitarist John Renbourn and it appeared on the B-side of her 1965 debut single, a cover of Paul Simon's 'The Leaves That Are Green'.

Instrumentally, it has Page on banjo, six and 12-string acoustic guitars and electric guitar. John Paul Jones is on mandolin and bass. While Plant unfolds a tale of medieval woe, the tension builds beautifully as Bonzo wades in, and Page adds an understated but frenzied Gibson run. One of their most adventurous outings and quite brilliant in its execution - lyrically and musically.
The version that featured on a rare advance promo single issued in the US by Atlantic has a slightly longer guitar fade out.

Live performances: Scarcely ever performed live by Zep, the only known performances were a one-minute extract played at the evening show at Madison Square Garden on September 19, 1970.The only other confirmed performances of the song are from May 3, 1971 Copenhagen, May 10, 1971 Liverpool and November 16, 1971, at Ipswich. Robert sometimes threw in some lines of this during 'Trampled Underfoot', remarking on its performance on the last night of the 1975 US tour in LA as being 'Trampled Under Gallows'. It was revived by

Page & Plant at their *MTV Unledded* London filming in 1994 and on their 1995/6 and 1998 world tours. It was also performed by Plant on his 2003 tour with Strange Sensation and on his *Band Of Joy* tour in 2010/11.

TANGERINE
Page
Studios: Headley Grange, Hampshire; Olympic, London; Ardent, Memphis

Jimmy provides an eight-second count-in to a mellow solo composition left over from his Yardbirds era. The melody of the tune derives from The Yardbirds track 'Knowing That I'm Losing You' which was recorded at their final recording sessions at Columbia Studios, New York in April 1968 and remains officially unreleased. Lyrically, this may have been a love song related to Page's dalliance with sixties songstress Jackie De Shannon. Page used a Giannini GWSCRA12 P Craviola acoustic for the Zep studio recording. Robert duets with himself on a double-tracked vocal, and Page layers on some tasteful pedal steel guitar.

Live performances: It joined the acoustic set on the Japanese dates in September 1971 and remained in the set on all tours up to the US dates in the summer of 1972. It was revived as a four-part harmony rendition for the Earls Court season in 1975, for which Jimmy pulled out the Gibson double-neck. Page & Plant revived it on their 1995/6 and 1998 world tours. Plant also performed it on his *Band Of Joy* 2010/11 tour, notably at the BBC Radio 2 Pop Proms concert at the Roundhouse in October 2010.

THAT'S THE WAY
Page, Plant
Studios: Headley Grange, Hampshire; Olympic, London; Ardent, Memphis

One of their very best performances and arguably Robert's best ever lyric, 'That's The Way' carried the working title of 'The Boy Next Door'. It was written at the cottage in Bron-Yr-Aur, and centres around the dissolution of a pair of star-crossed lovers. The lyrics were also influenced in part by the unrest Robert witnessed on their early 1970 US travels. The tale unfolds against a rush of acoustic guitars, and a moving horn-like electric solo from Jimmy. This was a direct product of the trip to Wales, as recalled by Page: "It was one of those days after a long walk and we were setting back to the cottage. We had a guitar with us and coming down the ravine we stopped and sat down. I played the tune and Robert sang a verse straight off. We had a tape recorder with us and got the tune down." In a recent interview in *Guitar World*, Page revealed that in the studio he overdubbed a dulcimer on the end of the track and also added bass parts.

Live performances: The band premièred it at the 1970 Bath festival, and it was a standard feature of the acoustic set during 1970/71 and up to the American tour in 1972. It was recalled for the Earls Court season in 1975. Page & Plant revived it at their *MTV Unledded* London filming and on their 1995/96 world tour. John Paul Jones performed and sung it on his 2001 tour dates.

BRON-Y-AUR STOMP
Page, Plant, Jones
Studios: Headley Grange, Hampshire; Olympic, London; Ardent, Memphis

A playful, folksy singalong, this was written at the cottage about Plant's dog Strider. Page gets in some fine picking, Bonzo adds spoons and castanets, and Jones plays an acoustic bass. The tune itself was initially written as a chord sequence on acoustic guitar termed 'Bar III'. It was also tried in an electric rockier arrangement at the commencement of the third album sessions in December 1969, when it was known as 'Jennings Farm Blues'.

Live performances: It was performed in the acoustic set from the UK dates in spring 1971 through to the American tour in 1972. A revamped arrangement with Jones on stand-up bass was used for the

Japan/UK/Europe 1972/73 dates. It was recalled in this format for Earls Court in 1975, and then as a medley with 'Black Country Woman' on the 1977 US tour.

HATS OFF TO (ROY) HARPER

Traditional; arranged by Charles Obscure

Studios: Headley Grange, Hampshire; Olympic, London; Ardent, Memphis

A Page/Plant studio jam, loosely based on Bukka White's old blues tune 'Shake 'Em On Down' with Page on authentic bottleneck guitar. The title is, of course, an acknowledgement of their admiration for the Manchester born singer-songwriter. Page and Plant first met Harper at the Bath festival in 1970 and became longstanding admirers.

Page would later record an album, *Whatever Happened To Jugula,* with Harper, issued in 1985. In 2011, Page reunited with Harper for his 70th birthday celebration concert at London's Royal Festival Hall.

The track was billed as a traditional tune and arranged by Charles Obscure - another inside joke. This originated from a lengthier studio jam that also incorporated Bukka White's 'Fixin' To Die' and Arthur 'Big Boy' Crudup's 'That's All Right' which has surfaced under the title 'Blues Medley' on various bootlegs.

Live performances: None.

LED ZEPPELIN IV

Atlantic Records - original issue 2401 01 2, November 12 1971 reissued as K 50008
UK Album Chart: No 1; US: No 2
Sales figures approx. and counting:
UK 1,800,000 - 6x Platinum;
US 32,000,000 - 32x Platinum

For a record that began life after the band had endured something of a crisis of confidence, Led Zeppelin's fourth album has done pretty well for itself. Worldwide sales to date rack up at 32 million and counting. In the US alone it has been confirmed as 32 times platinum, making it the third best selling album of all time in the US behind Michael Jackson's *Thriller* and The Eagles *Their Greatest Hits 1971 -1975* . These colossal sales figures vividly illustrate the fact that *Led Zeppelin IV* is the most accessible album of their catalogue and it continues to attract new listeners by the week. Few albums in the history of rock can rival its influence. The fact that much of the album was made in a mysterious, run-down 18th century workhouse in the middle of rural Hampshire only adds to its legendary status.

Back in December 1971, Led Zeppelin's fourth album was riding high on both the UK and US charts. Forty years on, along with other classic perennials such as *The Dark Side Of The Moon, Bat Out of Hell* and *Rumours,* it continues to occupy a special place as the people's Led Zeppelin album. By virtue of the inclusion of 'Stairway To Heaven', it's also the Zep album that has introduced a multitude of listeners to the delights of the band. New listeners picking up on *Led Zeppelin IV* were more often than not led to the path of the entire Zep catalogue – in this way the album has been the catalyst for the discovery of their music for many fans.

Surprisingly, given its sales longevity, *Led Zeppelin IV'* s origins can be traced to a time of uncertainty as to their standing in the rock landscape. To paraphrase a line from that much maligned song - there was still time to change the road they were on.

The story begins on the evening of Saturday September 19, 1970. The four members of Led Zeppelin had just taken a final bow before leaving the stage of New York's Madison Square Garden. It was the day after news of Jimi Hendrix's death had broken, a tragedy Plant had mentioned on stage. They had performed afternoon and evening performances at the prestigious venue – the final dates of a massively successful sixth American tour. These two shows alone had netted each of the four members $30,000 - not bad for six hours work. Their second album had been a fixture on the album charts on both sides of the Atlantic for nigh on a year, racking up sales of over a million in both territories. The previous June, the group's bill-topping appearance at the Bath Festival had cemented their reputation on home soil. Readers of the then hugely influential *Melody Maker* had just voted them as the top act in their annual pop poll, ending years of dominance by The Beatles.

There was little doubt that Led Zeppelin were now the biggest band in the world.

Then came the backlash...

In early October their eagerly awaited new album, *Led Zeppelin III*, was released on an unsuspecting public. Its bold agenda of combining the familiar, trademark heavy rock dynamics with more acoustic textures confused both the public and press alike.

Led Zeppelin III sold well initially, but it didn't have the across-the-board appeal of their first two albums. Never entirely at ease with the press, Page and Plant were particularly sensitive to the criticism. For Page, the third Zeppelin album signalled the beginning of a new era. "There is another side to us. This album is totally different to the others and I see this as a new direction."

Plant again: "Now we've done *Led Zeppelin III* - the sky's the limit. It shows we can change, we can do things. It means there are endless possibilities. We are not stale and this proves it."

Brave fighting talk - but quite how their following would react long-term to this new direction was at the time still in question. After the initial glow of success, they were at somewhat of a crossroads and their next album would prove crucial. Page later reflected: "With *Led Zeppelin III* we thought we'd made a great album - in fact we knew we had. At the time, though, it was said we had started playing acoustic instruments because Crosby, Stills & Nash had just come through and we were ripping them off. I know the record company expected us to follow up 'Whole Lotta Love'. But we never made a point of trying to emulate something we had done before."

Sensibly, they took their time in recording their fourth album. To recharge their batteries, manager Peter Grant refused all offers to tour over the coming months. This included turning down flat a cool one million dollars to appear on a New Year's Eve concert to be relayed across the world via satellite. Years later, Peter Grant noted: "I got approached for the band to perform a show in Germany on New Year's Eve 1970 that would be relayed to American cinemas. The offer got up to a million dollars, but I found out that satellite sound can be affected by snowstorms so I said no. The promoters couldn't believe it, but it just wasn't right for us."

In late October, Page and Plant returned to the idyllic cottage halfway up a mountain in South Snowdonia known as Bron-Yr-Aur. It was here that earlier in the year they had conceived many of the songs for *Led Zeppelin III*. This return visit again found them ensconced around the open fire with acoustic guitars in hand preparing material for the next record.

They already had a backlog of completed and work-in-progress ideas, amongst them a lilting, Neil Young-influenced tune titled 'Down By The Seaside'; a semi-acoustic country stomp called 'Poor Tom'; and an acoustic idea with idealistic lyrics waiting to be honed ('The Rover'). John Paul Jones had also been working on a brooding keyboard piece that would later emerge as 'No Quarter', while Page had begun demoing a lengthy instrumental track which started off tranquil but built to a crescendo.

Initially they considered a double album, and Page even toyed with the offbeat idea of issuing the album as four separate EPs.

In December they booked initial studio sessions at Island Studios. The Basing Street location was fast becoming the most in-demand studio in London and they had recorded much of *Led Zeppelin III* there the previous May. Jethro Tull were recording their *Aqualung* album at Island around the same time. Page, though, was also looking to record on location with The Rolling Stones' newly built mobile recording unit. Page noted: "We started off doing some tracks at Island then we went to Headley Grange, a place we had rehearsed at. We took The Stones' mobile. It was ideal. As soon as we had an idea we put it down on tape."

Plant reflected: "Most of the mood for the fourth album was brought about in settings we had not been used to. We were living in this falling down mansion in the country. The mood was incredible."

So on a cold January morning early in 1971, accompanied by a handful of roadies plus engineer Andy Johns (brother of noted producer Glyn Johns who had worked on the first Zeppelin album), Page, Plant, Jones and Bonham convened on the old workhouse to set up and record material for their fourth album. Parked outside was the Stones' mobile studio looking not unlike some vintage army intelligence unit. There exists cine footage taken by John Bonham of the band at Headley Grange. It centres mainly on panning around the outer buildings and grounds with Page and Plant on the lawn, Plant wearing a sky blue West Ham United away soccer shirt. He can be seen in the same shirt on one of their rare excursions away from the sessions – a date at the *Disc & Music Echo* Music awards in early February where they received the Best Group award.

Engineer Andy Johns recalled the idea behind going to Headley Grange in an interview with *Guitar World*: "I had just done *Sticky Fingers* with the Stones and we'd used the mobile truck on that. So I believe I suggested using the truck to Jimmy. We had used Mick's house at Stargroves, but Jimmy didn't want to stay there because Mick wanted too much money. Then Jimmy found this old mansion so we brought the truck there." They did eventually record at Stargroves the following year for the *Houses Of The Holy* album.

John Paul Jones has less positive memories of their stay at the Grange. "It was cold and damp. I remember we all ran in when we arrived in a mad scramble to get the driest rooms. There was no pool table or pub. It was so dull, but that really focused your mind on getting the work done."

With the album sessions completed by early February, Page took Andy John's advice and flew with Peter Grant and Johns to Sunset Studios in Los Angeles to mix the tracks. Just as they were flying into LA, the city suffered a minor earthquake, as Page recalled: "The funny thing is that on 'Going To California' you've got the line 'mountains and the canyon's started to tremble and shake' and curiously, as we landed, there was a mild earthquake. In the hotel room before going to the studio you could feel the bed shake."

Unfortunately, the mixdown did not go as planned, much to Andy John's embarrassment. "I convinced Jimmy to mix it in Los Angeles. We booked time at Sunset Sound, but the room that I'd worked in before had been completely changed. So we used another room there and mixed the entire album. We came back to London and played it back at Studio One at Olympic. Anyway, we put it on and it sounded terrible. I thought my number was up - but the others seemed to look to Jimmy, even though it was just as much my fault. So it had to be remixed again and that was difficult."

Despite all these problems, the resulting production was one of Page's finest. Rarely again did he so precisely capture the four strands of the group on record so clearly. It's a testament perhaps to how this relaxed style of recording, away from the distractions of the city, suited them. Looking back, it may well have been a wise move to have invested in their own mobile recording unit.

They had hoped to have the album out by late April 1971, but that was to prove impossible given that they had lined up a series of UK and European dates in the spring. Page and Johns mixed most of it again between their spring UK and European tour dates at Olympic Studios. The only mix from the Los Angeles trip that was deemed fit for eventual release was 'When The Levee Breaks.' The album finally went off to be cut at Trident Studios in London with more lacquers cut at The Beatles' Apple Studios in the mid-summer of 1971.

By that time they had already began previewing numbers from the album in their new stage set. The first airing of new material occurred on Friday, March 5 at Belfast's Ulster Hall, when 'Black Dog', 'Going To California', 'Stairway To Heaven' and 'Rock And Roll' were all played live for the first time. For the live performance of 'Stairway', Page had acquired a custom-built Gibson ES1275 double-neck guitar to play the six and 12-string passages the song requires. He had seen blues man Earl Hooker using such a guitar in the early sixties, Charlie Whitney of the group Family was another advocator of the Gibson double neck model.

The so called 'Back to the clubs' UK tour saw them return to venues such as London's Marquee where they had established their reputation in the early days. UK listeners to Radio One's John Peel *In Concert* programme were also privy to an exclusive airing of this new material. On Sunday 4 April Radio One aired a one-hour live show edited down from a full performance recorded three days earlier at the Paris Cinema in London. 'Going To California' and 'Stairway To Heaven' were the new numbers aired ('Black Dog' was also performed but not aired). For 'Stairway' this would be airplay number one - with another four million to follow during the next four decades.

In Europe a month later they previewed more songs from the fourth album. At an extraordinary gig at the KB Hallen in Copenhagen on May 3,'Black Dog', 'Going To California', 'Stairway To Heaven' and 'Rock And Roll' were joined by the only known live performance of 'Four Sticks' ("Well try something we've never done before... there's every chance that we will fall apart," Plant warned the audience) and a premiere of 'Misty Mountain Hop'.

With the album fully mixed and completed, and having survived a riot at a curtailed show in Milan early in July, their attention turned to the design of the album cover. Despite some reticence from Atlantic Records, the new album boasted a distinctive gatefold sleeve that had no mention of their name. When it came to a title for the album, Jimmy Page confounded the record label and the media by devising an idea that led to the unpronounceable series of symbols that would form the enigmatic title.

Page had set something of a precedent with the distinctive sleeve designs of their first three albums. Alongside Pink Floyd and Roger Dean's work with Yes, Zeppelin was established as the forerunners of imaginative album artwork. When it came to *Led Zeppelin IV* they did not disappoint; however, they faced heavy opposition with Atlantic Records over their insistence that their name should not appear anywhere on the sleeve. Robert Plant noted at the time: "There was a lot of opposition from Atlantic about it being untitled and we wanted a cover with no writing on it and the hierarchy of the record business is not into the fact that covers are important. So we said they couldn't have the master tape until they got the cover right."

The actual photo used for the cover was said by Page to have been discovered by Plant when they visited an antique shop in Reading. Describing it, Page said: "The old man on the cover carrying wood is in harmony with nature. He takes from nature. It's a natural cycle." The high rise flats that can be seen on the back cover were situated at Eve Hill in Dudley and were demolished in 1999. The striking inside cover illustration was based on The Hermit character tarot card as drawn by 19th century illustrator Pamela Colman Smith. A symbol of self-reliance and wisdom, it was drawn by Barrington Colby, a friend of Page and entitled *View In Half Or Varying Light*. Page later based his *The Song Remains The Same* movie fantasy sequence on this same image. He also came up with the typeface for the lyrics of 'Stairway To Heaven' which appeared on the inner sleeve. The cover was coordinated by Graphreaks. Atlantic in the US did get around the wordless album image by initially shrink wrapping the album with a sticker that carried the symbols and track listing. Zep's customary iron control could not prevent a bizarre version of the sleeve surfacing on a Russian pressing in the nineties that replaced the stick carrying old man with a contended Russian worker smoking a pipe.

Jimmy Page was also the instigator behind the enigma over the album's actual title. "After all this crap with the critics, I put it to everybody else that it would be a good idea to put something out that was totally anonymous," he explained later. "At first I wanted just one symbol but since it was our fourth album and there were four of us, we each chose our own. I designed mine and everybody else had their own reasons for using the symbol selected." Page's curious Zoso emblem has remained a vivid image ever since, as instantly recognisable to Zeppelin and rock fans in general fans as the Coca-Cola or Nike logos are in the world at large. On the album's inner sleeve, Sandy Denny, who duets with Plant on 'The Battle Of Evermore', is represented by an additional symbol of three pyramids.

The deployment of four symbols as the title for *Led Zeppelin IV* only added to their overall mystique and the saga of what they represent (if anything) still rages today on Zep internet forums and message boards. The four symbols were first introduced to the rock media via a series of teaser press adverts placed in the music papers in the weeks leading up to the album's release - each depicting a particular symbol alongside a sleeve of a previous Zep album.

The symbols for John Paul Jones and John Bonham were selected from Rudolph Koch's *The Book of Signs.* Jones's symbol - a single intersecting circle said to symbolize a person who possesses both confidence and competence – is difficult to draw accurately. John Bonham's three interlocking rings is said to represent the triad of mother, father and child. It was also, somewhat appropriately, given the late drummers penchant for alcoholic beverages, the logo for Ballantine beer.

Robert Plant's symbol was his own design, though it can also be traced to a book titled *The Sacred Symbols Of Mu* by Colonel James Churchward. The feather in the circle represents the feather of Ma'at the Egyptian goddess of justice and fairness and is the emblem of a writer. "The feather is a symbol on which all sorts of philosophies have been based," noted Plant. "For instance, it represents Red Indian tribes."

Jimmy also designed his own symbol. Often referred to as 'Zoso', there have been

various theories put forward surrounding its origin. Some point to it being used as early as 1557 in representing Saturn. It's also been noted that it is made up of astrological symbols for Saturn, Jupiter and perhaps Mars or Mercury. The symbol also appeared in almost identical form in a rare 19th century dictionary of symbols titled Le Triple Vocabulaire Infernal Manuel du Demonomane, by Frinellan (a pseudonym for Simon Blocquel), published by Lille, Blocquel-Castiaux in 1844. "My symbol was about invoking and being invocative," Page told journalist Mick Wall in 2001, adding "That's all I'm going to say about it."

These four distinctive symbols first unveiled over 40 years ago for *Led Zeppelin IV* are now synonymous with the band. As well as adorning many a T-shirt and poster design, they were incorporated into their *Remasters* and *Mothership* compilation artwork. The symbols have also lingered large within the presentation of the three surviving members: Page and Plant used their linked symbols as the logo for their 1995/6 tour, Jones incorporated his into the artwork of his 1999 *Zooma* solo album and Plant used the feather in a circle on the back cover sleeve of his *Band Of Joy* album. Page also employed his distinctive Zoso symbol for his link up with The Black Crowes in 1999 and as the sole imagery on the front cover of his recent Genesis Publications *Jimmy Page By Jimmy Page* book.

When the album was released, the wordless title caused much confusion. It appeared in the press under various names including *The New Led Zeppelin Album, Led Zeppelin IV, Four Symbols, Runes* and even *Zoso* - though some music papers did make the effort to reproduce the actual symbols themselves. Music trade papers used the symbols on their chart pages.

The band's hectic schedule that year continued unabated. In August they were back in America for their seventh US tour. Page was in buoyant mood and playing brilliantly. "Once the album was completed and mixed I knew it was really good," he said. "We actually went on the road in America before the manufacturing process was completed and somebody at Atlantic Records said, 'This is professional suicide for a band to tour without an album.' In retrospect that is rather amusing!"

The new material was already making an impact, and Page still recalls with pride the reaction they got to 'Stairway' when they performed it at the Los Angeles Forum for the first time. "We played 'Stairway' at the Forum before the album was out and around a third of the audience stood up and gave us a standing ovation. It was then that I thought, 'Actually this may be a better number than I'd imagined'."

Equally successful was a three-city, five-concert first visit to Japan. Here they performed some of the most enjoyable concerts of their career - away from the glare of the press and the intensity of America, they were able to stretch out and extend their set list, throwing in off-the-cuff versions of 'Smoke Gets In Your Eyes', Cliff Richards' 'Bachelor Boy', The Beatles' 'Please Please Me', and the only logged live performance of *Zep III's* 'Friends'. It's fair to say there were now two distinct entities to the group - the tight recorded unit as found on record and the improvisational and spontaneous live act that would go on to delight audiences around the globe.

After a short break, to round off a very productive year, Peter Grant booked a 16-date UK tour that nicely coincided with the eventual release of their long delayed, long awaited fourth album. It kicked off in Newcastle on November 11 and took in two memorable nights at London's Wembley Empire Pool.

Despite the delays and the negative reaction to the previous album, it was clear that the band's popularity had not declined at all. Demand for tickets was overwhelming. All 9,000 seats for their November 20 Empire Pool show sold out in under an hour. A

second was added and they could have easily slotted in a third had their schedule allowed it.

Their stage presentation now featured each of their four symbols - on Bonham's bass drum, Jonesy's organ, Jimmy's speaker cabinets, and Plant's feather symbol adorned the PA. Page also took to wearing a specially knitted jumper depicting his Zoso symbol. The set list now included 'Rock And Roll' in the main set (now under its correct title), alongside 'Black Dog', 'Stairway' and 'Going To California'.

Talking about the album to Chris Welch of *Melody Maker,* Bonzo was hugely enthusiastic: "My personal view is that it's the best thing we've ever done. I love it. It's the stage we were in at the time of the recording. The playing is some of the best we have done and Jimmy is like... mint!"

The culmination of the whole year's efforts were the two significant five-hour extravaganzas in London's Empire Pool on November 20 & 21 – the largest indoor UK audiences they had played to at that point.

After the disappointing press reaction to their third album, *Led Zeppelin IV* was very well received. Even *Rolling Stone,* never a great supporter of the band's work, relented. The review by Lenny Kaye, who would go on to become Patti Smith's guitarist, was surprisingly positive. "Out of eight cuts," wrote Kaye, "there isn't one that steps on another's toes, that tries to do too much at once. And [there are] a couple of songs that when all is said and done, will probably be right up there in the gold-starred hierarchy of put 'em on and play 'em again." Describing one of those tracks, 'When The Levee Breaks', Kaye added "Led Zep have had a lot of imitators over the past few years, but it takes cuts like this to show that most of them have only picked up the style, lacking any real knowledge of the meat underneath."

Led Zeppelin IV climbed to the number one spot on the UK chart on December 4,

1971, where it stayed for two weeks before being dislodged by T Rex's *Electric Warrior*. It went on to spend 61 consecutive weeks on the chart.

It was a similar story in America, though it was with some irony that Carole King's multi-million selling soft rock album *Tapestry* kept it from reaching number one.

Not that it really mattered - the airplay generated by 'Stairway To Heaven' ensured the album remained in the *Billboard* top 40 album chart for the next six months. Peter Grant steadfastly refused to issue the track as a single, knowing that restricting its availability to the LP alone would inevitably add to its sales.

From the adversity of the *Led Zeppelin III* backlash, Zeppelin triumphed. As a complete work, *Led Zeppelin IV* remains their most focused statement.

It's the product of a band on a quest for absolute musical freedom. Their ability to blend acoustic and electric influences within a rock framework is something Led Zeppelin did more successfully than any other act before or since. The eight cuts possess an economy and subtly that defines their sound. From Page's unimpeachable riffs, through Jones' musical invention, Plant's clarity of vocal to that titanic John Bonham drum sound - *Led Zeppelin IV* still emits a freshness that belies its age.

BLACK DOG
Page, Plant, Jones
Studios: Headley Grange,
Hampshire, with The Rolling Stones' Mobile;
Island, London
If *Led Zeppelin III* had created doubts in some corners as to their ability to still flex the power displayed on the first two albums, here was the perfect antidote. The moment Page warms up the Gibsons, this is one of the most instantly recognisable Zepp tracks.

The initial idea for the riff came from John Paul Jones after he had been listening to

Muddy Waters 1968 album *'Electric Mud'*. "I recall Page and I listening to Electric Mud by Muddy Waters. One of the tracks, 'Tom Cat', is a long rambling riff and I really liked the idea of writing something like that - a riff that would be a linear journey."

The almost impossible-to-copy rhythmic swing of the track (4/4 time set against 5/4) was a key indication of how far ahead of the rock game Zep were at the time. Bands such as Grand Funk Railroad were touted as being successors to Zep's heavyweight crown, but their riffing was devoid of the grace and timing of 'Black Dog'. Using Plant's a cappella call and response vocal technique between the riffs was an arrangement Page had picked up from Fleetwood Mac's 1969 hit 'Oh Well' (in 1999 Page performed 'Oh Well' on tour with The Black Crowes). The closing solo is constructed out of four overdubbed Les Paul fills. Page's fade out solo was a cleverly overdubbed and triple-tracked guitar pieced together by four different solos.

'Black Dog' takes its title from a black Labrador that hung around at the Grange.

Live performances: 'Black Dog' joined the set on the UK tour at Belfast's Ulster Hall on March 5, 1971. It was retained for each subsequent tour up to the 1973 US tour and was used as an encore medley with 'Whole Lotta Love' on the 1975 US tour and Earls Court. The track was only played twice in 1977 – both times as encores (on June 13 in New York and July 23 in Oakland). It returned with a vengeance for their 1979 Copenhagen/Knebworth dates and 1980 European tour (complete with rare spoken intro from Jimmy). Page & Plant revived it on their 1995/96 and 1998 world tours, and it was performed by Page with David Coverdale on their Japanese tour in 1993. Page & Plant performed a radical reworking of the song for the 1995 American Music Awards show and on the Andrew Denton TV show in Australia in 1994. John Paul Jones performed an instrumental of the song on his 1999/2001 tour dates. It was still a regular part of Plant's live shows with The Band Of Joy, albeit in a radically reworked arrangement. The song was also performed at the 02 reunion – the filmed video clip of which was officially sanctioned for screening on TV news programmes at the time.

ROCK AND ROLL
Page, Plant, Jones, Bonham
Studios: Headley Grange,
Hampshire with The Rolling Stones' Mobile;
Island, London
Another instantly identifiable Zeppelin anthem. This track came out of a jam with Rolling Stones' mentor Ian Stewart on piano. They had been trying out 'Four Sticks' when Bonzo played the intro of Little Richard's 'Good Golly Miss Molly'/'Keep A Knockin', and Page added a riff. Fifteen minutes later, the nucleus of 'Rock And Roll' was down on tape - displaying the full benefit of recording on location with the tapes ever running.

The jam session nature of the song's construction resulted in it being credited as a four man group composition, and when they played the track live during their UK, European and US dates later that year, Plant introduced it under the title 'It's Been A Long Time'. When it came to deciding the final track line-up for the album, they agreed this three-minute and 40 seconds of stomping rock'n'roll should be titled just that. So it became universally known as 'Rock And Roll' and it would go on to be a Zep concert favourite, taking its rightful place as an appropriate set opener from late 1972 through to 1975.   Much played in the post-Zep era – it was still a regular part of Plant's *Band Of Joy* set this year – it's also been subject of several cover versions, including a charity single performed by Full Metal Rackets featuring John McEnroe and Pat Cash. In 2002, they allowed the track to be used by General Motors for a series of US TV commercials for their Cadillac automobiles.

Live performances: A lasting part of their history, 'Rock And Roll' came in as an encore on the spring 1971 dates when it was referred to by Plant as 'It's Been A Long

Time'. It was inserted on a few dates of the 1971 US, Japanese and UK dates. When they revamped the set in late 1972 for the Japan and UK dates it was elevated to the opening number, probably because its first line - "It's been a long time since I rock and rolled" - was highly appropriate for a show opener. It retained this status on every show up to the Earls Court season in 1975. It became a medley encore with 'Whole Lotta Love' in America for the 1977 tour. For Knebworth '79 and Europe '80 it was an encore in its own right. Post-Zeppelin, it has enjoyed airings at Live Aid '85, at Hammersmith with Plant and Page in 1988, at Jason Bonham's wedding bash, and the Knebworth '90 Silver Clef reunion. Page performed it with David Coverdale on their Japanese tour in 1993 and Plant performed it on his 1993/4 world tour. Page & Plant revived the track on their 1995/6 and 1998 world tours. It was the final number played at the 02 reunion show in 2007. Plant also performed it on his tour with Alison Krauss and on his *Band Of Joy* tour in 2010/11.

THE BATTLE OF EVERMORE
Page, Plant
Studios: Headley Grange,
Hampshire with The Rolling Stones' Mobile;
Olympic, London
The tune for this was written by Page late one night at the Grange while he experimented on Jones' mandolin. Robert came up with a set of lyrics inspired by a book he was reading about the Scottish wars.

Zep and Fairport had long since enjoyed a healthy rapport with Fairport bassist Dave Pegg hailing from the same Black Country area and being a lifelong friend of Plant and Bonham. Zep had jammed with Fairport at the Troubadour in Los Angeles on their last US tour and all the group had partied with their singer Sandy Denny at the *Melody Maker* poll awards in London the previous September. A month later, Page and Plant went to see Sandy's new group, Fotheringay supporting Elton John at the Albert Hall. At Headley Grange, Plant sang a guide vocal, leaving out the response lines for Denny to insert. This engaging folk rock lament would prove to be a cornerstone of the completed album, and gave Sandy Denny the singular distinction of being the only outside musician ever to be credited as having sung on a Led Zeppelin album. At the time Sandy noted Plant's own prowess on the session: "We started out soft, but I was hoarse by the end trying to keep up with him," she said.

The song appeared in the 1992 grunge cult film, *Singles*, performed by The Lovemongers who featured Ann and Nancy Wilson of Heart. In 2008, Page performed a solo version on mandolin in the grounds of Headley Grange for the documentary film *It Might Get Loud* which also featured him working with The Edge and Jack White.

Live performances: 'Evermore' was only ever played live by Zeppelin on the 1977 US tour, with John Paul Jones taking on the dual vocal task. Page & Plant revived the track at their *MTV Unledded* London filming in 1994 in an ambitious arrangement with Najma Akhtar on vocals, and also on their 1995/6 world tour (with Akhtar guesting). Robert Plant performed it with Alison Krauss on their 2008 tour and for a special guest appearance with Fairport Convention at the Cropredy Festival in August 2008 (sharing vocals with Kristina Donahue, daughter of one time Fotheringay and Fairport guitarist Jerry Donahue).

STAIRWAY TO HEAVEN
Page, Plant
Studios: Headley Grange,
Hampshire with The Rolling Stones' Mobile;
Island, London
Couples have played it during their marriage services, radio stations still can't stop playing it, would-be guitarists learn their craft by it, and the Australians, led by Rolf Harris, have made a whole parody album industry out of it. Even evil messages were claimed to have been heard when it was played backwards.

There was a time, however, when 'Stairway To Heaven' was simply the longest track on Led Zeppelin's new album. They knew it was

good, but they could never have dreamt the sheer commotion that this eight-minute epic would cause over the ensuing decades. It's been both loved and loathed in equal measures.

'Stairway' started out as a fairly complete chord progression that Page brought in when they commenced recording at Island studios in December 1970. At Headley Grange the song developed around the log fire with Robert composing a set of lyrics full of hippy mysticism that told the tale of a search for spiritual perfection. The song's arrangement with Jones contributing bass recorder on the intro and Bonzo entering as the track built to a crescendo, came together very quickly. This left Jimmy to add the solo, for which he returned to the Telecaster, back at Island. For the live version he would invest in a custom-made Gibson SG double-neck guitar.

Page made three separate attempts at the solo - and rather than deploy the usual Gibson Les Paul, he returned to the battered old Telecaster (a gift from Jeff Beck) that he had used on the first Zep album. The result was one of iconic guitar solos destined to be air-guitared in the bedrooms of fans across the globe.

It's worth noting that comparisons have been made between the opening chord passages of 'Stairway To Heaven' and the two-and-a-half minute instrumental track 'Taurus' written by Randy California and recorded by Spirit on their eponymous 1968 album. Zeppelin performed as support act to Spirit on their first US tour date in Denver and were on the same festival bill on three occasions in the summer of 1969. Page also adapted a version of Spirit's 'Fresh Garbage' in their early 1969 set lists.

Zep musicologist Rikky Rooksby detects a slight resemblance between the two, but points to Zep's own 'Tangerine' from *Led Zeppelin III* being a more obvious link. "The rapid descending C/G/B-Am idea heard just before Plant sings 'to think of us again'," notes Rooksby, "is the main idea for the four middle verses in 'Stairway', albeit faster."

'Stairway' would go on to log over three million radio plays and rack up over a million sales in sheet music alone. It has also spawned UK top ten cover version hits for Far Corporation and Rolf Harris. Rolf's version was one of 26 versions performed on the Australian TV chat show *The Money Or The Gun* in the early nineties and subsequently featured on an album titled *Money Or The Gun – Stairways To Heaven* released in 1993.

By the late seventies, Plant had tired of the song and started to deride it publicly. "There are only so many times you can sing it and mean it," he said. "It just became so sanctimonious." His antipathy towards it resulted in a major backstage row with Page before their 1988 Atlantic Records 40th anniversary reunion at Madison Square Garden. Right up to them going on stage Plant was refusing to sing it, although he relented at the last minute. In the nineties, he returned to it only once – recording a short acoustic arrangement for a Japanese TV show with Page during a promotional visit for their 1994 *No Quarter - Unledded* album. Respectfully, on the night of their 02 reunion for the late Ahmet Ertegun on December 10, 2007, they paid due homage to the song, performing it in a dignified manner midway through the set, perhaps in an attempt not to give it any special significance which would have been the case had they performed it as the set closer, as in the seventies. Following the performance, Plant poignantly proclaimed to the audience: "Ahmet we did…''

Back in 1971, they were all justly proud of 'Stairway To Heaven', and Page views it as the apex of their career. Talking to Cameron Crowe of *Rolling Stone* in 1975, he said: "To me, I thought it crystallized the essence of the band. It had everything there and showed us at our best as a band and as a unit. Every musician wants to be able to do something of lasting quality, something which will hold up for years and I guess we did it with 'Stairway'."

Live performances: 'Stairway to Heaven' was premièred at the Ulster Hall, Belfast, on March 5, 1971 and was performed at every gig thereafter. It became the finale of the set from Brussels in 1975 to Berlin in 1980. Post-Zeppelin airings include the Live Aid '85 and Atlantic '88 reunions, plus instrumental versions by Page on the ARMS shows in 1983 and the 'Outrider' tour in 1988. Page employed the opening chords of the song to close the live version of 'Babe I'm Gonna Leave You' on their 1995/96 and 1998 Page & Plant world tours. They also performed a surprise edited acoustic duet version for a Japanese TV appearance in November 1994. That performance aside, after refusing to perform the song for almost two decades and 200-plus Page/Plant concerts, Robert finally conceded and the song was resurrected in an honest rendition at the 2007 02 reunion show.

MISTY MOUNTAIN HOP
Page, Plant, Jones
Studios: Headley Grange,
Hampshire with The Rolling Stones' Mobile;
Olympic, London
An uplifting outing written and recorded at the Grange, with Jones on electric piano and providing the central riff motif the song revolves around. As Jones revealed "I got up before everyone else one morning and I was playing around on the electric piano. When the others got up I played it to them and it went from there." Lyrically, it relates to Plant's days as a hash smoking hippie. John Bonham makes an exemplary contribution, dropping off the beat at the fade. This track has been a perennial live favourite of Plant in particular and was still part of his *Band Of Joy* set in 2011.

Live performances: It joined the set on the European tour in 1971 and was used as a link track for 'Since I've Been Loving You' from the Japan tour in 1972 up to the US tour in 1973. It was then dropped from the set, but did reappear at the Copenhagen/Knebworth '79 dates. Post-Zeppelin, it has been played by Plant on his solo tours, with Page at the '88 Atlantic reunion, on a guest spot at Hammersmith in 1988, and at the Knebworth Silver Clef show in 1990. Page & Plant revived it on their 1998 world tour and Page performed it with the Black Crowes on their 2000 US tour dates. Finally, it was performed at the 02 reunion concert in 2007.

FOUR STICKS
Page, Plant
Studios: Headley Grange,
Hampshire with The Rolling Stones' Mobile;
Island, London
A difficult track to record, this required many more takes than usual, and is so called because Bonzo employed the use of four drum sticks to create the relentless rhythm track.

Led by a brilliantly incessant Page riff and powered by Bonham's literal use of four drumsticks - hence the title - it meandered off into a spiralling acoustic section ("When the owls cry in the night") underscored by JPJ's then pioneering use of a VCS 33 synthesiser, and all mixed by Page to achieve maximum stereo split. "We tried different ways of approaching it. The idea was to get an abstract feeling. We tried it a few times and it didn't come off until the day Bonzo had a Double Diamond beer, picked up two sets of sticks and went for it. It was magic."

The successful take of 'Four Sticks' occurred the day after John Bonham had witnessed Ginger Baker's gig at the Lyceum on February 1. This particular gig featured a "drum battle" between Baker and jazz drummer Elvin Jones (who had been feuding in the music papers). Suitably inspired, Bonham came in the next day determined to show his erstwhile ex-Cream hero a thing or two. He more than succeeded.

This was one of the tracks they recut with members of the Bombay Symphony Orchestra in 1972. It also featured Jones on Moog synthesizer. Another song that has enjoyed deserved renewed attention in the 90's, being one of the most played Zep numbers on Page & Plant's 1995/96 world

tour and still a staple part of Plant's solo live set in 2006.

Live performance: The only documented live Zeppelin performance is on the 1971 European tour in Copenhagen; however, Page & Plant revived it at their *MTV Unledded* London filming in 1994 and performed it extensively on their 1995/6 world tour. Plant also performed it on his 2002-6 tours with Strange Sensation.

GOING TO CALIFORNIA
Page, Plant
Studios: Headley Grange,
Hampshire with The Rolling Stones' Mobile;
Olympic, London
Another acoustic beauty with some memorable Plant lyrics, heavily influenced by Joni Mitchell. This started out life as a song about Californian earthquakes and when Jimmy, Andy Johns and Peter Grant travelled to LA to mix the album, lo and behold, the mountains did begin to tremble and shake. Then it was known as 'Guide To California'. It also tells of an unrequited search for the ultimate lady. "It's terribly hard," Plant would often ad lib in the live rendition.

Live performances: It was introduced on the spring UK tour in 1971 and retained for all shows up to the next year's US tour. Then it returned to the set for Earls Court in 1975 and the 1977 US tour. Plant performed the track on his solo tours in 1988, 1993 and 2002 (and also at the Knebworth Silver Clef show in 1990). Page & Plant revived it on their 1995/96 and 1998 world tours.

WHEN THE LEVEE BREAKS
Page, Plant, Jones, Bonham,
Minnie.
Studios: Headley Grange, Hampshire with The Rolling Stones' Mobile; Sunset Sound, Los Angeles
On June 18, 1929, in New York, Memphis Minnie and Kansas Joe McCoy recorded a blues tune called 'When The Levee Breaks' which referenced the Mississippi river floods of 1927. Forty years later in leafy Hampshire, Led Zeppelin reconstructed the

song to form the spiraling finale of their fourth album. It had already been tried unsuccessfully at Island at the beginning of the sessions, but in Headley Grange it took on a whole new direction.

That unique drum sound was created by positioning Bonham's drums in the hallway of the house, known as the Minstrel's Gallery. Page was equally enthusiastic: "What you're hearing on the record" said Page "is the sound of the hall with the stereo mic on the stairs, second flight up. There were a lot of different effects in there. Phased vocal and a backwards echoed harmonica solo. I'd used backwards echo as far back as The Yardbirds' days." (The effect can be heard on The Yardbirds' track 'Ten Little Indians' from their *Little Games* album.)

That drum sound remains today the most sampled beat of all time. It was first sampled on the Beastie Boys track, 'Rhymin' & Stealin' and has since been used by Coldplay, Dr Dre, Sophie B Hawkins, St Etienne, Bjork and Eminem, to name but a few. It remains one of the most startling percussive statements ever committed to tape. The relentless, much sampled, pummelling drum sound that is the key

ingredient of the fourth album. Indeed, all over the album Bonham let loose with a percussive ferocity that remains at the heart of his legacy.

As Plant once observed: "John always felt that his significance was minimal, but if you take him off any of our tracks, the track loses its sex, its potency and its power. He had a heart of gold but he never had any idea of how important he was and he was very insecure because of it."

Live performances: Rehearsed for the 1975 tour itinerary, it was tried out at the Rotterdam and Brussels warm up dates, but survived only a handful of opening shows on the subsequent US tour before being discarded. Page and Plant revived it at their Corris Slate location *MTV Unledded* filming in 1994 and on their 1995/6 world tour. It was also performed with Neil Young and Michael Lee on drums at the 1995 Led Zeppelin Hall of Fame induction in New York

John Paul Jones performed an instrumental version of the song on his 1999 /2001 tour dates. Robert Plant offered his rendition with Strange Sensation on their 2005 tour and with Alison Krauss in 2008.

HOUSES OF THE HOLY

Atlantic K50014, March 28, 1973
UK Album Chart: No 1; US: No 1
Sales figures approx. and counting:
UK 300,000 - Platinum;
US 11,000,000 - 11 x Platinum

As 1972 dawned, Led Zeppelin's on the road schedule continued unabated. The original plan was for them to stop off en route for a date on February 14 in Singapore, but the authorities there refused them entry due to local regulations banning long hair on men. Unless they cut their hair, there would be no concert. There was no concert!

Instead, the band travelled via Air India, stopping off in Bombay. The six-date tour, comprising mostly open air shows, was a big success with record breaking attendances. Some 25,000 came to see them in Auckland, New Zealand with trains specially chartered in from the islands. The set list broadly picked up where they had left off last year with an ever expanding rock and roll medley, extending to include such numbers as 'Let's Have A Party'. Surprisingly, Zeppelin enjoyed generally good press coverage and snatches of the Sydney show and a press party were filmed and shown on national television.

On the way back from the tour, Jimmy and Robert stopped off in Bombay again and recorded 'Friends' and 'Four Sticks' with the Bombay Symphony Orchestra in the local EMI studios. It was these arrangements (never officially released) that would be the basis for the MTV *Unledded - No Quarter* reunion versions by Page & Plant some 22 years later.

In the early spring, the band reconvened to begin sessions for their fifth album. They again went for a non-studio location – this time opting to record at Stargroves, Mick Jagger's country estate in Berkshire. Both Jimmy and John Paul had by now installed home studios of their own, enabling them to demo their own songs; and Jimmy was therefore able to present complete arrangements of 'The Rain Song' with its strange tunings and *chiaroscuro* dynamics, and another guitar extravaganza then known as 'Many Many Times' - soon to retitled 'Over The Hills And Far Away'. Jones, meanwhile, had honed 'No Quarter', a track first tried out earlier at Headley Grange, into a brooding, quivering, synth-styled mantra.

Once installed in Stargroves, other songs came from rehearsing together. These sessions on location, together with a further bout of recording at Olympic Studios in May, proved so productive that some numbers didn't even make the final *Houses Of The Holy* line-up. 'Black Country Woman', 'Walter's Walk', 'The Rover' and even the title track would all appear on later Led Zeppelin albums.

Eddie Kramer was again called in to engineer the sessions. He also took various photos during the sessions including shots of them outside on the lawn recording 'Black Country Woman'. "I can't recall whose idea it was to go outside," recalls Kramer, "but I was always into experimenting, and as soon as it was suggested I was off out with the microphones. Bonzo was magnificent at those sessions. We recorded 'D'yer Ma'ker' and got a great sound with Bonzo in one room, a sort of conservatory. The thing is with Bonzo, you could record him on a cigarette lighter and he would still have sounded fantastic. I can remember Bonzo, Plant, Page and Jones out on the lawn listening to playbacks of 'D'yer Mak'er' and 'Dancing Days' all walking like Groucho Marx in sync, with back steps and forward steps in time to the music."

These tracks in particular vividly illustrated the good to be alive feel of the period.

They were back for another American tour in early June. This month-long 17-date stretch that followed two little-publicised warm-up dates in Holland and Belgium may have been the lowest profile tour of all Led Zeppelin's American visits, but as the belated official live set *How The West Was Won* revealed years later - in performance terms it was possibly the best.

Vastly overshadowed by The Rolling Stones' US tour of the same period, they found themselves performing some of their most adventurous shows to little press acclaim. The exception was a perceptive piece by Roy Hollingworth for the *Melody Maker* which went out under the headline "Led Zeppelin - The Forgotten Giants?"

While in New York in June, they spent time mixing down tracks that had been recorded at Olympic Studios in England the previous month. The track 'Houses Of The Holy' was also laid down at the New York sessions, though it did not make the final fifth album selection. The tour itself had plenty of preview extracts from this 'work in progress' fifth album – 'The Ocean', 'Dancing Days', 'The Crunge' (inserted in 'Dazed And Confused'), and 'Over The Hills And Far Away'. 'Black Country Woman' (recorded at the fourth album sessions and later to appear on *Physical Graffiti*) also received a try out - a policy that was in stark contrast to the inflexibility of the sets from their latter era. With the acoustic segment still intact, the shows were beginning to run into three hour marathons. The off-the-wall song selections of these dates made for some of the most interesting of their entire career, particularly in light of the fact that much of the tour went unrecorded in the press.

Being ignored by the press was certainly not lost on them and in a rare interview at the

time John Paul Jones summed up their frustrations. "Here we are slaving away constantly getting incredible reactions and nobody back home seems to care," he said. John Bonham added: "It's the Stones this.., the Stones that... it made us feel we were flogging our guts out and for all the notice we were being given we might as well have been playing in Ceylon. Kids in England didn't even know if we were touring the States. It comes across as though we're neglecting them, which of course we're not."

It would be an entirely different story on their next visit in 11 months time. Grant began to realise that it was time to hire a proper PR team and recruited BP Fallon in the UK and, later, Danny Goldberg from the respected Solters, Roskin & Sabinson agency, for the US.

There was no real let-up in their hectic touring schedule during this period. Following a second Japanese tour, they played their longest ever UK tour comprised of 24 dates, after which they spent a month in Europe. There were security problems in France when rioting fans at Lyons caused dates in Marseilles and Lille to be cancelled. Musical developments included the constantly evolving 'Dazed And Confused' marathon that would further extend in the US and 'Whole Lotta Love', the continuing springboard for all manner of rock and roll fun. Zeppelin were clearly enjoying themselves - even if the delayed release of *Houses Of The Holy* had met with some indifferent response in the press.

In an interview at the George V hotel during their two-show residence in Paris in April 1973, Plant defended the album: "So there's some buggers who don't like the album. Good luck to 'em. I like it and a few thousand other buggers too." And in a comment that would have a hollow ring about it in future years, Plant went on to state: "We're playing better than we've played before. It's working that does it. The British tour, then three weeks off and then a solid blow over here. It's easy to get stale and some bands reach a peak and think that's it. The old country house bit and a year off. It doesn't work that way. There's only one way to function and that's on stage. We've reached a high and we ain't going to lose it. And no bad album review is going to change that."

The distinctive sleeve design was the product of a meeting between the Hipgnosis sleeve design team of Sorm Thorgerson & Aubrey Powell, and Jimmy, Robert and Peter Grant. Jimmy had admired the Hipgnosis design on Wishbone Ash's album, *Argus*.

However, the meeting got off to a bad start when Storm's initial suggestion of a cover concept with a tennis racket illustration was misinterpreted by Page as a slur on the band suggesting their music was literally a racket.

Aubrey Powell of Hipgnosis recalls that both the Nazca lines in Peru and the geological rock formation at the Giant's Causeway in Northern Ireland were considered for location shooting, with the Giant's Causeway in Ireland eventually being chosen. Powell took two children along and based his image on a science fiction book called *Childhood's End* by Arthur C. Clarke, in which children climb off the end of the world.

The outer photos were shot in black and white in appalling conditions, while the inner sleeve was taken at nearby Dunluce Castle. The two child models, Stefan and Samantha Gates, were featured naked climbing the mountain. Remembering the shoot, Stefen said: "For the Zeppelin cover we went to Ireland during the troubles. I remember arriving at the airport and seeing all these people with guns. We stayed in this little guest house near the Giant's Causeway and to capture the so-called magic I've heard people saying they put wigs on several children. But there was only me and my sister and that's our real hair. I used to love being naked when I was that age so I didn't mind. I'd whip off my clothes at the drop of a hat and run around having a great time, so I was in my element. My sister was older so she was probably a bit more self-conscious."

All the shots were later airbrushed, though original instructions for the children to be gold and silver were amended by accident to a more atmospheric purple. This elaborate printing technique delayed the original January 5 release date to late March. Following in the tradition of the fourth album, it was an artistic statement that gave little indication of the musical content within. This, of course, only added to Led Zeppelin's increasing mystique. After the furor of the wordless fourth album, Grant did allow Atlantic to add a wraparound band to UK copies of the sleeve. Surprisingly, this tactic survived well into the Eighties.

Houses Of The Holy ushered in the golden middle period of Zeppelin supremacy. By the time of its release on March 28, 1973, Led Zeppelin were unquestionably the most popular live band in America. Along with The Rolling Stones and The Who, they formed a mighty triumvirate of great British bands who bestrode the rock concert industry like colossi.

After the usual long delay due to the inevitable sleeve problems, *Houses* tied in nicely with a tour of Europe that was closely followed with a two-legged assault on America. In fact, the week the album ascended to the top of the American chart, Led Zeppelin opened their US tour by playing two mammoth dates. In Atlanta they drew 49,000 on May 4, while the next day a staggering 56,800 packed into the Tampa Stadium in Florida. This gave them the distinction of attracting the largest audience ever for a single act performance, beating the previous record held by The Beatles for their 1965 Shea Stadium show. It was a record that they themselves would top at the Silverdome in Pontiac, Michigan four years later.

Despite receiving some decidedly mixed reviews, the album entered the UK chart at number one, while in America its 39-week run on the *Billboard* Top 40 was their longest since the first album.

The headline preceding the normally supportive Chris Welch's review in *Melody Maker* - "Zeppelin lose their way" - was one of many mixed reactions to the album. In the main, the press criticism was leveled at the tongue-in-cheek nature of 'The Crunge' and 'D'yer Mak'er'.

Once again they had not travelled down the expected path, and in pleasing themselves they may have not pleased the critics. But their ever increasing following, as the 1973 US tour testified, was still with them every step of the way. The album was a massive seller in the US during the first six months of release. In retrospect, *Houses Of The Holy* holds its ground with the middle period releases quite admirably. While the barnstorming effect of the early era was now levelling off, and though devoid of the electricity of *Zeppelin I* and *II*, the sheer diversity of the third album, and lacking the classic status of the fourth, *Houses Of The Holy* nevertheless found its rightful niche. In doing so, it laid several foundations on which they would expand their future collective musical aspirations.

THE SONG REMAINS THE SAME
Page, Plant
Studios: Stargroves, Berkshire with The Rolling Stones' Mobile; Olympic, London
This shimmering Page extravaganza was originally conceived as an instrumental under the working title 'The Overture'. When they came to rehearse the track at a location in Puddletown, on the River Piddle in Dorset, Plant added lyrics and they renamed it 'The Plumpton And Worcester Races'. Finally it was recorded at Stargroves in May 1972 as 'The Song Remains The Same'. Page has revealed he played a Fender electric 12-string, with Les Paul overdubs and standard tuning. On stage he used the Gibson double neck.

The finished article is an uplifting barrage of six-stringed picking and chording, over which Plant's slightly speeded-up vocal track chronicles their travels and observes that the common denominator to it all is that if you

give, you get back, in fact 'The Song Remains The Same'. John Paul Jones also puts in some fluid bass lines. A long term on stage favourite, and held in such high esteem that it would go on to become the title of their feature film.

Live performances: A 28-second instrumental of the track appeared within 'Dazed And Confused' at a gig in Auckland on February 25, 1972. It was premièred in full on the Japanese tour in October 1972. Throughout the tour, Plant introduced the then untitled track as 'Zep', 'The Overture' and 'The Campaign'. The track remained in the set for every live gig up to Earls Court in 1975, and the live arrangement always dove-tailed into its studio counterpart, 'The Rain Song'. From the US tour in 1977 up to the 1979 Copenhagen and Knebworth shows, the track was employed as a suitably vibrant set opener in its own right. It was then rested for the European '80 dates. Page & Plant revived it on their 1995/96 world tour. It was also performed again at the 02 reunion show in 2007.

THE RAIN SONG
Page, Plant
Studios: Stargroves, Berkshire with The Rolling Stones' Mobile; Olympic, London; Electric Lady, New York City
This was one of the new songs for *Houses* that benefited from the recent installation of a studio console at Jimmy's Plumpton home. A new Vista model, it was partly made up from the Pye Mobile Studio which had been used to record the group's 1970 Albert Hall show and The Who's *Live At Leeds* album.

Page was able to bring in a completed arrangement of the melody for which Robert matched some sensitive lyrics. This track also marks the debut of the John Paul Jones one-man orchestra. He layers on a drifting string symphony created by a mellotron, an early sampling keyboard synth. The working title for this song was said to be 'Slush', a reference to its easy listening mock orchestral arrangement. Page recalls that the song was a direct response to a comment made to him by Beatle George Harrison who stated they never did any ballads. "So I wrote 'The Rain Song' – in fact, you'll notice I even quote 'Something' in the song's first two chords." The acoustic playing here features unorthodox tuning on the six-string.

Live performances: The song came into the set as a dual performance with 'The Song Remains The Same' and was retained in this format on every subsequent tour up to Earls Court in 1975. When 'The Song' became the set opener, 'The Rain Song' was dropped for the 1977 dates; however, it was resurrected as a solo piece for the Copenhagen, Knebworth and Europe 1979/80 gigs. It was another number which required the Gibson double-neck guitar on stage. Page & Plant revived it at their *MTV Unledded* London filming in 1994 and on the Japanese/Australian leg of their 1995/96 world tour.

OVER THE HILLS AND FAR AWAY
Page, Plant
Studios: Stargroves, Berkshire with The Rolling Stones' Mobile; Electric Lady, NYC
This opens with some superbly interwoven acoustic playing before shifting gear for an electric chorus that finds the Jones/Bonham rhythm bond as steadfast as ever. Plant, meanwhile, waxes hippily about that open road (and that Acapulco gold). A cut that displays all the colour and light of the group's maturing musical landscape. The weird sounding ending was achieved by a combination of reverb guitar and Jonesy's keyboard effects. The original master tape box had this listed under the title 'Many Many Times'.

Archive footage of this track being performed live at Seattle in 1977 and Knebworth in 1979 was used for an officially distributed video of the song used to promote the 1990 *Remasters* releases.

Live performances: One of the new songs to be introduced on stage way ahead of the album's release. This track came in on the

1972 US trip. Usually employed in the early part of the set to provide Page with a chance to warm up the Gibson, it stayed with them for each tour up to the Copenhagen/Knebworth shows in 1979. Jimmy performed it on his solo *Outrider* tour in 1988 and Page & Plant revived it on three occasions during their 1995/6 world tour.

THE CRUNGE
Bonham, Jones, Page, Plant
Studios: Stargroves, Berkshire with The Rolling Stones' Mobile;
Olympic, London; Electric Lady, New York City
'The Crunge' came out of a Bonham inspired spontaneous jam at Stargroves. Jimmy came in with a funk riff (and a chord sequence he'd had kicking around since 1970), stepping on and off the beat, rendering the whole thing completely undanceable. This spurred Robert to come up with a set of lyrics that parodied the James Brown/'Take it to the bridge' school of funk mannerisms. With tongue firmly planted in cheek, they named this non-dance cult 'The Crunge' and even thought about illustrating the 'dance steps' on the cover. The track is preceded by studio chat between Jimmy and engineer George Chkiantz which can be heard just as Bonzo comes in on the intro.

Live performances: It was never performed as a track in its own right, 'The Crunge' was initially incorporated during 'Dazed And Confused' on the 1972 US tour, and more commonly within 'Whole Lotta Love' up to the 1975 dates. It was mainly put in as an ad-libbed instrumental, though on occasions did receive a full Plant vocal - notably on the March 24/25 1975 LA Forum dates where on the latter night it was sequenced together with James Brown's 'Sex Machine'.

DANCING DAYS
Page, Plant
Studios: Stargroves, Berkshire with The Rolling Stones' Mobile; Electric Lady, NYC
Built around another classically incessant Page riff, Plant captures the intended 'good to be alive' vibe with a smiling vocal, as he

sings about those lazy hazy summer nights. Eddie Kramer recalls them dancing out on the Stargroves lawn during the playback· of this track. It summarises the positive atmosphere of the time perfectly. This was the first track from the album to be offered for radio play by Atlantic. It was premièred on Saturday March 24, 1973, on the Radio One Rosko lunch time show.

Live performances: First aired during the 1972 US tour notably at the Seattle Coliseum on June 19 when it was played twice: first in the main set, then as an encore! It was subsequently performed on the Japanese/UK tour. Discarded for the '73 US tour, it made a surprise return on the '77 US tour, this time as part of the acoustic medley with 'Bron-Y-Aur Stomp'. A complete acoustic version was also performed at the June 27 Forum show in 1977. It was revived by Page & Plant on their 1995/6 world tour.

D'YER MAK'ER
Bonham, Jones, Page, Plant
Studios: Stargroves, Berkshire with The Rolling Stones' Mobile; Electric Lady, NYC
Another number constructed out of rehearsals at Stargroves. Bonzo came up with the song's structure, which set out to capture a Fifties doo-wop feel (hence the Rosie & The Originals sleeve credit) and what began as a mock fifties spoof *à la* Ben E. King then twisted into a reggae off beat. By retaining this slight off-beat on the tempo, the subtle reggae influence emerged, which the critics were quick to jump on. The title referred to an old English music hall joke along the lines of "My wife's gone on holiday'' – "Jamaica? No, she went of her own accord!''

'D'Yer Mak'er' seems to have become a controversial issue within the band. Jones has asserted his disdain for the number, feeling it started off as a joke and wasn't thought through carefully enough.

Robert Plant was keen to issue it as a single in the UK. Atlantic even went as far as

distributing advance promo copies to DJs, but the others did not share Plant's enthusiasm for its release. However, producer Jonathan King tried his luck with a cover version recorded by the obscure Betty Joe on the Bell label. It failed to dent the UK charts.

Live performances: Though never performed live in its entirety, Plant did throw in lines from the song during the 'Whole Lotta Love' medley *circa* 1973/75, notably at the March 21 date in Hamburg on the 1973 European tour and final night at Earls Court on May 25, 1975.

NO QUARTER
Jones. Page, Plant
Studios: Stargroves, Berkshire with The Rolling Stones' Mobile; Olympic, London; Electric Lady, New York City
This brooding Jones creation had been tried a year earlier at Headley Grange. Now slowed down in tempo, and with added synth, bass and piano effects, it took on a dark, mysterious texture. Plant's vocals are superbly treated, while the instrumental passage, where Jones' grand piano merges with Page and Bonham's understated rhythmic touches, is a sequence of high drama and quite breathtaking in its delivery.

One of their foremost studio achievements, outtake versions that have emerged on the bootleg CD *Studio Daze* offer much insight into the song's construction, and again demonstrate Bonzo's vital contribution to the feel of the track. On the instrumental backing track outtakes, he lays down exquisite spacey snare fills for Jimmy and Jonesy to work around. The guitar solo effect was achieved by direct injunction and compression.

Live performances: Not surprisingly, this particular journey became a centrepiece of their live shows. Thus, from its introduction to the set on the 1973 US tour, it developed into a marathon Jones showcase, played at every show through to Knebworth in 1979. At the LA Forum on March 25, 1975, Page, Jones and Bonham took the song into a very atypical jazz arrangement, quite unlike any other version in that era. On four occasions during the 1977 US tour, the song included a full version of B. Bumble & The Stingers' 'Nut Rocker'. It was deleted from the set on the scaled down Europe shows of 1980. Plant reintroduced the number to his 'Manic Nirvana' tour in 1990. Page & Plant revived it in an acoustic arrangement at their *MTV Unledded* location filming in Dolgoth Wales in 1994 and on their 1995/6 tours (while they returned it to a more traditional, electric setting for their 1998 world tour). John Paul Jones performed it in an instrumental version on his 1999 tour dates and Plant briefly used it as a set opener with Strange Sensation in 2005. The song was performed once again at the 02 reunion show in December 2007.

THE OCEAN

Bonham, Jones, Page, Plant
Studios: Stargroves, Berkshire with The Rolling Stones' Mobile;
Olympic, London; Electric Lady, New York City

"We've done four already but now we're steady and then they went..." John Bonham's thick Midlands accent rings in this delightful closing rocker. 'The Ocean' refers to Zeppelin's ever growing and ever faithful army of fans and the auditoriums they were filling. "Has the ocean lost its way, I don't know," he reflects, going on to explain his devotion to his daughter, Carmen ("She is only three-years old"). At around one minute and 41 seconds there is a subliminal sound of what appears to be a telephone ringing.

Page and Co. meanwhile strut out another memorable riff that would later inspire a few thousand sales of Beastie Boys albums. The closing doo-wop finale is a further joy. "So good!" shouts Plant and he's so right. The live performance of this track drawn from their 1973 Madison Square Garden gigs is one of the stand out moments from the 2003 Led Zeppelin DVD set.

Live performances: This came into the set as early as the 1972 summer tour. It was an encore during the UK tour dates of 1973. It was further employed on the European trek in the spring, and the summer tour of the US (and deleted thereafter). During Plant's solo tours samples of the track and the 'la-la-la-la-la-la' chorus were inserted into 'Tall Cool One'. Page quoted from the song's riff during his live version of 'Custard Pie' on the 1988 *Outrider* tour.

PHYSICAL GRAFFITI

Swan Song SSK 89400, February 24, 1975
UK Album Chart: No 1; US: No 1
Sales figures approx and counting:
UK 600,000 - 2x Platinum;
US 16,00,000 - 16x Platinum

After the lengthy non-stop touring schedule of 1972/3, Led Zeppelin took stock of their situation and took an 18-month long sabbatical from live appearances. "We've been coming to different conclusions and decisions and we've got mixed up in a rather gargantuan film," commented Plant at the time. "Nothing's preconceived right now. We'll work a bit and then we'll take a break. That's the way it works - that's Led Zeppelin right now."

However, even before a note had been rehearsed for the album they faced a major problem. John Paul Jones told Grant that he was becoming disillusioned with his role and the constant rigours of touring. He'd been seriously thinking of quitting and had even considered applying for the job of choirmaster at Winchester Cathedral. Grant hushed up the crisis, told Jones to take a few weeks to think about it, and gave the studio time over to Bad Company so they could record their debut album. Grant recalls: "It was kept low key. I told Jimmy, of course, who couldn't believe it. But it was the pressure. He was a family man, was Jonesy. By that time, the security thing in the US was getting ridiculous. We started getting death threats. It got very worrying after that

and I think that's how we lost a little of the camaraderie. Eventually, I think he realised he was doing something he really loved. It was never discussed again."

John Paul agreed to take part in the rescheduled album sessions. Musical inspiration immediately followed with the initial recording of a Bonham/Page demo titled 'Driving To Kashmir', which would become known simply as 'Kashmir'. This Eastern influenced epic would develop into a centrepiece of their future stage set.

Once reunited, it was a case of pooling ideas. Mostly what they had were, as Robert later described them, 'the belters'. "We got eight tracks off," he explained in the spring of 1974, "and a lot of them are really raunchy. We did some real belters with live vocals, off-the-wall stuff that turned out really nice."

Similar to the sessions for the previous two albums, the location recording technique gave them ample time to develop material along the way. Plant again: "Some of the tracks we assembled in our fashioned way of running through a track and realising before we knew it that we had stumbled on something completely different."

A distinct character of these sessions is the throatiness of Robert's vocals. Talking to *The Scotsman* newspaper in 1988, Plant said: "Fifteen years ago I had an operation on my throat and couldn't speak for three weeks." If Robert had got his dates right, the period he was talking about was the autumn/winter of 1973/4, and this may explain why his voice was less than crystal clear for the sixth album sessions.

Those eight tracks, engineered by Ron Nevison, extended beyond the length of a conventional album and this prompted them to construct a double set. This was achieved by reassessing the material recorded for earlier albums, from which seven further tracks were added. The whole package was mixed down by the late Keith Harwood at

Olympic, and released as *Physical Graffiti* in 1975. It was a massive outpouring of Zeppelin music that proved to be the definitive summary of their studio work.

At the time, a return to the live arena was still a long way off. Grant decided it would be best not to tour at all in 1974; instead, they busied themselves with the completion of a sixth album and continued working on the film. Peter Clifton took over the project after the band grew dissatisfied with Joe Massot's original rushes. Massot signed off with the famous comment: "They thought it was my fault Robert Plant had such a big cock!"

Grant also renegotiated their Atlantic deal and set up their own Swan Song record label, with Zeppelin, Bad Company, Maggie Bell and The Pretty Things as the initial stable of artists. This was inaugurated with launch parties in New York and Los Angeles in the early summer on 1974. In LA, they gained an audience with Elvis Presley following his Forum concert. A UK launch duly followed at Chiselhurst Caves in the Autumn.

There was no shortage of concert offers during the layoff. Promoter Freddie Bannister jumped the gun by announcing he had secured Zeppelin to headline the first Knebworth Festival due to be staged on July 20 - only for Grant to decide otherwise. An offer to headline a festival in Munich on July 29 for a show that would be relayed via satellite to 10,000 theatres in America by ABC TV, was also given the thumbs down.

However, the group members were not entirely out of view on the live front. There were a few jam sessions and cameos, mostly with old friend Roy Harper and Swan Song label mates Bad Company. All the group were in attendance at the Wembley Stadium show headed by Crosby, Stills, Nash & Young which featured Plant favourite Joni Mitchell. Page and Bonham later jammed with Stills and Young at an after-show party at London's Piccadilly.

By late September, the new album had been mixed and completed, and Page revealed it would be a double set: "We have more material than would fit in with a single album. So we figured it was time to put out a double set and include some tracks we have in the can. It seems like a good time to do that now."

With Swan Song now active, the feature film project on the back burner (soon to be dubbed by Grant as "The most expensive home movie ever made"), and a major new double album ready for release, Grant began piecing together a major new touring schedule for 1975.

As *NME*'s Nick Kent astutely observed after meeting up with them at initial rehearsals at the Liveware Theatre in London's Ealing in late November: "The barley has been harvested. The heifers too have been put out to pasture and the Scalextrix sets have been stored away for the time being. Led Zeppelin are once again fully operative, girding their collective loins for another American tour after what has undisputedly been their longest period of musical inactivity. Atlantic records is excited, and every juvenile devotee throughout the USA who teethed his taste for rock on those first Zepp outings is excited..."

"1974 didn't happen. 1975 will be better," Jimmy Page observed in November 1974. The lay off had been their longest to date - but a vital one. Armed with a new double album set, *Physical Graffiti*, ready to be issued on their newly inaugurated label Swan Song, Led Zeppelin began a new chapter in their history with the announcement of a long-awaited US tour.

This tenth US visit was a lengthy two-leg affair, preceded by two January warm up dates in Rotterdam and Brussels. In line with the developing rock concert presentation, this tour was on a much grander scale and incorporated a massive light show with a neon lit 'Led Zeppelin' backdrop. Krypton laser effects were employed for Page's violin bow interlude, and for the first time, Bonzo was on a high-rise rostrum.

The early part of the tour was dogged by ill health. Jimmy was forced to develop a three-finger technique after slamming his hand in a train door prior to leaving England. Plant also struggled with a bout of flu while Bonham suffered stomach pains. Only Jones survived intact. "Nothing exciting ever happens to me!" he dryly commented at the time.

Due to Page's hand restrictions, 'How Many More Times' was drafted in as a replacement for 'Dazed And Confused' up until early February. After it returned at Madison Square Garden on February 3, Plant began using the spacey middle section - previously reserved for their version of Scott McKenzie's 'San Francisco (Be Sure To Wear Some Flowers In Your Hair)' - as a vehicle for other bizarre interpretations. As the tour progressed, these would include Joni Mitchell's 'Woodstock' and Ben E. King's 'Spanish Harlem'.

This new stage show also featured plenty of new material, with 'Kashmir', 'In My Time of Dying', and 'Trampled Underfoot' quickly established as live standards. The set list was constructed to represent, as Plant would put it: "Every colour of the spectrum" - a cross section of their six and a half year development. 'Stairway To Heaven', now established as the most in-demand track on US radio, closed every performance.

Off stage, there were the by-now-customary rumblings, even before the tour commenced. A proposed February 4 date at the Boston Gardens was cancelled by the local Mayor after fans rioted as they waited in line for tickets. A headlining appearance due for March 8 at Florida's West Palm Beach Speedway was also thwarted by officialdom.

Refreshed by a ten-day break in mid-February, Zeppelin really hit their stride during March. By that time, *Physical Graffiti* was ensconced on top of the *Billboard* chart and their five other albums also re-entered the Top 200 - confirmation of their now undisputed position as the world's top rock attraction. The final flurry of shows, culminating in three nights at their old

stomping ground, the LA Forum, saw them scale new heights of on-stage improvisation with the set now stretching to three hours. "My voice was getting so good by the end, I felt I could sing anything!" observed Plant shortly after the tour ended.

It was another hugely successful conquest of America - even if the early part had been hindered by their physical state. As they left the stage for the final time on the last night in LA, Plant excitedly announced: "If there's anyone here from England... Well, we're coming back, baby!"

By then the *Physical Graffiti* album had topped the charts on both sides of the Atlantic. The sleeve design is one of their most elaborate. It features a photograph of a New York City tenement block, with interchanging window illustrations. The album designer, Peter Corriston, was looking for a building that was symmetrical with interesting details, that was not obstructed by other objects and would fit the square album cover. He said: "We walked around the city for a few weeks looking for the right building. I had come up [with] a concept for the band based on the tenement, people living there and moving in and out. The original album featured the building with the windows cut out on the cover and various sleeves that could be placed under the cover, filling the windows with the album title, track information or liner notes."

The two five-story buildings photographed for the album cover are located at 96 and 98 St Marks Place in New York. The same location was used for the Rolling Stones video for 'Waiting On A Friend'.

To enable the image to fit properly with the square format of the album cover, the fourth floor (of five) had to be cropped out, making them appear as four-story buildings in the image. Mike Doud assisted on the inner sleeve typography. The interchanging window illustrations featured photos of the band in drag taken at a party on their 1973 US tour along with random images such as the Lunar moon landings and the Queen's Coronation.

The title *Physical Graffiti* was coined by Page to illustrate the whole physical and written energy that had gone into producing the set. The release date was timed to coincide with their 1975 American tour campaign which commenced in January. Minor delays kept it from appearing until late February. When it did appear on February 24 the demand was staggering.

Physical Graffiti made what had by now become Led Zeppelin's customary entry at number one on the UK chart, while America just went *Graffiti* mad. It entered every US chart at number three - then a record for a new entry - before lodging itself at the top for six weeks. Even more remarkable was the fact that all five previous Zepp albums returned to the *Billboard* chart. No other rock act had ever been so well represented.

It had been two years since their last album, but the waiting had been worth it. Led Zeppelin had delivered. Given the luxury of the double format, *Physical Graffiti* mirrors every facet of the Zeppelin repertoire. The end result is a finely balanced embarrassment of riches. Through light and shade, from a whisper to a scream, this one has it all.

CUSTARD PIE
Page, Plant
Studios: Headley Grange,
Hampshire with Ronnie Lane's Mobile;
Olympic, London
One of the belters from Headley Grange, 'Custard Pie' is a prime knockabout rocker with a vintage Page riff, finely undercut by J.P. on clavinet. As well as tapping the Bukka White songbook for the 'shake 'em on down' refrain, other sources of inspiration can be traced to Sonny Terry's 'Custard Pie Blues', Blind Boy Fuller's 'I Want Some Of Your Pie' and Big Joe Williams' version of the song, 'Drop Down Mama'. Plant throws in a bluesy mouth harp to aid the effect, Page filters a piercing solo through an ARP synthesiser,

and it all dances off to a pleasing fade. 'Drop down!' squeals Plant and Bonzo duly obliges with a typically robust attack on the bass drum. Page revealed on his web site that this had the working title of 'Drop Down Mama'.

Live performances: Although rehearsed for the 1975 set, 'Custard Pie' never received a public Zeppelin airing. Years later, Plant would redress the balance by incorporating a chorus of the song onto the end of the live version of 'Tall Cool One'. Page also produced his own live version on the Outrider tour during the same year. It was also performed at the Jason Bonham wedding reunion in 1990. Page & Plant revived it on their 1995/6 world tour and Page performed it with the Black Crowes on their 1999 US tour dates.

THE ROVER
Page, Plant
Studios: Stargroves, Berkshire, with
The Rolling Stones' Mobile; Olympic, London
A track that dates back to 1970, 'The Rover' was rehearsed as an acoustic blues piece before being recorded at Stargroves with Eddie Kramer for the fifth album. When it didn't make the final *Houses Of The Holy* selection, Page returned to it in 1974, overdubbing and re-mixing the basic track with Keith Harwood. The curious "Guitar lost courtesy Nevison... Salvaged by the grace of Harwood" sleeve credit would appear to be a reference to certain mixing difficulties they may have had here - Nevison being engineer Ron Nevison.

'The Rover' possesses a stirring melodic base, from which Plant waxes idealistically about the need for solidarity, and Page strings together one of his most perfectly constructed solos.

Live performances: Though elements of the song were heard on stage during 1972 and 1977, no complete version was ever played; however, the song was rehearsed in full, as can be heard on the remarkable soundcheck rehearsal tape commonly attributed to July 6, 1973 at Chicago Stadium and now available on the bootleg CDs *Round And Round* and *Tribute To Johnny Kidd And The Pirates*. The rehearsal took place before the opening date of the second half of the tour. "In those days we used to play songs that were totally unrelated to the current tour during rehearsals. In fact, loads of songs were born in the rehearsal jam session," Page said in 1990. 'The Rover' was occasionally used as an insert during 'Babe I'm Gonna Leave You' by Page & Plant on their 1995/96 world tour.

IN MY TIME OF DYING
Bonham, Jones, Page, Plant
Studios: Headley Grange,
Hampshire with Ronnie Lane's Mobile,
Olympic, London
A traditional song that can be found on Bob Dylan's first album, the lyrics can be traced back to a 1927 recording by Blind Willie Johnson entitled 'Jesus Make Up My Dying Bed'. This impressive arrangement has one the most powerful drum sounds ever committed to tape (recorded in the same way as 'When The Levee Breaks'); the point where Page straps in for a peerless bottleneck frenzy backed by Jones and Bonzo at the nerve centre has to be one of the most scintillating moments in the whole of the Zeppelin catalogue. The intensity is quite frightening. It eventually winds down via a studio cough from Bonzo. "That's gotta be the one hasn't it?" inquires the drummer from behind the screens. Indeed it was...

A stunning live delivery of this track drawn from their May 1975 Earl's Court shows can be seen on the 2003 Led Zeppelin DVD.

Live performances: It was brought in to the revamped set for all their 1975 dates and used again on some of the 1977 US tour where it was alternated with 'Over The Hills And Far Away'. It was a number that Plant was unsure of performing after his 1975 car crash, due to its fatalistic lyrical theme. Post-Zep, it was performed by Page on his solo Outrider tour, with David Coverdale on their tour of Japan in 1993, and with the Black Crowes on their 1999/2000 US tour. The

track was also performed by Plant occasionally on his 1993 US tour. Plant did insert lines from the song within the 'Calling To You'/'Whole Lotta Love' medleys on their 1995/6 world tour and within How Many More Times on their 1998 world tour. The performance of the song at the 02 reunion show in December 2007 was one of the evening's highlights.

HOUSES OF THE HOLY
Page, Plant
Studios: Olympic, London; Electric Lady, New York City
Another fifth album overspill, this title track was recalled for the double set and required no further re-mixing, having been tied up by Eddie Kramer as far back as the Electric Lady sessions in June 1972. It's a strident mid-tempo exercise with the same smiling friendliness in its grooves as can be heard on 'Dancing Days'. This similarity may have accounted for its absence on the *Houses Of The Holy* album. In order to create the layered guitar intro and fade, Jimmy used a Delta T digital delay unit.

Live performances: It was never performed live by Zeppelin. Plant did occasionally sing lines from the song within an arrangement of Garnet Mimms 'As Long As I Have You' on his Priory of Brion gigs in 2000.

TRAMPLED UNDERFOOT
Jones, Page, Plant
Studios: Headley Grange,
Hampshire with Ronnie Lane's Mobile;
Olympic, London
Page revealed on his official web site 'On This Day' feature recently that recording commenced on February 20, 1974 after they had completed 'Ten Years Gone'. The working title was 'Scotch And Coke'. Much rehearsal went into perfecting the relentless semi-funk riff that dominates this driving tale of the motor car and its relation with the sexual act, a theme inspired by Plant's affinity for the Robert Johnson track 'Terraplane Blues' recorded in 1936. Jones' clavinet and Jimmy's wah-wah and backwards echo make for a formidable partnership. Jones use of the

clavinet was inspired by Stevie Wonder playing one on 'Superstitious' and Billy Preston's 'Outta Space'.

Plant's vocals are a little too back in the mix (a characteristic on most of the Headley Grange tracks) but not enough to dim the overall incessant effect, which remains quite irresistible. Special UK singles of this track were pressed for promotional purposes in time for the Earls Court shows and it became a US top 30 hit reaching number 28 on the *Billboard* chart.

Live performances: Another Zeppelin concert showpiece, this track was played on every live show from 1975 through to the last gig in Berlin in 1980. For some of the 1977 US shows it became an encore number. In 1988, it was revived by Plant for his Now And Zen tour, including a memorable guest performance by Jimmy at Hammersmith in April. Page & Plant included it on their 1998 world tour and John Paul Jones performed it on his 1999 solo tour dates. They performed the track once again at the 02 reunion show in December 2007.

KASHMIR

Bonham, Page, Plant
Studios: Headley Grange,
Hampshire with Ronnie Lane's Mobile;
Olympic, London
This particular epic grew out of two separate Page riffs which he combined when he and John Bonham demoed it late in 1973. Robert wrote the lyrics on the road to Tan Tan while holidaying in South Morocco immediately after the 1973 US tour. The song's working title was called 'Driving To Kashmir'. Plant would later refer to it as 'The pride of Led Zeppelin'.

When it came to recording in early 1974, J.P. scored a suitable Eastern string arrangement. Kashmir's real beauty of course, lies in Page's Moorish chord riff that carries the song towards those desert wastelands. There is an ethereal, slightly discordant and somewhat eerie quality to this music that hints at the mysteries of the

East, and seems derived from musical signatures not normally found in the standard Western scale. Page has revealed that outside session musicians were brought in to add strings and horns, a rare occurrence on a Zeppelin session.

Unquestionably the most startling and impressive track on *Physical Graffiti*, and arguably the most progressive and original track that Led Zeppelin ever recorded, 'Kashmir' went a long way towards establishing their credibility with otherwise skeptical rock critics. Many would regard this track as the finest example of the sheer majesty of Zeppelin's special chemistry. The song enjoyed further success in 1998 when Page utilised the basic riff of 'Kashmir' for a collaboration with rapper Puff Daddy. This new version used on the *Godzilla* soundtrack reached number two in the UK singles chart. This arrangement has been much deployed as TV and radio background link music notably on the *X Factor*. Jimmy can be seen performing and explaining how the song came together in 2008 on a soundstage in front of Jack White and The Edge for the *It Might Get Loud* documentary film.

Live performances: The song made its debut in Rotterdam on January 11, 1975 and was performed on every subsequent gig up to the final show in Berlin on July 7, 1980. From the 1977 US dates onwards, 'Kashmir' led out of Jimmy's 'White Summer'/'Black Mountain Side' solo guitar spot, for which he switched to playing a Dan Electro guitar. Post-Zeppelin, it was aired at the Atlantic Records 40th birthday celebration at Madison Square Garden. Jimmy also slotted in a few riffs of this epic during the 'Moonlight Midnight' medley on his Outrider tour and performed it with David Coverdale on their Japanese tour in 1993.

Page & Plant performed it at their *MTV Unledded* London filming in 1994 and on their 1995/96 world tour. The song was generally regarded as the outstanding performance of the 02 reunion show in December 2007.

IN THE LIGHT
Jones, Page, Plant
Studios: Headley Grange,
Hampshire with Ronnie Lane's Mobile;
Olympic, London

This was another creation that was honed down from various ideas. Rehearsal versions offer alternate lyrics such as 'In The Morning' while a complete outtake that has surfaced leads with the refrain 'Take Me Home'. On his website Page said the working title was 'Everybody Makes it Through'. Opening with a drone-like keyboard effect from Jones, the track travels down more than one tempo change, as Robert sings with great passion about the need for eternal optimism. The fade-out is another wonderful example of the interplay enjoyed by Jimmy and Bonzo, as a mass of overdubbed guitar parts filter around some exemplary percussion. Jimmy would later cite this as his favourite track on the whole album.

Live performances: Surprisingly enough, this was never attempted live; it was, however, used as an intro link to 'Nobody's Fault But Mine' on some of Plant's Now And Zen American shows in 1988. Plant did insert lines from the song within the Calling To You/Whole Lotta Love medleys performed with Page on their 1995/6 world tour and within How Many More Times on their 1998 world tour. Page performed it with The Black Crowes on their 2000 US dates and Plant performed the song in full on the Scandinavian and US tours with Strange Sensation in 2001.

BRON-YR-AUR
Page
Studios: Island, London; Olympic,
London

A short winsome acoustic solo, this was written at the cottage in South Snowdonia in 1970 during the preparation for *Led Zeppelin III*. The track was used as a background soundtrack in the sequence in *The Song Remains The Same* movie as they travelled in limos to Madison Square Garden.

Live performances: Briefly part of the acoustic set on the sixth American tour August/September 1970.

DOWN BY THE SEASIDE
Page, Plant
Studios: Island, London; Olympic,
London

This was another song written at Bron-Yr-Aur in the spring of 1970. Originally conceived as a Neil Young-influenced acoustic strum-along (with Robert playing guitar), this electric arrangement was recorded at the time of the fourth album sessions. It features some lively electric piano, a sensitive Plant vocal, and an unexpected rise in tempo halfway through. The manner in which Page and Bonham turn away from the tranquil landscape of the song to take it all up a gear, and then slip back to the original lilting theme with effortless ease, is a master-stroke of controlled dynamics. Plant's lasting affinity for the song led him to record a new version in 1994 with Tori Amos for inclusion on the official Led Zeppelin tribute album *Encomium*.

Live performances: It was never performed live by Zeppelin, but Plant did insert lines from the song within the 'Calling To You'/'Whole Lotta Love' medleys with Page on their 1995/6 world tour.

TEN YEARS GONE
Page, Plant
Studios: Headley Grange,
Hampshire with Ronnie Lane's Mobile;
Olympic, London

Jimmy had honed the guitar orchestration at his Plumpton home studio ready to record. Robert added the moving narrative about an age-old love affair that still cuts deep. The emotional content of this piece is further emphasized by the subtle Page embellishments incorporated into the song, particularly a series of overdubbed guitar parts, all in perfect harmony. It stands as one of their finest arrangements.

Live performances: The song was brought in for the 1977 US tour. Jones originally played the melody on acoustic guitar, but then introduced a special three-necked guitar that encompassed bass pedals, mandolin and six- and 12-string acoustics. It was played again on the July 24 Copenhagen warm-up show and at the August 4 Knebworth show in 1979. The problems encountered in setting up Jones's multi-faceted instrument probably accounted for its omission at the second Knebworth concert and at the first Copenhagen warm-up. Page & Plant performed it for one show only on February 15, 1996 in Osaka, Japan. Page resurrected it for his 1999 and 2000 US tours with the Black Crowes.

NIGHT FLIGHT
Jones, Page, Plant
Studios: Headley Grange,
Hampshire with The Rolling Stones' Mobile;
Olympic, London
This track was a bright rollercoaster rocker from the sessions at Headley Grange for the fourth album. Lyrically, it reflected Plant's thoughts on the threat of nuclear war. Plant's strident vocals are crystal clear and supported by some turbulent drumming. Page, meanwhile, puts in some swirling Leslie guitar, playing off a warm organ sound supplied by JPJ. An outtake with extra backing vocals on the middle-eight section remains in the vaults. Although never played live in the Zep era, it can be heard in a rehearsal version from the presumed July 6, 1973 Chicago soundcheck. A version by the late Jeff Buckley can be heard on the expanded edition of his *Live At Sin-e* set.

Live performances: Never played live with Zep, but was resurrected 23 years after its release by Page & Plant and played at their Molson Beer competition winners only London ULU show on October 30, 1998. Plant also performed it with Strange Sensation on their Scandinavian/US tour in 2001.

THE WANTON SONG
Page, Plant
Studios: Headley Grange,
Hampshire with Ronnie Lane's Mobile;
Olympic, London
Original tape boxes have this track listed as being titled 'Desiree' – possibly a namecheck

for Desiree Serino, the future spouse of fellow Swan Song act Bad Company drummer Simon Kirke.

'The Wanton Song' is lit up throughout by a simple but quite brilliant Page riff that grinds the listener into submission. His guitar effects include the use of backwards echo during the solo and refrain, and also playing through a Leslie speaker to create the organ effect. Jones and Bonham back up with a barrage of noise with equal panache.

Live performances: The bridge of the song is another piece of Zeppelin music that can be heard clearly on the Chicago July 6, 1973 soundcheck tape. It was played on the European warm up dates in early 1975 and some of the opening 1975 US tour dates and then discarded. Extensively performed by Page & Plant as a set opener on their 1995/6 and 1998 world tours and on an appearance on the 'Later With Jools Holland' TV show in 1998. Page also performed it with the Black Crowes on their 2000 US tour dates and on the *Jay Leno Tonight* TV Show.

BOOGIE WITH STU
Bonham, Jones, Page, Plant,
Stewart, Mrs. Valens
Studios: Headley Grange, Hampshire with the Rolling Stones Mobile; Olympic, London
In an interview prior to the fourth album release, Plant revealed that one of the tracks on the album was 'Sloppy Drunk', on which he was quoted as saying, "I play guitar and Jimmy plays mandolin - you can imagine it being played as people dive around the maypole."

He was likely to be referring to 'Boogie With Stu', which was the result of a Headley Grange jam session with Ian Stewart from the Rolling Stones camp on barrel house piano (hence the Stu reference in the title) and Page on mandolin. Recorded at the same session as 'Rock And Roll' during their fourth album sessions in 1971 ,this was basically a re-write of Ritchie Valens 1950s hit 'Ohh My Head' – itself a variation on Little Richard's 'Ohh My Soul'. The slapping percussive effect (reminiscent of the intro to

Simon & Garfunkel's 'Cecilia') on A guitar came from an overdub session with the ARP guitar synth. The song was credited to all the band plus Mrs. Valens and Ian Stewart. Allegedly, the credit to Valen's mother, Connie Valenzuela, was due to the fact that they had heard she had never received a royalty for her son's hits. Ironically, Valens' publisher, Kemo Music, filed suit for copyright infringement and an out of court settlement was reached. Page told *Guitar World*: "What we tried to do was give Richie's mother credit because we heard she never received any royalties from any of her son's hits and Robert did lean on the lyrics a bit. So what happens? They try to sue us for the whole song."

Live performances: Never performed live.

BLACK COUNTRY WOMAN
Page, Plant
Studios: The garden at Stargroves, Berkshire with The Rolling Stones' Mobile; Olympic, London
Ever on the look-out for off-the-wall recording locations (Plant once tried to record some vocals out in the quadrangle of Headley Grange and had to flee from a gaggle of geese that attacked him!), the boys took to the garden at Stargroves for this session in the spring of 1972. The resulting take was nearly shelved when a plane cruised overhead, but as the opening dialogue reveals, it was all captured for posterity. Prior to release, 'Black Country Woman' was sub-titled 'Never Ending Doubting Woman Blues'. This was a reference to a final spoken tag left off the finished version which had Robert proclaiming: "What's the matter with you mama, never-ending, nagging, doubting woman blues."

Live performances: This was first performed at the June 19, 1972 show in Seattle. It didn't make a return appearance until 1977, when it was then merged into a medley with 'Bron-Y-Aur Stomp'. Plant played it on his 1988 *Now And Zen* tour and revived it 20 years later on his 2008 tour with Alison Krauss.

SICK AGAIN
Page, Plant
Studios: Headley Grange, Hampshire with Ronnie Lane's Mobile; Olympic, London
And finally... a mid tempo-rocker based on Plant's still vivid tales of the 1973 US tour and the teenage groupies known as the LA Queens that surrounded them. It's powered by a series of Page runs and some ferocious Bonham hammering that assist in conjuring up the required images. Juicy and muscular, and inevitably tight but loose, 'Sick Again' is a fitting exit. Listen carefully and you can hear Bonzo coughing out loud after Page's sonic finale. The live performance of this track drawn from their Knebworth 1979 shows is another stand out moment of the 2003 DVD release.

Live performances: This track held the distinction of being the second number performed on all the 1975 and 1977 tour dates. On the 1977 tour it was preceded by a link from 'The Rover'. It was rehearsed at Bray Studios during the summer of 1979 for its return to the set, but it only made three out of the four '79 shows. It's likely that it was excised from the first Copenhagen warm up show due to the power failure delay. Page performed it with the Black Crowes on their 1999 and 2000 US tour dates.

PRESENCE

Swan Song SSK 59402, April 5, 1976
UK Album Chart: No 1; US: No 1
Sales figures approx. and counting:
UK 300,000 - Platinum;
US 3,000,000 - 3x Platinum

It was never Led Zeppelin's intention to record a seventh album in 1975. Up until the summer of that year they were riding on a crest of a wave.

A few weeks after Led Zeppelin completed their 1975 US tour with three sold out dates at the LA Forum, Jimmy Page, Robert Plant and Peter Grant met in New York to discuss the group's future plans. The meeting with Grant and their accountants confirmed something they had known for a while. A period of tax exile was essential for them to protect their vast earnings. Grant quickly established a base for his operation, renting promoter Claude Knobs' house in Montreux, Switzerland. A touring plan was drawn up that would see them return to the US to play a series of major outdoor dates in August and then move back to Europe and then onto South America before returning to perform in Europe in early 1976.

Page and Plant wanted to spend time travelling together during the summer before the American dates. In early May, they returned to the UK to prepare for the forthcoming Earls Court stint. The subsequent London concerts consolidated Zeppelin's position as the world's top band

as they delivered some of the longest and most intense performances of their career. During those shows Plant threw in more than one barbed comment regarding their upcoming forced exile: "Somebody voted for someone and now everybody's on the run. You know Dennis (Healey, then Chancellor of the Exchequer)... no artist in the country anymore... he must be dazed and confused..."

After Led Zeppelin played their final night at Earls Court on Sunday May 25, Plant comments somewhat ironically: "This is our last concert in England for some considerable time. Still there's always the eighties." His parting shot was equally to the point. "If you see Dennis Healey tell him we've gone..."

The next day Plant and wife Maureen flew to Agadir. Three weeks later, Jimmy met up with him in Marrakesh where they spent several nights at the local folk festival. They then travelled down to the Spanish Sahara looking to go to Tafia. Confrontations between Spain and Morocco at the time prevented them from going much further in that part of the country. So they travelled by car back up through Casablanca and Tangier, meeting up with the rest of the group in Montreux. A date was set in mid-August for them to meet up in Paris to begin rehearsing for the US tour which would commence on August 23 with two massive dates at the Oakland Stadium near San Francisco.

Before then, Plant and family took a holiday on the Greek island of Rhodes, planning to join Phil May of The Pretty Things. Page went to Sicily to view a farmhouse once owned by Aleister Crowley and returned to London for work on the film. As Page commented "We were all going to meet up five days later... then there was the accident and we were just stopped in our tracks."

The accident that would dictate a whole new direction occurred on Monday, August 4. A hired Austin Mini, driven by Plant's wife Maureen, left the road and crashed into a tree. On impact Robert suffered multiple injuries to his right leg and elbow, Maureen a broken pelvis and fractured skull. Plant's children suffered minor injuries and Jimmy's daughter, who was with them, escaped with bruising. Plant was taken to a Greek hospital where, with the aid of an interpreter, he tried to explain who he was. Plant recalled: "I had to share a room with a drunken soldier who'd fallen over. He kept uttering my name and singing 'The Ocean' - it was bizarre." Luckily, Jimmy's girlfriend Charlotte got word to Richard Cole in England who immediately flew out with two Harley Street doctors in a private jet owned by the civil engineer Sir Robert McAlpine.

Peter Grant was immediately informed and wired promoter Bill Graham to cancel the already sold out Oakland Stadium shows. Additional dates lined up for Tempe, Kansas City, Atlanta, Louisville, New Orleans, Denver, Pasadena Rose Bowl, and University of Oklahoma in Norman Oklahoma were also cancelled.

Cole arranged for the Plant family to fly back to England via Rome. Knowing a stopover in the UK would adversely affect his tax status, a plan was hatched to move Robert to Jersey. Heavily encased in plaster, Peter Grant ensured his flight would be as comfortable as possible: "I bought the seats in the front and then had them removed. There was a bit of a row, but I got the captain to make sure we could unscrew the seats before we took off. That way Robert got the space he needed."

After recuperating at a house owned by noted Jersey lawyer Dick Christian, the entourage moved out to Los Angeles. It was here they made a crucial decision. Rather than spend the time wallowing in self pity, it was decided they would use this period to record a new album.

Robert's own morale had been severely tested during the weeks since the accident and having to leave his wife behind made him understandably depressed. "Time goes very slowly when you get up every day and you can't kick a ball... kick a roadie or even your drummer."

On September 14, the entourage showed up at the Renaissance Pleasure Fair in Navato, 30 miles north of San Francisco. Plant was carried round in a sedan chair. They were eventually joined in LA by John Paul Jones and John Bonham. Full scale rehearsals were soon underway in SIR Studios in Hollywood.

The material they were constructing had an immediate edge to it. It was back to basics. Page did bring in a few riff structures he had kept under wraps for some time (notably the riff pattern used on the then unreleased 'Walter's Walk' which was layered onto 'Hot's On For Nowhere') but mostly they started from scratch. The slow blues 'Tea For One' began as a bluesy skit with Plant singing the lines to 'Hoochie Coochie Man' and 'Minnie The Moocher'. Old standards such as 'Stop Me Talking' were also used to warm up the rehearsals. With little material pre-planned, the lyrics for these new songs were heavily influenced by recent events. The lengthy 'Achilles Last Stand' was built around the travels Plant had experienced with Jimmy back in the summer. His depressive state in Malibu gave rise to the venomous theme of 'For Your Life'. "That was a bitter treaty with rock 'n' roll," he commented later. "The girls who in 'Sick Again' had been wonderful were now suddenly... well they were hung on the balance of a crystal paying through the nose."

Talking about the strangeness of the times, Plant recalled later: "I was just sitting in that wheelchair and getting morose. 'Tea For One' was very personal. I couldn't get back to the woman and children I loved. It was like... is this rock 'n' roll thing really anything at all?"

Whilst in Los Angeles, they ventured out to see Donovan's Santa Monica show and met up with Paul Rodgers and Boz Burrell from Bad Co. Jimmy checked out Michael Des Barres' new band Detective, and a deal was set up for them to sign for Swan Song. There were familiar reports of Bonham's bad behaviour on the LA club circuit and drugs were never very far away.

By late October they were ready to record. Knowing the American tax situation was now likely to catch up with them, they ventured back to Europe, selecting Musicland Studios in Munich as the place to record.

Once underway (they were a week behind schedule when one of them turned up late), the Munich sessions went supremely well under the guidance of engineer Keith Harwood. In just a mere 18 days they had the whole thing complete. Page: "We hardly went out from the studio. 'For Your Life' was made up there and then on the spot. So was 'Hot's On For Nowhere' and the structure for 'Achilles'. I built it piece by piece and got it in one. I'm really pleased with the solo on 'Tea For One'. It's so held back. Seven minutes long and at no point does it blow out."

There was a moment of drama when Plant slipped over a wire in the studio, landing on his bad ankle, but luckily he was OK. Plant recalled: "I've never known Jimmy to move so quickly. He was out of the mixing booth and holding me up, fragile as he might be. It was a bit rash of me to be bopping about but the track we were doing was so brilliant." With The Rolling Stones due in to begin recording after them, Page asked Mick Jagger for two extra days to finish the project - putting in one 14-hour session to finish the overdubs before their time was up, much to the Stones amazement. Jimmy: "That was the ultimate test of that whole lifestyle. It was incredibly fulfilling. The band went away leaving me and Keith Harwood the engineer to do all the overdubs. We had a deal between us: whoever woke up first woke the other up and we'd continue the studio work." The new album was completed the day before Thanksgiving. The next day, Plant called the Swan Song office in New York to tell them the news - even suggesting they should title the album *Thanksgiving*. That idea was later dropped in favour of *Presence* after consultations with Hipgnosis on the artwork.

With the album completed, it was back to the serenity of Jersey; however, the performing bug was beginning to kick back in. On December 3, Bonzo and John Paul Jones sat in with Norman Hale, the resident pianist at Behan's Park West, a local establishment (Hale was a former member of The Tornados). They promised to return the next week with the whole band. So on December 10, Led Zeppelin made a surprise 45 minute appearance at the club with Hale on piano. Their last show at Earls Court had been seen by some 18,000; just 350 witnessed this return to something like active duty.

Reflecting on this surprise gig a few weeks after, Plant commented: "No one really knew who we were and we had this great piano player. After about 15 minutes of Eddie Cochran and Little Richard repertoire, we got right into a long blues thing. Suddenly all the stops and dynamics we subconsciously activate on stage came out. We were very happy with each other. I was sitting on a stool and every time I hit a high note I stood up but not putting any weight on my foot. I made sure I sat almost behind Bonzo, wedged between the piano and the drums, but then I felt myself edge forward a little bit... then after the third number I was wiggling the stool past the drums and further out. Once we got going we didn't want to stop. They kept flashing the lights on inside the place... 'Get them off they've done enough!'"

This impromptu appearance fuelled rumours that they would soon be back on stage in a touring capacity. Plant, however, was still in the early stages of a full recovery. In Paris on New Years Day he took his first steps unaided. "It was one small step for man," he said soon after, "and one giant leap for six nights at Madison Square Garden."

In January, he was in New York giving interviews, looking very fit with a restyled haircut. Plant exclaimed: "I know it's a real punk thing to say, but it's just good to be alive. This is the longest, most pensive period of my life. I had no choice but to question everything after the accident. My mind, which at first was taken up with repairing the physical, was then taken up with the musical. As such there's a lot of determination on this new album."

Page and Bonham were also over for the trip - a boisterous Bonzo bursting on at the end of Deep Purple's show at the Radio City Hall to proclaim to the crowd in an inebriated state, "Hi, I'm John Bonham from Led Zeppelin and we've got a new album coming out soon!" With the glint now firmly back in Plant's eye, the entourage journeyed to their old hunting ground of Los Angeles, checking out, amongst others, the all girl group, The Runaways. With the infamous cover art now complete, Jimmy returned to the UK to give a round of promotional interviews upon the album's early April release. Page: "The whole testimony of the new album is that it proved to us once and for all that there was no reason for us to split up. I can't think of many groups who have been going as long as we have who still have that spontaneity about them. I'm very optimistic about the future."

For the *Presence* album sleeve they again collaborated with Storm Thorgerson and Aubrey Powell of the Hipgnosis design team. Hipgnosis were already renowned for the distinctive images that adorned *Dark Side Of The Moon*, *Wish You Were Here* and Zep's own *Houses Of The Holy*.

For *Presence* they went right out on a tangent. The concept came about after a group meeting between Hipgnosis, Peter Grant and George Hardie (a fine art designer who had worked on the first Zeppelin sleeve). It was apparent to Storm and Powell that Zeppelin projected an almost unseen *presence* of power - the brief was to translate that presence into a visual illustration.

The front cover photograph of the family at the table was shot in a studio in Bow Street, London. It was intercut with backdrop images of the Earls Court boat show. The back cover photo of a school girl was modelled by Samantha Giles, who had previously been seen deployed as one of the children

climbing up the mountain on the cover of *Houses Of The Holy*. The style of all the photographs they used was deliberately dated - some of them were taken from photo libraries of *Life* and *Look* magazine. The photos were then enhanced with the laying on of a black object. *The Object*, as it was copyrighted by Swan Song, was a black obelisk 12 inch high figure originally mocked up by George Hardie and then completed by model maker Crispin Mellor.

Storm Thorgerson remembers: "What we came up with was the idea of placing an item from one time or another into a surrounding from another time. So we chose all those pictures from the forties and fifties and contaminated them with the presence of the black obsessional object. The black object stands as being as powerful as one's imagination cares it to be, and we felt Zeppelin could rightfully feel the same way about themselves in the world of rock music. So, in those scenes, *The Object,* as we dubbed it, was essential to all parts of the society. And those people in the scenes were trying to discover what *The Object* was - and how its presence was felt. I think the whole sleeve concept was very appropriate for Zeppelin. The band are a very powerful band, musically and socially, and the black object is a definite thing of power. Its pervasive presence and mystery appealed very strongly to them."

Jimmy was in agreement with most of their ideas: "It came out of that conversation when Hipgnosis said we had a very positive force. The fact that four people can create an effect. There's definitely a presence there - and that was it. They came up with *The Object* and wanted to call it *Obelisk*. I held out for *Presence*. You think about more than just a symbol that way."

Plant: "I'm glad people are wondering what it means. The most I can say though is that everybody should work it out for themselves - it's not hard to work out, especially for our Kubrickian fans." Plant's comments seemed a clue that *The Object* was Zeppelin's miniature modified version of the monolith featured in Stanley Kubrick's *2001: A Space Odyssey*.

The Kubrick 2001 theme was also taken up by an hilarious *Earth News* American radio special broadcast in the US at the time of the album's release. The dialogue ran as follows: "*The Object* is black... and twisted and obviously worse for wear and tear since its original appearance in 2001. To look at it on the pictures decorating the new Led Zeppelin album, it would seem *The Object* is now back in the year 1950 or thereabouts. Robert Plant has contemplated *The Object,* perceiving in it the messages that others might discover in The Pyramids of Egypt. 'It's been ever present throughout time,' he told us. 'We just took one moment in time in which to illuminate its presence in society.' *The Object* may not be welcome everywhere - it appeared recently in the home of John Bonham who told us this story: 'While I was away, my wife received one of these *Objects* in the post and put it on the table. There was a tape machine running, recording the children singing, and when they played it back, there was another sound on the tape altogether, so there's something to think about. In fact, Pat put it outside the house; we won't have it in the house at all.' So be forewarned. If Led Zeppelin's music is sounding a little strange to you lately, it may be because of that *Object* on the cover. If so, follow the lead of John Bonham's wife and put the album sleeve out of the house."

Swan Song planned a grand publicity stunt to launch the album. One thousand black *Objects* were manufactured - the plan was to simultaneously place them outside strategic world buildings such as The White House, The Houses Of Parliament and Downing Street. However, a leak of the album's design to *Sounds* in early March led to the cancellation of that idea. *The Object* models were eventually distributed to various journalists and media people, and are now very highly collectable Zep artefacts.

In the UK, the whole speculation of the meaning of the sleeve design was taken up by *Sounds* who asked readers to write in with their own explanations. Thirty years on, one can only marvel at the eccentric reaction that all of this *Object* scrutiny prompted. It was another episode in the grand Zeppelin guessing game. Did it really mean something, or was it all part of their playful desire to add to the mystique?

Whatever it was, you can hardly imagine anyone getting so worked up about a mere sleeve design in this miniature CD jewel box age. Back then, these matters inspired a great deal of interest, as anyone weaned on double gatefold sleeves in the Hipgnosis/Roger Dean/Island era will testify.

Unlike their previous two albums, this time they did put their name and title on the front cover - albeit embossed within the white sleeve, similar to The Beatles' 'White Album'. The original ship out of the album in the UK had the sleeve encased in a shrink-wrapped outer package with the title and name in black with a red underlined border. In the US, the shrink wrap added the album song titles.

Perhaps fittingly, the sleeve was subsequently victim of a very clever parody concocted by popular satire rockers of the time, Albertos Y Lost Trios Paranoias. In a superb spoof on the artwork of the official Zeppelin UK ads, the group advertised their new album with the illustration of *The Thing* - an upright version of *The Object* all under the slogan "The Albertos Give It To You Straight".

In the UK, the album went gold on advance sales alone and was the fastest selling album in the Atlantic group's history up to that point. It was an instant number one. In the US, it made the biggest leap in *Billboard*'s then chart history, moving from 24 to the top spot in its second week of release. By and large, it was favourably received by the critics and fans alike.

On May 16, Page and Plant were back on stage at the LA Forum, jamming with Bad Company for an encore performance of 'I Just Wanna Make Love To You'. "I want to get back on stage so much," said Plant after the show. Despite constant rumours during that summer of 1976, Grant declined all offers, awaiting Plant's full fitness in the new year. The attention instead turned to the long awaited release of *The Song Remains The Same* movie and soundtrack. These events seemed to somewhat overshadow the *Presence* album, and sales drifted off. It did seem that the majority of fans were content to store the strange looking sleeve away, preferring the thrill of the film and its accompanying live album.

When it came time to rehearse for their 1977 tour though, it was the number that in his *Sounds* review Jonh Ingram said would be "A motherfucker live" that they immediately got to work on. 'Achilles Last Stand' went on to become a centrepiece of their comeback US tour which commenced in the spring of 1977. "*Presence* was our stand against everything. Against the elements and chance," Plant told *NME*'s Roy Carr from the Manticore rehearsal studio early that year.

At the time, Jimmy Page certainly saw the album as a watershed: "All our pent up energy and passion went into making it what it was. That's why there was no acoustic material there. The mechanism was perfectly oiled. We started screaming in rehearsals and never stopped."

A soap opera of events surrounded its emergence as they turned inner turmoil into something constructive. The atmosphere that surrounds the whole record is one of urgency and fight. It needs to be listened to with the knowledge of just exactly what they were going through at the time. Then its true power is undeniable. This isn't the Led Zeppelin record for musical diversity. But it is the record for sheer out and out muscle and thrust.

The urgency and spontaneity made little time for the experimentation of the past. So there were no boogies with Stu, no hat's off to Harpers, no funk or reggae parodies - no mellotrons or synths.

The result of the basic bass/drums/guitar/vocal approach was to give the record a very live feel - leading to the conclusion that *Presence* is the nearest they got to capturing over a complete album the unpredictable edge and power of their on-stage performances within a studio.

Presence was perhaps Zeppelin's lesson in immortality. In a year that had seen them taste immense success in both the US and the UK, they suddenly found themselves in a position of rare vulnerability, and out of it made a record that once again saw the original catalyst of the group back at the helm. *Presence* is stock full of Jimmy Page's guitar rages. Rarely before or since had he dominated an album so convincingly. For that reason alone it's a vital part of the story. In recent years, it has rightly received the acclaim it deserves. *Presence* portrays the real heart and soul of Led Zeppelin more vividly than anything else they released.

 ### ACHILLES LAST STAND
Page, Plant
Studio: Musicland, Munich

'Achilles Last Stand' is a glorious 10-minute opening salvo that finds all the musicians pushing their talents to the limit. John Bonham's drumming is at once both explosive and inventive, driven along by an irresistible chugging Jones' bass line. All this acts as a perfect lynchpin for Page to weave his magic. His playing, constantly overdubbed, is simply magnificent, scaling the song's basic two-pronged structure with amazing dexterity.

"There were basically two sections to the song when we rehearsed it," Page recalled in 1977. "I know John Paul Jones didn't think I could succeed in what I was attempting to do. He said I couldn't do a scale over a certain section, that it just wouldn't work. But it did. What I planned to try and get that epic quality into it so it wouldn't just sound like two sections repeated, was to give the piece a totally new identity by orchestrating the guitars, which is something I've been into for quite some time."

The title itself is an oblique reference to Plant's injuries - Achilles being immortal but for the heel. Plant unravels a bizarre tale here inspired by his and Page's travels across Africa immediately after the Earls Court shows. With its theme of movement, meeting and positive outlook, his lyrics act as a perfect foil for the relentless pace of the track 'Achilles Last Stand' is an absolutely crucial performance and one that remains as vital today as it did when it took shape inside Musicland back in 1975. An impressive live delivery filmed and recorded at their Knebworth shows in 1979 can be seen on the official 2003 Led Zeppelin DVD.

Live performances: The first number to be rehearsed when they regrouped in late 1976 for the 1977 US tour, 'Achilles' held its place in the set throughout 1977, Copenhagen and Knebworth 1979, and into 1980 with one curious exception - their last show in Berlin on July 7, 1980. Page expected to use the Gibson double-neck when it came to performing this epic live, but found it worked fine with just the Gibson Les Paul. Page & Plant revived it for their 1995 US tour on the opening dates in Pensacola and Atlanta.

 ### FOR YOUR LIFE
Page, Plant
Studio: Musicland, Munich
There's much to admire here both lyrically and musically. Built on a grinding penetrating riff, it finds Plant in understandably reflective mood as he relays the trails of cocaine addiction - at around 5:30 the sound of snorting through a straw adds an aural effect to the bleak lyrical theme.

Much of the basic track was created inside Musicland as they went along. The whole affair has a very live in the studio feel with the four of them captured in perfect unison The simply stunning solo (one of his absolute best) from Page marks the recorded debut of a new part of his guitar arsenal - a 1962 Lake Placid blue Fender Stratocaster (supplied by ex-Byrd Gene Parsons), later to be employed on stage during 1979/80 and with The Firm. Not instantly appealing, 'For

Your Life' seeps into the consciousness with repeated hearings. This was once one of the most overlooked track in the Zep catalogue but not anymore.

It has enjoyed renewed acclaim following its live debut delivery at the 02 reunion concert in 2007.

Live performances: Never performed live in the Zep era. Page did rehearse the song in an instrumental arrangement for the Japanese tour with David Coverdale in 1993 but it was not performed live at the time. Finally the track received a live airing at the 02 reunion in December 2007, the only song in the set that had not previously been performed on stage.

 ### ROYAL ORLEANS
Bonham, Jones, Page, Plant
Studio: Musicland, Munich
Royal Orleans is the name of a hotel in New Orleans located at 621 St. Louis Street which was often favoured by the group in their touring heyday and is the setting for this whimsical 'road fever' lament. Lyrically, it tells the humorous and allegedly true story of John Paul Jones pulling a drag queen at the hotel and not noticing until the vital moment. Note the reference to looking like Barry White. All this is played out against a short, sharp riff injection, from which Page throws in some funky lines and Bonzo takes to the bongos. Royal Orleans 'road fever' lyrical content would suggest it was a composition that Plant had written some time previous to this period.

When the entire *Presence* album was premièred on the Alan Freeman show on Radio One on April 3, 1976, the version of this track had an edit in the middle of the solo. This could have been cut to accommodate radio timings, or perhaps this version was taken from an early mix of the album used for pre-release promotion.

Live performances: Never performed live.

LED ZEPPELIN
FROM A WHISPER TO A SCREAM

1944

January 9
James Patrick Page born in Heston,
Middlesex.

1948

May 31
John Henry Bonham born in
Redditch, Worcestershire .

1948

August 20
Robert Anthony Plant born in
West Bromwich, Staffordshire.

1946

January 3
John Paul Jones
(Baldwin) born in
Sidcup, Kent.

1963

January
Jimmy Page's first
appearance on record,
a session for Jet
Harris & Tony
Meehan's 'Diamonds'.

1965

February
Jimmy Page releases a
solo single - 'She Just
Satisfies'/'Keep Moving'.
John Bonham joins A
Way Of Life.

1967

April
Robert Plant joins The
Band Of Joy – later to
be followed by John
Bonham.

1966

May
Jimmy Page records Beck's Bolero
with Jeff Beck, John Paul Jones,
Nicky Hopkins and Keith Moon – tal[k]
of forming a band has Moon stating
they would go down like a 'lead
zeppelin'. The track is released as th[e]
B-side to Beck's 'Hi Ho Silver Lining[']
hit the following May.

June
Jimmy Page joins The Yardbirds,
initially on bass but soon switched t[o]
dual lead guitar with Jeff Beck. His
first performance with the group is o[n]
June 21 at London's Marquee Club.

1962

Jimmy Page joins
Neil Christian &
The Crusaders.

1968

July
Jimmy Page, Chris Dreja and Yardbirds manager Peter Grant see Robert Plant play with Obs-Tweedle in Walsall. Plant is offered the vocalist job in the new Yardbirds line-up. Chris Dreja decides not to carry on as bassist and Page calls in John Paul Jones. John Bonham completes the new Yardbirds line-up on Plant's recommendation.

August
First Page, Plant, Jones and Bonham rehearsals in Chinatown, London.

September/October
Led Zeppelin's debut album recorded at Olympic studios.

October
Page and manager Peter Grant decides to change the group name to Led Zeppelin, a phrase coined by Keith Moon during the Page 'Becks Bolero' sessions.

October 25
The debut 'Led Zeppelin' gig at Surrey University in Battersea Park Road, London.

1970

January 7
UK tour commences in Birmingham.

1969

January 12
Led Zeppelin debut album issued in America.

February
Led Zeppelin's debut album enters the *Billboard* Top 40.

March 23
First BBC radio session airs on John Peel's *Top Gear* show.

March 28
Led Zeppelin debut album issued in UK.

1974

May 7
The group's own record label Swan Song Records launched with all members in attendance at two receptions in New York and Los Angeles. During these celebrations the group attend Elvis Presley's LA Forum concert and gain an audience with him after the show.

1971

March 5
British tour commences at Belfast Ulster Hall. 'Stairway To Heaven' is played live for the first time.

July 5
European tour dates ends with a curtailed show at Milan's Vigorelli Stadium due to a crowd riot.

November 12
Led Zeppelin IV album released.

Do what thou wilt . . .
But know by this summons
That on the night of the Full Moon
of 31st October, 1974

Led Zeppelin

request your presence
at a
Halloween Party
to celebrate
Swan Song Records'
first U.K. album release
'Silk Torpedo'
by

The Pretty Things

in
Chislehurst Caves,
Chislehurst, Kent.
Celebrations will commence
at 8.00 p.m. . . .

Swan Song Records

Distributed by Atlantic Records

1972

November
Fifth album mixed and completed. Announcement of their longest ever UK tour of 25 dates prompts 100,000 ticket sales in one day.

1973

March 28
Houses Of The Holy released.

May 5
56,800 attend Led Zeppelin's second show of their ninth US tour at Tampa Stadium. This sets a record for the largest attendance for a one-act performance, previously held by The Beatles for their Shea Stadium show in 1965.

1979

August 20
In Through The Out Door released.

1977

July 24
The second Oakland Coliseum date – their last ever US show.

July 26
Robert learns of the sudden death of his five-year-old-son Karac due to a stomach infection. The remaining seven US dates are cancelled.

1980

September 25
John Bonham found dead at Jimmy Page's Windsor home after a drinking bout, following rehearsals for the impending US tour.

1976

April 5
Presence released.

October 19
The Led Zeppelin film *The Song Remains The Same* receives its world première at Manhattan's Cinema One in New York.

October 22
The Song Remains The Same soundtrack double album released worldwide.

1980

December 4
Led Zeppelin issue the following press statement: "We wish it to be known that the loss of our dear friend, and the deep respect we have for his family, together with the sense of undivided harmony felt by ourselves and our manager, have led us to decide that we could not continue as we were."

1985

July 13
Jimmy Page, Robert Plant and John Paul Jones reunite for an appearance at the Live Aid concert at JFK Stadium in Philadelphia.

1990

October 29
The *Remasters* box set and compilation released.

1982

November 22
Coda released.

1988

May 14
Page, Plant and Jones reunite for appearance at the Atlantic 40th Anniversary show at Madison Square Garden, New York.

November
Led Zeppelin
manager Peter
Grant dies of a
heart attack.

1997

November 24
Led Zeppelin *BBC
Sessions* released.

1998

April
Jimmy Page and
Robert Plant's *Walking
Into Clarksdale* album
released.

1995

February 26
Page and Plant commence world tour
in Pensacola, Florida.

1998

December 10
Final Page & Plant appearance
concert at the Amnesty
International benefit show in
the Palias Omnisports Bercy
Paris – future planned shows in
Japan are cancelled after Plant
decides to end the association.

2007

June
Page, Plant, Jones and Jason Bonham commence rehearsals in London for a planned reunion show.

December 10
Led Zeppelin re unite for a concert in aid of Ahmet Ertegun at the 02 Arena London.

2003

May 26
Led Zeppelin *DVD* and *How The West Was Won* live set released.

2008

September
Robert Plant states that he has no plans to work with Page and Jones on a reunion.

2005

February
Page and Jones attend the Grammys in Los Angeles to receive Led Zeppelin's Lifetime Achievement award.

2009

January
Jimmy Page's manager Peter Mensch ends Zeppelin reunion speculation by stating "It's over – if you didn't see them in 2007 you missed them. It's done."

NOBODY'S FAULT BUT MINE

Page, Plant
Studio: Musicland, Munich

Here's another track in a long line of Zep derivative blues mergings. Rarely though, did they ever dress up an old blues tune as effectively as this Blind Willie Johnson song from the late twenties. It's led by a dynamic sonic introduction with Page's technological phased riffing playing off Plant's moanings. It goes on to stomp its way through a series of impeccably timed rhythmic shifts - a masterclass of the Jones/Bonham team work. Plant is outstanding throughout, stuttering the lyrics to build the tension and blowing a mean harmonica behind Page's soloing. The Page/Plant credit here is a little misleading as Blind Willie Johnson may well have been under the impression that he wrote the lyrics back in 1928, a fact Robert acknowledged when introducing the track on stage in Copenhagen in 1979.

Live performances: A welcome addition to the set on the 1977 US tour, it remained a stage favourite through to the Copenhagen, Knebworth and Europe dates in 1979/80. It was also revived by Plant for his solo tours in 1988 and 1990. Page & Plant performed it in a bluesy jug band arrangement at their *Unledded* location filming at Corris Slate in 1994 and on their 1995/6 world tour. Page also played it with The Black Crowes on their 1999 and 2000 US tour dates.

CANDY STORE ROCK

Page, Plant
Studio: Musicland, Munich

This is a basic fifties rockabilly skit with a heavily echoed Plant vocal aping Elvis clone, Ral Donner. Plant again: "That was a saving grace and me being Ral Donner - the guy who wanted to be Elvis... and now was. The bridge section is pure Ral and Jimmy's guitar playing is incredible. The whole band moved into another gear on that. Bonzo's and Jonesy's rhythm playing went beyond mere pop music, beyond jazz and rock'n' roll. It was just inspired. The middle section can be traced back to live performances of the *Houses Of The Holy* track 'Over The Hills And Far Away' where Page, Jones, and Bonham would frequently drift of into a similarly paced improvisation. This track was selected as the overseas single from the album backed with Royal Orleans and was issued in France, Germany, Portugal, Spain, Japan, Australia, New Zealand (as a part of a limited 10 singles box set), Canada and America.

Live performances: The track was never performed live by Zeppelin, but Page & Plant did perform an ad hoc version at their Wembley Arena gig on July 26, 1995. The rockabilly nature of the track finally led Page & Plant to play it in full at their Montreux Festival appearance during the Night Of Sun Records show on July 7, 2001.

HOTS ON FOR NOWHERE

Page, Plant
Studio: Musicland, Munich

The track described by noted *NME* scribe Charles Shaar Murray at the time as "What the Glenn Miller Orchestra would have sounded like had they have been a murderously heavy four piece rock band."

It indeed does swing in a light and upbeat atmosphere somewhat at odds with the aggressive and questioning lyrical theme. The basic structure can be traced to the rehearsal sessions for the sixth album as well as the '75 era live versions of 'Dazed And Confused'. Plant unfolds more tales from Malibu, taking a swing at his close friends in the process and throwing in plenty of 'oohs' and 'ahs' for good measure. He later revealed that the accusations leveled at "friends who would give me fuck all" were aimed at Page and Peter Grant who for some reason had incurred his displeasure.

Page, meanwhile, makes full use of the tremolo arm on the new blue Strat, as he pulls out a ridiculous twang in the middle of a delightful solo. From the moment Plant shouts, "Oh, I lost my way home!" Bonzo roars in with some decorative fills, and Page takes it all out on a blistering babble of notes.

This track's odd time signature was echoed some 17 years later in the impressive Page/David Coverdale collaboration 'Pride And Joy'.

Live performances: Zeppelin never performed the song live. Page eventually performed it on his US tour with The Black Crowes in 2000.

TEA FOR ONE
Page, Plant
Studio: Musicland, Munich

A relaxed blues winds up the proceedings. Lyrically, Robert reflects on the post-accident period when he was separated from his wife Maureen.

Talking about the strangeness of the times, Plant recalled later: "I was just sitting in that wheelchair and getting morose. Tea for One' was very personal. I couldn't get back to the woman and children I loved. It was like... is this rock'n'roll thing really anything at all?"

The track grew out of pre-production rehearsals in Hollywood - an early version emerged on a rehearsal tape - the basic structure of the song being hammered up by Plant with 'Minnie the Moocher' lyrics. In its completed version, 'Tea For One' successfully recaptured the spirit of their earlier, self-penned blues epic 'Since I've Been Loving You'. The solo by Page is beautifully restrained.

Live performances: It was never performed live by Zeppelin. A few chords of the song were played live by Page during their Earls Court shows in 1975. Plant would occasionally insert lines from the song within the live version of 'Since I've Been Loving You' during Page & Plant's UK tour in 1995. It was finally given a live airing by Page & Plant on the Japanese leg of their 1995/96 world tour.

SOUNDTRACK FROM THE FILM THE SONG REMAINS THE SAME

Swan Song 89402, October 22, 1976
UK Album Chart: No 1; US: No 2
Sales figures approx. and counting:
UK 300,000 - Platinum;
US 4,000,000 - 4x Platinum

When Led Zeppelin undertook their 1973 US tour they graduated from being a mere rock band to something of an institution in America. By the end of the exhausting two-legged, three month trek (for which they grossed over $4,000,000), few kids in the United States would not have heard of the four Englishmen now breaking attendance records previously set by The Beatles.

Grant did his groundwork with this one, hiring PR consultant Danny Goldberg to ensure that this time around nobody took the spotlight away from his boys. He also knew that the demand to see their live show was bigger than ever, and he booked stadium venues without hesitation.

The two opening dates established the trend: 49,236 at Atlanta Braves Stadium on May 4 and 56,800 at Tampa Stadium a day later. This latter show smashed The Beatles' 1965 Shea Stadium attendance record for a single act performance.

Goldberg did his job by securing a well documented quote after the May 4 date from the Mayor of Atlanta: "This is the biggest thing to hit Atlanta since the première of *Gone With The Wind*." The attendance records quickly came to the attention of the US mainstream press. They also hired their own luxury jet, a Boeing 720B known as The Starship, which came complete with LED ZEPPELIN emblazoned on the fuselage.

Their stage show was further developed with the introduction of laser effects, dry ice, backdrop mirrors, hanging mirror balls and even a Catherine wheel pyrotechnic effect for Bonzo's gong at the show's climax. "We felt the denim jeans trip had been there for a long time," said Plant. "It was time to take the trip a little further and these ideas fit perfectly with the mood of the new songs and the excitement of the old."

On-stage developments included rapturous nightly receptions for 'Stairway To Heaven' due to increased audience awareness of the song from massive FM radio airplay. Jones's 'No Quarter' was developing into a showpiece all of its own, and the no-nonsense medleys in 'Whole Lotta Love' made for breathless finales.

From the start, the 1973 tour developed into one of their most enjoyable visits. George Harrison caught up with them in LA and was amazed by the length of their show. "Fuck me... with The Beatles we were on for 25 minutes and could get off in 15!" he told the band.

Plant suffered some vocal problems in early July, but in general their performances throughout the tour were consistent. The confident mood within the camp inspired them to decide to film the latter stages of the tour. "It all started in the Sheraton Hotel, Boston," remembered Grant. "We'd talked about a film for years, and Jimmy had known Joe Massot was interested - so we called them and over they came. It was all very quickly arranged."

Massot hurriedly assembled a crew in time for Led Zeppelin's last week of the 1973 tour. He started with the band in Baltimore on July 23, 1973 and subsequently filmed the group's three concert performances at Madison Square Garden on the nights of July 27, 28, and 29, 1973. The film was entirely financed by the band and shot on 35mm with a 24-track quadraphonic sound recording. The live footage in the US alone cost $85,000. This would prompt Peter Grant to comment that the project was, "The world's most expensive home movie."

Back in the UK during the Autumn of 1973, Joe Massot and his film crew spent time with all four group members and Peter Grant to film location sequences. Each of the members acted out a fantasy role. Grant and Cole were portrayed as Mafia style henchmen; Page re-enacted the Tarot card illustration of their fourth album sleeve, climbing a mountain near Loch Ness in December. Plant went to Raglan Castle in Wales to film a King Arthur-style scene. Jones cavorted around his Sussex home as a ghostly Lord of the Manor, and Bonham, somewhat less pretentiously, was featured drag racing at Santa Pod and riding his Harley around Blackpool. Unhappy with the progress of the film, Grant had Massot removed from the project and Australian director Peter Clifton was hired in his place in early 1974. Clifton found that there were gaps in the concert footage, suggested that they reconstruct the stage and film more footage at Shepperton Studios. This took place during August 1974. There had been plans to shoot some more film on their intended 1975 and 1976 dates, but Robert Plant's car accident in August 1975 put that to rest. So with short term plans for live gigs an impossibility, Page used this period of inactivity to tie up the movie and soundtrack, using the footage shot with Joe Massot and employing Peter Clifton to arrange the technical aspects.

The film soundtrack was mixed at Electric Lady Studios in New York and Trident in London. Page patched together differing versions of the songs to complete a double album of recordings from the Madison Square Garden gigs.

The movie poster and sleeve design depicted a run down picture house, which was based on Old Street studios, a London rehearsal theatre they used to perfect the 1973 US stage act prior to touring. The sleeve notes were penned by *Rolling Stone* journalist Cameron Crowe.

The film was premièred in New York at Cinema 1 on October 19, with the album hitting the stores on October 22. It reached number one in the UK but had to settle for second place in the States.

Both the album and movie were met with mixed reviews. The fact that the recordings were now three years old hindered the overall effect of the album as Zeppelin's stage act had moved on considerably from 1973. As a soundtrack to the film it was an adequate representation of how they were in 1973, but by Page's own admission the New York shows had been good but not "magic". Though it was not known at the time, they had far better live material lining their archives, notably the 1972 Long Beach and LA Forum shows that would eventually form the *How the West Was Won* album.

At the time, fans were content to soak up the vintage offerings of these 1973 recordings. The album was well sequenced and recorded, and as such did good business around the globe. It acted as an aural example of their on stage craft at a time when they were unable to tour due to Plant still recovering from his car smash injuries. Some 30 years hence, Page would revisit this much maligned project to mixed results.

ROCK AND ROLL
Bonham, Jones, Page, Plant
The perfect set opener. For the live version Plant sings in a lower key.

CELEBRATION DAY
Jones, Page, Plant
In the movie, 'Rock And Roll' is edited into 'Black Dog'. The album, however, has the authentic link into 'Celebration Day'. Strangely edited out of the film, this underrated stage number sounds spot on. Jimmy is particularly impressive weaving a cluster of notes towards the outro.

THE SONG REMAINS THE SAME
Page, Plant
An excellent live take with Page switching to the double-neck. In the film, it accompanies Plant's Arthurian fantasy sequence, snippets of which he would later use as a backdrop to 'Immigrant Song' on his 1990 solo tour.

THE RAIN SONG
Page, Plant
This dovetails from 'The Song Remains The Same', as was the custom during this era. This version includes some delicate Page strumming and precise Bonham dynamics. At times, though, the mellotron quivers a little unsteadily.

DAZED AND CONFUSED
Page
Stripped of the on-stage visuals, this marathon loses its appeal somewhat. There are some high spots, the 'San Francisco' sequence, the bow interlude with its stereo panning and the guitar-vocal interplay. Elsewhere, it becomes excessive and lumbering.

NO QUARTER
Jones, Page, Plant
This is the album's standout performance. Everything works perfectly here, from Jones' revolving opening through to a simply divine Page solo. A slightly different version appears in the film.

STAIRWAY TO HEAVEN
Page, Plant
'Stairway' had yet to take on truly epic proportions during this era, and it followed 'Dazed And Confused' in the set. Such was the excitement of the number that the audience often drowned out the intro to 'Stairway'. Madison Square Garden was one such venue. Though the album version gives little away, the live outtakes reveal Plant trying to settle the audience down. The intro link retained for the album has Plant saying: "This is a song of hope." It edits out his next line: "And it's a very quiet song... so shurrup!"

MOBY DICK
Bonham, Jones, Plant
Here's another track that loses most of its impact without the visual footage. In the movie it makes a perfect accompaniment to Bonzo's profile. On record it goes on much too long. A far better idea here would have been to insert the 'Heartbreaker' segment that precedes 'Whole Lotta Love' in the film, run through to the 'Whole Lotta Love' track and then add 'The Ocean' as an encore. Both these tracks were left on the splicing block.

WHOLE LOTTA LOVE
Bonham, Jones, Page, Plant
In the film, as in all the shows on the tour, 'Whole Lotta Love' segued in from 'Heartbreaker'. Here it's edited to appear as a track in its own right. Complete with Jimmy on backing vocals, 'The Crunge' sequence, the theremin attack, and 'Let That Boy Woogie', it sustains the interest.

The following tracks appeared in the film but are not featured on the original 1976 album: 'Black Dog', 'Since I've Been Loving You' and 'Heartbreaker'. Jimmy's solo piece from *Physical Graffiti*, 'Bron-Yr-Aur', is also heard in the film. Another number, copyrighted as 'Autumn Lake', is played on a hurdy gurdy by Page in an early pre-concert sequence.

IN THROUGH THE OUT DOOR

Swan Song 59410, August 20, 1979
UK Album Chart: No 1; US: No 1
Sales figures approx. and counting:
UK 300,000 - Platinum;
US 6,000,000 - 6x Platinum

In late July 1977, Led Zeppelin arrived in California to perform two open air shows in Oakland. They were riding high on the back of a lengthy and successful American tour. All that evaporated in the space of a few days. Firstly, manager Peter Grant and John Bonham were involved in a backstage fight with members of promoter Bill Graham's staff at the first Oakland show. This would result in them both being given suspended sentences. A few days later in New Orleans, Robert Plant heard the devastating news that his six-year-old son Karac had died back in England from a mysterious virus. The tour was immediately cancelled.

Aside from a few interviews from Jimmy Page denying they were splitting, nothing was heard from the group for the next nine months. Eventually in May 1978, the first seeds of a Led Zeppelin comeback were sown at another stately English building near the Forest of Dean. Clearwell Castle, previously used by Deep Purple, was the location chosen for the first group get-together.

Robert's decision to return to the Zeppelin fold was greatly influenced by John Bonham,

who cajoled him to get back to doing what he did best. "I didn't want to leave my family," reflected Robert. "And I also didn't know if it was worth it. John came over and told me all the reasons it was worth it. He had the history with me outside of the success. He was the only one who hugged me and helped me at all. He said, "C'mon, we are going to go down to Clearwell and try some writing."

At this stage nothing substantial emerged from the three week stint of rehearsals. They did work on a new composition entitled 'Carouselambra' and a riff exercise dubbed 'Fire'. Jones himself was unsure of the sessions as he stated years later, "Getting back together at Clearwell was a bit odd. I didn't really feel comfortable." Jimmy Page was more upbeat, saying: "That was basically a period of saying 'Hello' to each other musically once again. We hadn't played together for so long, and Clearwell was the first actual playing we'd done for what seemed like an eternity. It was really just limbering up."

Plant was also optimistic, stating: "I started to play again, and I realised that I still possessed something that really turned me on."

Plant did begin his return to the stage with three low key guest appearances. First he sat in with local Midlands band, Melvin's Marauders (aka Melvin Giganticus and the Turd Burglars) at the Memorial Hall in Wolverly; then while on holiday in Ibiza in August, Robert jammed with Dr. Feelgood and Atlantic Records executive Phil Carson at the Club Amnesia. On September 16th Robert turned up at the Birmingham Town Hall to see Dave Edmunds perform and joined him during the encore.

In October, John Bonham and John Paul Jones took part in an all-star recording session held at Abbey Road's Studio Number 2. On the invitation of Paul McCartney, they joined McCartney's Wings and a host of musicians including, Dave Gilmour, Hank Marvin, Kenny Jones, Ronnie Lane, Gary

Brooker, Tony Ashton and Pete Townshend, to record two tracks, 'Rockestra Theme' and 'So Glad to See You Here', as part of what McCartney dubbed 'The Rockestra'. The tracks were later included on the Wings album *Back To The Egg*. The same month the group resumed rehearsals at Ezyhire, a North London studio. This time there was a clear purpose: the plan was to begin preparing new material for a new album. On November 6 the band flew to Stockholm for a series of Monday through Friday recording sessions at Abba's Polar Studio, which would result in the *In Through The Out Door* album released the following year. Every Friday afternoon the band would fly back for the weekend and then return on the Monday.

For these sessions John Paul Jones emerged with various keyboard-led ideas and was anxious to apply them in the studio on his new GX1 keyboard synth set-up. He recalled: "I was one of the first to get one I think - it was Stevie Wonder and myself. The sound you could get out of it was, at the time, very inspiring."

Thus, tracks such as the previously mentioned 'Carouselambra' were dominated more by Jones than anyone else. The fact that he and Robert were often at the studio first led to their influence being felt strongly. "The band was divided between people who could turn up at recording sessions on time and people who couldn't," claimed JPJ. "I'd got the GX1 installed and I wasn't just going to look at it. I worked really hard on 'In The Evening' and 'Carouselambra'. It was a transitional period. It was a chance to see what else we could do."

Page was reported as being distant and less enthusiastic, showing particular indifference to Plant's mellow leanings on 'All My Love'. "Jonesy started working more closely with Robert," recalls Page. "I wasn't that keen on 'All My Love'. It just didn't seem us. In fact, Bonzo and I both felt it was a little soft, that album. We wanted to make a more hard driving rock album after that."

Page's spark however, was certainly in evidence on 'Wearing And Tearing' - a raucous punk tempered number that didn't make the final album but subsequently showed up on the posthumous *Coda* set in 1982. Page and Plant both checked out concerts by Jerry Lee Lewis and Duane Eddy while in Stockholm – perhaps lending inspiration to the rockabilly influenced 'Hot Dog' and 'Darlene'.

Years later, Jimmy would defend his role at the time: "There are people who said 'Jimmy wasn't in good shape' or whatever. But what I do know is that *Presence* was recorded and mixed in three weeks and *In Through The Out Door* was done in a little over three weeks. So I couldn't have been in that bad a shape. I'd have never been able to play and I wouldn't have been able to keep my head together to do this that and the other."

The sessions may have been on the tense side, but by early December they had ten numbers completed and the band returned to the UK in time for Christmas. Early in 1979, Page and Jones returned to Polar for further mixing and the album was duly completed with further work at Jimmy's Plumpton Studio.

It was rumoured they would undertake a series of dates in Europe at the end of February 1979. The album, tentatively titled *Look,* according to one source, was said to have a provisional release date of February 12. It was also reported that Robert Plant would warm up for the tour by playing small club dates with local Midlands band, Little Acre. These reports all proved somewhat premature; however, there was more on stage activity in the spring. On March 26, Robert joined Bad Company for the second show of their three-night stint at the Birmingham Odeon. He was back a week later on April 3, this time with Jimmy and Bonzo in tow, and they performed 'I'm Going Down'. Later in the month, Plant performed again with the Midlands part-time pick-up band Melvin's Marauders for an appearance at a Stourbridge wine bar.

Meanwhile in Hertfordshire, promoter Freddy Bannister had been looking for a big name to headline the 1979 Knebworth show. Initially, he had ideas to approach both The Eagles and Pink Floyd, but after the disappointment of failing to capture Zeppelin for the 1974 festival, Bannister was eager to land the band. Five years on the timing was right. Peter Grant was keen for them to come back in the best possible manner.

With a new album ready for release, all that was required to seal their return to active duty was a return to live performances. Due to Plant's reluctance to return to America, their scope was somewhat limited. The dilemma they faced was which way to move forward. The whole operation had become just too big. Page's experiences of overflowing audiences from the 1971 club tour ruled out any small dates. They had played the biggest indoor arena in the UK (Earls Court) four years earlier. As Peter Grant saw it, they had to come back in the grandest style.

As he told this writer years later, "We didn't want to start all over again so I said, 'Fuck doing a tour. We're the biggest band in the world so we better get out there and show them we still are.' I said Knebworth was the gig and I reckoned we could sell out two dates. I was absolutely confident."

The initial agreement with Bannister was for two dates, though it was agreed only one would go on sale. Grant also stipulated that the Showco lighting rig would have to be flown over from Texas at a cost of nearly £200,000. Their fee for performing was reported to be the largest ever paid to one single act at that time – a reputed £1 million.

On Tuesday May 22, Led Zeppelin formally announced their return to the UK stage. The news was exclusively revealed by Anne Nightingale on BBC TV's *Old Grey Whistle Test.* They would headline the Knebworth Festival to be staged within the grounds of the Stevenage stately home on August 4.

On Saturday June 9, Radio One's *Rock On* programme broadcast an exclusive interview with Robert Plant - his first in two years. It was conducted by Trevor Dann backstage at London's Palace Theatre following a Dave Edmunds concert he had attended. Robert gave little away, deflecting the questions with sometimes ambiguous answers: "I think the music will speak for itself. It will stand up there as it always has done. Things always change with Zeppelin, that's why after two years we can still get together and play. We are what we are when we walk on to the stage and play. It's not a question of are we heroes anymore? Heroes are in books, old books."

In early June, all four members of the group convened on the Knebworth site for a formal photo session with the Hipgnosis design team - later used on the official Knebworth posters. Promoter Freddy Bannister took several weeks to sort out the line-up for the two dates and both went on sale with only Zeppelin as the officially named attraction. Artists rumoured to be playing included Dire Straits, Little Feat, Joni Mitchell, Ian Dury, Roxy Music, JJ Cale, Bob Seger, The Boomtown Rats, Aerosmith, BB King and Van Morrison. Eventually, Fairport Convention were confirmed for the August 4 date and (somewhat bizarrely) Chas & Dave, Southside Johnny & The Asbury Dukes and Todd Rundgren's Utopia for both weeks. Fairport's appearance on the August 4 show was their penultimate before disbanding (at least for a while).

At one point The Marshall Tucker Band was also confirmed to appear, but they dropped out at the last minute with Commander Cody & His Lost Planet Airmen stepping in. The second on the bill spot was taken by Grant's choice of The New Barbarians, a part time pick-up band fronted by Ronnie Wood and Keith Richards. They had planned to perform at both gigs but they had to scrap the August 4 date due to Rolling Stones' recording commitments. Given some of the big names touted as being readied for the event, the actual line up was disappointing.

Zeppelin rehearsed for their big comeback at Bray Film Studios in Berkshire, close to where Jimmy lived in Windsor, spending three weeks in Bray on and off.

In a tactic that echoed Peter Grant's original launch of the band in 1968, Led Zeppelin flew to Copenhagen on July 23 to perform two warm up shows for the big event. The venue chosen for the band's first gig in two years was the obscure Falkoner Theatre in Denmark's capital. With a capacity of just 2,000, the low-key nature of these warm-up shows made it still possible to buy tickets at the door. The first night was dogged with technical problems. The enormous lighting rig that the band had hoped to install was too big for the venue. This resulted in the persistent blowing of the generator, which led to long delays.

The show eventually ended at 1 am the next morning. Predictably, there were first night nerves as they worked on the set list that would be presented to the massive crowds due at Knebworth in twelve days time. From the new album there were debuts for 'Hot Dog' and 'In The Evening'. The next night they returned to turn in a more consistent set.

Robert Plant would later have mixed feelings about the Knebworth comeback: "I wasn't as relaxed as I could have been. There was so much expectation there and the least we could have done was to have been confident enough to kill. We maimed the beast for life, but we didn't kill it. It was good, but only because everybody made it good. There was that sense of event. It was an incredible thing really. I patrolled the grounds in a jeep on the night before the first gig and people had pushed down the stone pillars to get in early. It was a phenomenally powerful thing."

Both Knebworth shows were professionally recorded on The Rolling Stones' mobile studio with George Chkiantz engineering and filmed for the backdrop video screens that were used on both dates. There was a plan for the footage to be used in a TV special - which is one of the reasons why the group wore the

same clothes on both dates. Nothing came of that, although the August 11 'Hot Dog' clip was quickly edited for use as an in store promo trailer for the new album.

In 2003, the official DVD compiled by Dick Carruthers and Jimmy Page included a superb seven song compilation of performances from their first Knebworth show on August 4 consisting of 'Rock And Roll', 'Nobody's Fault But Mine', 'Sick Again', 'Achilles Last Stand', 'In The Evening', 'Kashmir' and 'Whole Lotta Love' – with fan Andy Bank's cine film incorporated.

At the time of its release in 2003 Page commented: "The reality of Knebworth was that it was fantastic. We had to come in by helicopter and you could just see this huge sea of people. It was astonishing. Everything about those two Knebworth shows was a big deal, and it came across in some very evocative areas within the music. I had seen bits of it here and there over the years, but what I managed to find was extraordinary stuff that I never knew existed." Plant added: "If you see and listen to 'Achilles Last Stand' at Knebworth it's still absolutely spectacular."

Whilst Zeppelin's return to the stage was viewed as a triumph by their vast following, behind the scenes there was a less savoury atmosphere. First, there was a minor dispute over the potential filming rights of the event with Bannister under pressure to sign a waiver of any rights to him should they release anything after the event. There was also a dispute over payments which forced Bannister's Tedoar company into liquidation.

Away from the controversy of the business aspect of Knebworth, there was the matter of the release of the new Led Zeppelin album. In what may have looked like a rare lapse of marketing strategy, the album missed the concert deadline, appearing a week after Knebworth on August 20. Not that it made a scrap of difference. The record, eventually titled *In Through The Out Door* because, as Jimmy put it, "That's the hardest way to get back in", was rapturously received around the world. It made number one in the UK in its first week and number one in America in its second. It also instantly topped the charts in Japan, New Zealand, Australia and Germany. In the first ten days of release its sales topped two million.

It was in America though, that the real sales phenomena occurred. Its release was heralded as a saviour to the then flagging US record industry. It generated massive store traffic as it held the top spot for seven weeks. Even more remarkable was the renewed demand for previous Zep albums. Atlantic shifted a staggering one million back catalogue albums during September 1979, a situation that resulted in Led Zeppelin's entire catalogue appearing on the *Billboard* Top 200 during the weeks of October 27 and November 3. This beat the previous record for most albums on the chart set in 1975 held by... you guessed it, Led Zeppelin.

What made these figures all the more staggering was that during Led Zeppelin's absence from the music scene during the previous two years punk rock had emerged, and a central philosophy of punk was its contrary stance to - and general loathing of - massively popular 'stadium' bands like Led Zeppelin who, it was claimed, were now redundant in the new era. The success of both the Knebworth concerts and this album proved otherwise.

The album came packaged in no less than six different covers. Easily their most ambitious to date, the brief to Hipgnosis was simple enough. They all felt the album to be fresh, new and direct. The album sleeve was to indicate just that. Designer Aubrey Powell felt some of the music had a barrel-house, bayou bar, late night blues feel to it. On Page's suggestion, he worked on a bar room scene, travelling to New Orleans to gain some reference. They visited the Old Absinthe Bar at 400 Bourbon Street, just around the corner from the Royal Orleans hotel.

On his return, the Hipgnosis team built a New Orleans bar room scene at Shepperton

studios, shooting six different scenes. Peter Christopherson handled the lighting and Richard Manning transformed the images shot in the bar into prints, giving them a sepia tone so that they looked like vintage photos. The six different album covers are all of the same scene, but from the points of view of the six people in the bar - other than the central seated character, a heartbroken man who had just received a "Dear John" letter.

To indicate that freshness or a new lick of paint as Powell described it, an area was wiped clean on each print. This outer stroke led Jimmy to request that the inner sleeve be prepared in such a way that it would colour when water was applied.

Finally, Peter Grant insisted all the sleeves be shrink-wrapped into a brown paper bag so that no buyer would know which sleeve he would be receiving, and also to prove that you could stuff a Led Zeppelin album into a paper bag and it would still sell. And of course it did. Complete sets of the differing sleeves labeled on the spine A to F are now much sought after.

Musically, *In Through The Out Door* was dominated by John Paul Jones. Disappointingly, the album suffers from a less than crystal clear production, and in hindsight, contained more than its quota of filler material. 'In The Evening' was indication they could still strut with the best of them. The samba influenced 'Fool In The Rain' explored new territory, 'Carouselambra' was a lengthy epic in the 'Achilles' tradition, and Plant's vocals on the heartfelt 'All My Love' were outstanding.

There were three other performances from the 1978 Polar sessions that did not make the album: 'Ozone Baby', 'Darlene' and 'Wearing And Tearing', all three of which would eventually surface on *Coda* in 1982. If some of the harmony of the band had evaporated for those sessions, looking back, Robert did not hold John Bonham responsible: "On the contrary. It was the four of us, but I don't think it was as Led Zeppelin.

It might have been for a myriad of reasons. But if you listen to how Bonzo is contributing to the various pieces of music from 'Fool In The Rain' through to 'I'm Gonna Crawl' and 'Carouselambra', he was weaving with as much dexterity and finesse as the early days. The rest of us might have been struggling at that point but Bonzo still had it."

In November it was announced they had scooped seven awards in the annual *Melody Maker* readers poll – again a remarkable show of faith from their following in an era dominated by the emergence of punk and new wave. Against many odds Led Zeppelin seemed ready to take on the challenge of a new decade, though quite how they would slot in to the changing musical climate was unclear.

IN THE EVENING
Jones, Page, Plant
Studios: Polar Music, Stockholm;
Plumpton, Sussex
To illustrate the feeling of rebirth, Page pulls out the old violin bow to create a dramatic opening segment. From there on, this is a very satisfying flexing of the muscles. Plant's opening lines are said to have been influenced by Marty Wilde's 1961 hit, 'Tomorrow's Clown', which has the opening line "In the evening when the lights are low." The belated release of Page's early 70s soundtrack to the Kenneth Anger film *Lucifer Rising* in 2012 offered indication as to where Page first came up with the drone like intro sound.

Jimmy also used a gizmatron (an effect invented by Lol Creme and Kevin Godley of 10cc) device to increase distortion and create the slamming door effect heard at the onset of the solo. Plant's arrogant strutting vocal is undercut by a majestic cascading riff that ricochets off every wall. When the whole thing slows up momentarily, some shimmering minor chords and fluid bass take control. Then it's headlong into a powerful fade. A performance that pushed its chest out as if to say... take that. Clearly Led Zeppelin still had... it.

Live performances: Premièred at the Copenhagen shows, and in for Knebworth where it stood out as a stunning new creation, entering the set for Page's visual violin bow segment. It was also used on the Over Europe 1980 tour where Page played the string-bending blue Strat on this track. Plant then revived the number to great effect on his *Now And Zen* solo tour in 1988. He also performed it with Fairport Convention at their 1992 Cropredy Festival. Page & Plant performed it extensively on their 1995/6 world tour and on the opening night only in Zagreb on their 1998 world tour.

SOUTH BOUND SAUREZ
Jones, Plant
Studios: Polar Music, Stockholm;
Plumpton, Sussex
This was one of the first tracks to be recorded at Polar Studios on November 15, 1978. With its rollicking piano intro, this is a track that conjures up the Louisiana/New Orleans bar room feel of the sleeve. Plant's vocals are somewhat strained, but the track is enlivened by a measured Page solo and the doo-wop fade out.

Live performances: It was never performed live.

FOOL IN THE RAIN
Jones, Page, Plant
Studio: Polar Music, Stockholm
During the summer of 1978, the World Cup was played out in Argentina against a variety of samba-inspired TV soccer themes. Those South American themes were still ringing in the ears of Plant and Jones when Led Zeppelin reconvened to plan this album. Thus the idea emerged to layer on their own samba halfway through the hop-skip riff arrangement of this tune. Crazy as it sounds, it works beautifully right through JP's street whistles to Bonzo's delightfully constructed timpani crashes. Back at mid-tempo, Jimmy puts in quite an exquisite solo. A most successful alliance that grew out of Plant's insistence that new territory had to be investigated if they were to sustain his own personal commitment - a point thrashed out

at their rehearsal sessions at Clearwell Castle in May of 1978. 'Fool In The Rain' became their sixth US Top 40 hit when it reached number 21 in January 1980.

Live performances: The track was never performed live in the Zep era; however, Plant did perform a version of the song with Pearl Jam's Eddie Vedder at the Hurricane Katrina Benefit show at the House Of Blues in Chicago on October 5, 2005.

HOT DOG
Page, Plant
Studio: Polar Music, Stockholm
'Hot Dog' is said to be about groupie Audrey Hamilton with whom Plant allegedly had a brief dalliance on their 1977 US tour. Musically, it grew out of their London pre-production rehearsals, where as usual they began by running through old Elvis Presley and Ricky Nelson material from the fifties. A rockabilly country hoe-down, it was obviously great fun to record and did develop into a crowd pleaser on the European tour (though it sounded a little mystifying on its Knebworth première).

Live performances: Brought in for Copenhagen and Knebworth and retained for all the 1980 Over Europe dates. An official promo video of this track, filmed at Knebworth, was made available by Swan Song to the record industry in America.

CAROUSELAMBRA
Jones, Page, Plant
Studio: Polar Music, Stockholm
Driven along relentlessly by Jones's keyboard thrusts, 'Carouselambra' is a typically grandiose Zeppelin marathon. It was first conceived in rehearsal at their Clearwell Castle get-together in May 1978. This is one of the only tracks cut in the studio that employs the Gibson double-neck guitar, which can be heard to great effect by Page during the slower middle section.

Lyrically, this is a typically mystical affair made even more obscure by a very muddy mix that all but buries Plant's vocal.

Allegedly, it harkens back to the past to act as a shroud for a contemporary Plant observation of a person who, in his words, will one day realise it was written about them and proclaim... "My God! Was it really like that?"

'Carouselambra' covers a lot of ground during its 10-minute duration, and though the less than crystal clear mix restricts its majestic quality somewhat, the intentions here remain honourable. Last word to Plant: "I rue it now because the lyrics on the track were actually about the environment and that situation. The whole story of Led Zeppelin in its latter years is in that song... and I can't even hear the words!"

Live performances: It was never played live in the Zep era. They had planned to work on an arrangement of this for the prosed fall US 1980 tour. It certainly had the scope to be a compelling live piece. A section of the song was incorporated into 'In The Evening' by Page & Plant on their 1995/6 world tour.

ALL MY LOVE
Jones, Plant
Studios: Polar Music, Stockholm; Plumpton, Sussex
As can be observed from the composing credits, this came from an occasion when Plant and Jones arrived at the studio first. A very successful attempt to write a melodic, love song, the lyrics are full of poignancy as Robert reflects on his late son Karac inspiring him to turn in a superb vocal performance. Jones' classical keyboard solo is another revelation, while Jimmy adds some subtle acoustic picking. 'All My Love' mirrors the reflective and mellow mood Plant found himself in during 1978.
Page was a little unsure about the direction they went in with this track: "Bonzo and I both felt *In Through The Out Door* was a little soft. I wasn't really that keen on 'All My Love'. I was a little worried about the chorus. I could just imagine people doing that wave and all that. And I thought that's not us. In its place it was fine but I wouldn't have wanted to pursue that direction in the future."

A superb, extended alternative outtake of 'All My Love' has surfaced on bootlegs. It clocks in at seven minutes and two seconds and has a complete ending, with Plant echoing his "I get a bit lonely" sentiments in an arrangement that was later employed on the 1980 live version. The original two inch master reel of this outtake as recorded at Polar Studios on November 14, 1978 is labeled 'The Hook', a working title which probably refers to the commercial nature of the song. In 1980, singer Patty Boulaye recorded a cover version on the Polydor label.

Live performances: The only previously untried number inserted into the 'Over Europe' tour in 1980. It became one of the best received performances of the whole tour. Lines from the song were included by Page & Plant within the Calling To You/Whole Lotta Love medleys on their 1995/96 world tour. In 2011, Plant performed the song live on the Band Of Joy tour.

 I'M GONNA CRAWL
Jones, Page, Plant
Studios: Polar Music, Stockholm; Plumpton, Sussex

The final track on the album is enhanced by yet another major Jones contribution, this time a smooth synthesized string arrangement. 'I'm Gonna Crawl' is a relaxed and confident slow blues. Plant saw this as an attempt to capture the laid-back approach of the mid-Sixties work of Wilson Pickett, OV Wright and Otis Redding (with Pickett's 'It's Too Late' being a particular reference point). Some forceful Bonham sparring with Page brings a typical dynamic quality to the proceedings, while Jimmy is at his bluesy best on the solo. A pleading Plant vocal that peaks at 4 minutes 41 with the most screaming angst brings the track to a satisfying finale.

Live performances: Never performed live.

CODA

Swan Song A0051, November 22, 1982
UK Album Chart: No 4; US: No 6
Sales figures approx. and counting:
UK 60,000; US 1,000,000 - Platinum

Despite the layoffs, negative press reaction to their Knebworth shows, and the derision heaped down upon them by the newly popular punk bands ("Led Zeppelin? I don't need to hear their music - just looking at their album sleeves makes me want to throw up," said Paul Simonen of The Clash), the loyalty expressed by their still massive fan base indicated that this particular dinosaur was far from extinct. The problem faced by Peter Grant was how to capitalise on their sustaining power while Robert Plant refused to tour America. "We had to go back if the group was to continue, as that was where a sizeable amount of the market was," recalled Grant years later. To rejuvenate the camp, a plan was hatched to tour central Europe (avoiding the UK) over a two week period in the early summer of 1980.

After a couple of revisions to the itinerary, the tour kicked off in Dortmund on June 17 under the slogan "Over Europe 1980" and took in 14 dates spanning Switzerland, Holland, Belgium, and Germany. The early shows displayed a strong air of determined rejuvenation as they romped through a streamlined set that effectively disposed of much of the excessive improvisation of the past. There was a worrying night in Nuremberg on June 27 when they had to abandon the show after John Bonham collapsed with

exhaustion after three numbers. This was a result of nervousness and bad eating habits more than any drink or drug related issues.

Press coverage was minimal, draping a mystique over this tour (particularly in the US). This Europe jaunt did provide enough motivation for Plant to reconsider his decision on America. "I didn't put any pressure on him and he kept saying to Bonzo, 'What's G said about America?' I hoped being up there on stage would give him the necessary lift to do it," said Grant.

At the time, it would seem Plant harboured secret reservations about the long term future of the group. "By the time we got to the *In Through The Out Door* album, I was so furtive," he admitted in 1995. "And I think Jimmy was too. Maybe if we had communicated then as we do now, perhaps we could have gone on working together. In that period, I was beginning to think that I could do fresh things outside of the group."

Torn between opting out and letting the others down, Robert decided to continue in the band. As they were walking across the airport tarmac on their return to the UK in early July Robert told Grant that he would be willing to tour the US in the fall - but for a maximum of four weeks only.

A relieved Grant set about getting the wheels in motion for a campaign that would be dubbed "Led Zeppelin - The 1980's Part One". The group split for their customary summer recess, ready to reconvene at Page's Windsor house in September to prepare for their return to America.

On September 5, Swan Song issued the following press statement under the heading: "LED ZEPPELIN - THE 80's PART ONE." Grant: "I knew we couldn't cover everywhere in four weeks which was Robert's condition, but once we got over there and got back into the swing I thought we'd be fine. So it was Part One of what I hoped would be further visits."

The basic plan was to cover the Midwest and Northeast of America in October and

November, and return to the US for a West Coast tour early in 1981. The UK was pencilled in for the spring. On September 11, Swan Song announced the first run of dates - the itinerary would take in 19 shows commencing in Montreal on October 17 and ending with four nights at Chicago Stadium over November 10, 12, 13 and 15.

On September 24, John Bonham left his Worcestershire home to meet up with the rest of the group for initial rehearsals at Bray Studios. He began drinking quadruple measures of vodka at a stop off in a pub on the way and this binge continued when the group assembled at Bray. Bonzo had been feeling tentative about going back to America - the Bill Graham incident still hung heavy on his mind - and as ever he was nervous about preparing for a tour.

Realising there would be little in the way of serious rehearsing completed that night, Page and Plant called an early evening halt. They all returned to Page's Windsor home.

Bonham fell asleep around midnight. In the morning of September 25, Page's aide Rick Hobbs checked on Bonham's room at around 8 am. He appeared to be sleeping fine. At 1.45 pm roadie Benji Le Fevre and John Paul Jones entered Bonham's room to check on him again. He did not stir and on checking his pulse, John Bonham was found to be dead, a victim of water logging of the lungs through inhaling vomit following a drinking session that had included 40 measures of vodka. The verdict later recorded at the inquest was accidental death. He was just 32.

It was a tragic waste and on December 4 the group made the logical announcement that they "could not continue as they were".

During 1981 there was much speculation within the inner Swan Song sanctum over whether a final album would be delivered. The original Swan Song contract signed with Atlantic in 1974, called for five albums. With no intention of keeping the group together in any form, contractual and business reasons

therefore led Page, Plant and Jones to go ahead with a final album project.

The intention was to profile their 12-year career with a collection of quality left-over tracks. Page began shifting through the tapes at his Sol recording studio in Berkshire during the summer of 1981. After completing the *Death Wish II* soundtrack, he called in Robert and Jones to mix, and in some cases overdub, the eight selected tracks. The album had a working title of *Early Days And Latter Days,* and was compiled for release early in 1982. Its eventual release was held over until Robert's debut solo set *Pictures At Eleven* hit the shops in the summer.

The sleeve involved collating a selection of off-stage group photos to form a centre spread collage. Ideas thrown around at a meeting this author had with Page and Plant in March 1982 to discuss this projected sleeve ranged from using stills from their Knebworth rehearsal video filmed at Bray studios in June 1979, to digging up some celebrated 'road fever' pics from the 1973 US tour. Both of those ideas (in the latter case not surprisingly!) were ultimately vetoed. The final 30 photographs were eventually housed in a grey outer sleeve simply engraved with the words Led Zeppelin and *Coda*, an appropriate revised title, defined in the dictionary as, "An independent passage introduced after the main part of a movement."

Coda was released on November 22, 1982, with little pre-publicity. There was a low-key advertising campaign employing posters with a symbolic illustration of nine mysterious discs. In the UK, only the traditional crop of seasonal TV-advertised titles prevented it from reaching the top spot. It entered and stayed at number four. In America *Coda* reached a credible sixth on the *Billboard* chart.

The release of *Coda* neatly tied up the loose recorded ends and it remains an enjoyable and affectionate summary of the Led Zeppelin era - chronicling their studio development during the years 1969 to 1978 - with plenty of previously unheard surprises along the way.

WE'RE GONNA GROOVE
Ben E. King,
Live: Royal Albert Hall London,
Studio overdubs: The Sol, Berkshire
On the original sleeve notes of *Coda*, this cover of the 1969 Ben E. King hit known as 'Groovin' was listed as being recorded on June 25, 1960 at Morgan Studios during sessions for *Led Zeppelin II*. However this was amended on the *Complete Studio Sessions* liner notes as being sourced from the live recording made at the Royal Albert Hall on January 9 1970 (with sub-octivider guitar effects and overdubs added at the Sol Studio in 1982).

The live source was confirmed when the footage was released on the 2003 official DVD. It's a tremendous performance of the track which was used as the set opener on their early 1970 live performances. John Bonham's contributions are exemplary here.

Live performances: The set opener of the UK, European and US dates from January to April 1970, it was then discarded in favour of 'Immigrant Song'. Revived by Page & Plant as an insert into the Calling To You/Whole Lotta Love medleys on their 1995/96 world tour. Plant also performed the song in it's original 'Groovin' arrangement during his Priory Of Brion gigs in 1999/2000

 POOR TOM
Page, Plant
Studios: Olympic, London; The Sol,
Berkshire
One of the *Led Zeppelin III* leftovers from the June 1970 sessions at Olympic, 'Poor Tom' is another product of the trip to Bron-Yr-Aur. A semi-acoustic bluesy jugband work-out, it's propelled along by John Bonham's New Orleans influenced straight eight shuffle drumming and Plant's bluesy harmonica. The basic tune is similar to Prodigal Son written by Robert Wilkins and recorded by The Rolling Stones on their 1968 album *Beggars Banquet*.

Live performances: Never performed live.

 I CAN'T QUIT YOU BABY
Willie Dixon
Studio: Live: Royal Albert Hall
London; mixed at The Sol, Berkshire
This is listed on the *Coda* sleeve as being recorded "During sound rehearsal at the Royal Albert Hall London January 9, 1970". However, the release of the footage of this track from the gig on their official DVD in 2003 reveals this to be incorrect. The take shown on the DVD from the Royal Albert Hall is virtually identical to this version. (Though for this *Coda* outing it has been remixed and edited.) It can assumed therefore that Page had mixed it from the original Royal Albert Hall live recording.

Live performances: It was included in the set from 1968 through to the fifth US tour in 1970 and revived as part of the 'Whole Lotta Love' medley for the Japan, UK and Europe dates 1972/3. It was rehearsed for the Atlantic reunion show in May 1988, but not played. Page & Plant performed it on their first reunion prior to their *MTV Unledded* filming at the Alexis Korner benefit show at the Buxton Opera House on April 17, 1994. Occasionally used as an insert within 'Babe I'm Gonna Leave You' by Page & Plant during their 1995/96 shows and as an insert within 'How Many More Times' on their 1998 world tour. Jason Bonham sang the opening lines to this song prior to 'Misty Mountain Hop' at the 02 reunion show in 2007.

 WALTER'S WALK
Page, Plant
Studios: Stargroves, Berkshire, with
The Rolling Stones' Mobile; The Sol,
Berkshire
An unexpected gem, this one was laid down in May 1972 with Eddie Kramer and left off *Houses Of The Holy*. 'Walter's Walk' is a tense, unmelodic rocker spearheaded by a solid Page riff. The overall sound here shares little of the crispness of most of the *Houses* material. Only the drumming brings to mind that particular era. It obviously didn't fit into the game plan of the time, but emerges as a dense and intoxicating outing.

This existed only as a basic backing track until the band put *Coda* together. Plant added a new vocal that was recorded at The Sol Studios in early 1982.

Live performances: Never performed live in its entirety, the basic structure of 'Walter's Walk' was, however employed during 'Dazed And Confused' on their 1972 Australian and US tour dates (as can be heard on the *How The West Was Won* set).

OZONE BABY
Page, Plant
Studios: Polar Music, Stockholm;
The Sol, Berkshire
It's back to November 16, 1978 for an *In Through The Out Door* left-over. 'Ozone Baby' has an affable exuberance spurred on by Plant, who smiles through the whole thing. Up-tempo and friendly, its charm is further enhanced by a fluttering Page solo and some harmonised vocal effects.

Live performances: Never performed live - though elements of the riff can be heard in live arrangements of 'Dazed And Confused' on their 1975 US tour.

DARLENE
Bonham, Jones, Page, Plant
Studios: Polar Music; The Sol,
Berkshire
Recorded two days later in Stockholm, this is a basic rock 'n' roll inspired jam. Starting out as a jerkily riffed, playful exercise with tinkling Jones piano and off beat drumming, it develops into a rousing fade out with Page pulling out some classic James Burton licks.

Live performances: Never performed live.

BONZO'S MONTREUX
Bonham
Studios: Mountain, Montreux; The Sol, Berkshire
John Bonham had often talked about recording an all percussion track and during their tax exile in the late summer of 1976 he and Page met at Montreux Studios for sessions engineered by John Timperley. The resulting percussive showcase was an

amalgamation of overdubbed bass drums, snare drums, tom toms, timpani, timbale, congas, backwards echo and Harmonizer. Page had recently acquired an Eventide Cloek Works Harmonizer and working with keyboards he achieved the steel drum effects.

Live performances: Never performed live.

WEARING AND TEARING
Page, Plant
Studios: Polar Music; The Sol, Berkshire
A final Tuesday rendezvous with Led Zeppelin in the Abba studios. Recorded on November 21, 1978, 'Wearing And Tearing' is the number Page and Plant had threatened would keep up with the punk rock bands in London. It was also the track nearly made available to the 300,000-plus Knebworth attendees in 1979.

This is the riotous rocker that would have given The Sex Pistols and Clash a run for their money. This vibrant Plant plea for the right cure takes off at breakneck speed, side-stepping periodically to let Plant a cappella the lines *à la* 'Black Dog'. It gets more and more frantic with Page playing at a frightening pace, supported by that ever steady Bonham/Jones rhythm section. The intensity accelerates until the song heats up to an abrupt ending. It was the track Plant and Page graced Knebworth with 11 years on from 1979 when they performed it live together at the Silver Clef show in 1990.

Live performances: Never performed live in the Zeppelin era, though it was slated for inclusion in the set for their cancelled US fall tour in 1980. As previously mentioned, it was performed live by Plant with Page at the 1990 Silver Clef winners Knebworth 1990 show. The 1990 live delivery of the final track on the tenth Led Zeppelin album proved yet again the sheer potency of their material when in the hands of the original composers. For a few short minutes the song really did remain the same...

PART II

OTHER COMPILATIONS & LIVE RECORDINGS

LED ZEPPELIN REMASTERED 1990

LED ZEPPELIN

Atlantic 7567821441/2/4 (six albums, four CDs, four cassettes), October 15, 1990
UK Album Chart: No 48
Sales figures approx. and counting: UK 30,000; US 2,500,000 - 2x Platinum

Whole Lotta Love/Heartbreaker/ Communication Breakdown/Babe I'm Gonna Leave You/What Is And What Should Never Be/Thank You/I Can't Quit You Baby/Dazed And Confused/Your Time Is Gonna Come/Ramble On/Travelling Riverside Blues/Friends/ Celebration Day/Hey Hey What Can I Do/White Summer-Black Mountain Side/Black Dog/Over The Hills And Far Away/Immigrant Song/The Battle Of Evermore/Bron-Y-Aur Stomp/Tangerine/Going To California/Since I've Been Loving You/D'yer Mak'er/Gallows Pole/Custard Pie/Misty Mountain Hop/Rock And Roll/The Rain Song/Stairway To Heaven/Kashmir/Trampled Underfoot/For Your Life/No Quarter/Dancing Days/When The Levee Breaks/Achilles Last Stand/The Song Remains The Same/Ten Years Gone/In My Time Of Dying/In The Evening/Candy Store Rock/The Ocean/Ozone Baby/Houses Of the Holy/Wearing And Tearing/Poor Tom/Nobody's Fault But Mine/Fool In The Rain/In The Light/The Wanton Song/Moby Dick-Bonzo's Montreux/I'm Gonna Crawl/All My Love

REMASTERS

Atlantic Zep 1/7567804152/4 (triple album, double CD, double cassette), October 29, 1990
UK Album Chart: No 10
Sales figures and counting approx. UK 600,000 - 2x Platinum

Communication Breakdown/Babe I'm Gonna Leave You/Good Times, Bad Times/Dazed And Confused/Heartbreaker/Whole Lotta Love/ Ramble On/Since I've Been Loving You/Celebration Day/ Immigrant Song/Black Dog Rock And Roll/Battle Of Evermore/ Stairway To Heaven/The Song Remains The Same/D'yer Mak'er/No Quarter/Houses Of The Holy/Trampled Underfoot/ Kashmir/Nobody's Fault But Mine/Achilles Last Stand/All My Love/In The Evening (Cassette and CD versions also include Misty Mountain Hop/The Rain Song)

The release of these two separate Led Zeppelin retrospective collections in the space of two weeks in October 1990 rounded off a year in which the group's popularity reached heights unparalleled since the mid-Seventies. The excitement that greeted the appearance of the *Led Zeppelin Remastered* project emphasised how much the group - and the timeless and eclectic quality of their music - had been missed during the 'disposable pop' atmosphere of the eighties.

The whole exercise was a tremendous success, both critically and commercially. Reviewers who had previously been cold towards Led Zeppelin felt obliged to reconsider their opinions in the light of their influence and the obvious fact that so many of those groups that followed in their wake were noticeably inferior in every department. And for a boxed set costing almost £50, sales throughout the world were extraordinary. Much of this may have been due to the fact that Led Zeppelin's catalogue had never been shamelessly exploited in the same way that, say, The Who or The Stones' had been. That there had never been a Led Zep *Best Of* compilation before - and the aftermath of its eventual release - was surely a further indication of the astuteness of Peter Grant's long term management strategies regarding quality control.

It had been no secret that Jimmy Page was deeply unhappy with the earliest Led Zeppelin CDs that Atlantic issued without consulting him. Originally produced for vinyl, the music suffered in transit: subtle frequencies in the sound spectrum were lost and the 'ambient' sound that Page had worked so hard to create by the sensitive placement of microphones in the studio was also lost. Small wonder, then, that when Atlantic approached him to remaster the tapes for a compilation collection, he jumped at the idea. Studio time was booked at New York's Sterling studios where Page spent a week in May 1990 with engineer George Marino digitally restoring the bulk of Led Zeppelin's catalogue from the original two-track master tapes.

The plan was to compile a multi-track box set collection for which Page drew up a possible listing for Plant and Jones to sanction. "I really wanted to improve the overall sound spectrum," Page was quoted on the official press release. "Basically it's the same picture with a different frame."

John Paul Jones added: "The songs sound as fresh today as they did when first recorded, and the new positions in the running order seem to put them in a totally different light."

The original compilation concept was to package 54 tracks in a deluxe box with accompanying booklet of photos and essays. Atlantic's European distributors East West also managed to clear a separate edited version of the set for Europe only. This condensed version, virtually a greatest hits package aimed squarely at the lucrative Christmas market, appeared under the title *Remasters* as a 24-track, triple album and 26-track, double CD and cassette on October 15. A full marketing campaign including a TV advertisement was prepared as the Zepp catalogue finally succumbed to the Nineties commercial treatment. Plant, Page and Jones did retain part of their original strategy in vetoing the planned release of 'Stairway To Heaven' as a UK single.

The *Remasters* set was deleted in the UK in the summer of 1991, and since it contains one track not on the box set ('Good Times Bad Times'), it is sure to be a future Zep vinyl collectable. After a period of withdrawal, the set reappeared on catalogue in 1992 on CD and cassette. It was also eventually issued in America as a three-CD set with a bonus *Led Zeppelin Profiled* official interview promo CD. The real gem for Zeppelin enthusiasts was the October 29 appearance of the 54-track box set, simply entitled *Led Zeppelin* and spread over six albums, four CDs and four cassettes.

Despite certain faults - the dearth of selections from *Physical Graffiti*, no chronological live tracks or alternate studio takes, and the factual errors in the visually superb accompanying booklet (Live Aid in 1987!) - this set does stand as a lasting testament to the diverse musical styles Led Zeppelin approached from 1968 to 1980. Beautifully packaged with a typically enigmatic design featuring the shadow of an airship over those mysterious cornfield circles (which perhaps suggested that Led Zeppelin were somehow responsible for - or at least knew *something* about - their appearance in the first place), it's wonderful to hear so many tracks all at one sitting. For those very familiar with their catalogue, the new sequencing is also a joy - as 'Heartbreaker' switches instantly to 'Communication

Breakdown', 'Over The Hills And Far Away' juxtaposes against 'Immigrant Song' and 'The Song Remains The Same' drifts into 'Ten Years Gone'. Note too, the slightly longer intro to 'Nobody's Fault But Mine' with an extra opening Page guitar riff, and the fact that many timings on the original albums were well out (e.g. 'Kashmir' is now correctly listed as being 8.31 in duration, and not the long presumed 9.41).

And there are some new delights. The little heard *Led Zeppelin III*-era 'Hey Hey What Can I Do', previously available only on a long-deleted UK Atlantic sampler album, and as the B-side to the 1970 'Immigrant Song' US/European single, retains all its original summer of 1970 semi-acoustic warmth. It's also great to hear the spiraling blues slide of the BBC *Top Gear* 1969 radio remnant 'Travelling Riverside Blues' - a Page/Plant Robert Johnson interpretation. Nostalgic memories also prevailed on the live BBC take of 'White Summer/Black Mountain Side' from June 27, 1969. Jimmy also included an affectionate Bonzo tribute, an amalgamation of 'Moby Dick' and 'Bonzo's Montreux', produced with the aid of Synclavier programming at Atlantic's Synclavier suite.

All in all, the overall sound quality is greatly enhanced, with Page adding a new punch and clarity remastered from the original analogue tapes.

The reception the box set received exceeded even Atlantic's own high expectations. By the end of 1992 it had shifted over a million units worldwide, making it the best selling historical retrospective package of its kind, an extraordinary testament to Led Zeppelin's ongoing power, influence and popularity.

The previously unreleased material is analyzed below.

TRAVELLING RIVERSIDE BLUES
Page, Plant, Robert Johnson
Recorded at the Aeolian Hall, London
One of the legendary Zepp BBC

performances recorded on June 24, 1969, by John Waters at the BBC's Aeolian Hall in New Bond Street. This was one of the few BBC tracks on which Page was able to dub extra guitar tracks. An adaptation of an old Robert Johnson tune, it was initially aired on John Peel's *Top Gear* show on Sunday June 29, 1969, under the title 'Travelling Riverside Blues '69'. Its renown in collecting circles was largely due to the fact that it was a special recording intended only for radio broadcast. It was interest from US radio interviewers and fans during his *Outrider* tour that led Page to negotiate with BBC Enterprises for its release on the boxed set. A video promo with outtake footage from *The Song Remains The Same* was cut together for use by MTV and other interested TV outlets.

The track itself is a superb remnant from mid-1969, and remains for me one of their most complete performances, not least for Page's wonderful slide guitar work and Plant's teasing ad-libs ("Ahh why doncha come in my kitchen"). A superbly packaged one track promo CD single was issued for radio play in the US, which resulted in the track reaching number seven on the *Billboard* Top 50 chart in November 1990 (culled from national album rock radio airplay reports). In my extensive collection, this promo CD takes pride of place as my favourite CD single of all time.

Live Performances: Never performed live.

WHITE SUMMER/BLACK MOUNTAIN SIDE
Page
Recorded live at the London Playhouse Theatre for BBC radio
This recording comes from the live broadcast made from the Playhouse Theatre on June 27, 1969, for the pilot programme of Radio One's *In Concert* series. Zeppelin's involvement came about after Jimmy told producer Jeff Griffin that Zeppelin had enjoyed recording for *Top Gear*, but felt the scope of the session didn't allow them sufficient time to display what the band

could achieve. Griffin told Jimmy he was trying to get a one hour concert special off the ground and invited Zep to record the pilot programme. This broadcast subsequently aired again under the title *One Night Stand* on August 10 set the seal on the long running *In Concert* series which began a regular spot the following January.

The 1969 *In Concert* show has been much bootlegged and many fans will have already been familiar with the 'White Summer'/'Black Mountain Side' segment. The version presented here has a 15 second edit from the complete recording.

Live Performances: It was a staple set inclusion of the mid-'69 to early '70 dates, and gives Page an opportunity to indulge in the CIA tuning, accompanied on timpani and other assorted percussion by John Bonham. It was revived for the 1977 US tour (in an arrangement that segued into Kashmir), the Copenhagen warm ups, Knebworth and Over Europe 1980 tour.

HEY HEY WHAT CAN I DO
Page, Plant, Jones, Bonham
Studio: Island, London
This track has long been a much sought after Zep rarity and its inclusion on the box is most welcome. A product of the easygoing summer of 1970 sessions at Island Studios, having been conceived in rehearsal at Bron-Yr-Aur and Headley Grange, it is one of the most relaxed and commercial group compositions of this era, managing to balance the new found mellowness with the familiar dynamics. Note for example how Robert places just the right emphasis on the line "Gotta little woman and she won't be true," and just when you expect a switch to the cranked up Marshall amps, they allow the song to slip back into a warm country flavoured mandolin led melody. The collapsing finale recalls the finish of 'In My Time Of Dying'. A semi-acoustic groove recorded during the *Zep III* sessions, it may have been considered as a contender for their standalone single idea first mooted in late 1969. It eventually emerged as the B

side to the many American and foreign issues of the 'Immigrant Song' single. It was then issued on the Atlantic sampler album *The New Age Of Atlantic* in the spring of 1972.

Live Performances: It was never performed live by Zeppelin; however, Page & Plant did perform the song on the US leg of their 1995 world tour. Page performed it with The Black Crowes on their 1999 US tour dates and Plant occasionally performed the song with Strange Sensation on their 2002 tour.

MOBY DICK/BONZO'S MONTREUX
Page, Jones, Bonham
Studios: Mirror Sound, Los Angeles, Mayfair, New York, A&R, New York (Moby Dick); Mountain, Montreux, The Sol, Cookham (Bonzo's Montreux)
Although strictly speaking this is not really new or unheard material, the amalgamation is. It came about after Jimmy scanned the lists the others had compiled and found both these titles prominently featured. The idea to combine elements of both tracks came after he'd checked the tempo on a metronome. During the remastering period, Jimmy booked into the Atlantic Synclavier Suite in New York and, with help from John Mahoney, pieced the two tracks together using Synclavier programming. The result is an affectionate blend of two of Bonzo's most illustrious moments.

BOXED SET II

Atlantic 82477; September 1993
UK chart position: No. 56

Good Times Bad Times/We're Gonna Groove/Night Flight/That's The Way/Baby Come On Home/The Lemon Song/You Shook Me/Boogie With Stu/Bron-Yr-Aur/Down By The Seaside/Out On The Tiles/Black Mountain Side/Moby Dick/Sick Again/Hot Dog/Carouselambra/South Bound Saurez/Walter's Walk/Darlene/Black Country Woman/How Many More Times/The Rover/Four Sticks/Hats Off To (Roy) Harper/I Can't Quit You Baby/Hot's On For Nowhere/Livin' Lovin' Maid (She's Just A Woman)/Royal Orleans/Bonzo's Montreux/The Crunge/Bring It On Home/Tea For One

Due to the success of the first *Remasters* project, Jimmy Page responded to Atlantic's request that he work on the balance of tracks left off the set in readiness for a second box set release in 1993. After completing the mastering of the Coverdale/Page album at New York's Sterling Studios in the autumn of 1992, Jimmy immediately set to work on the second *Remasters* set, again working with engineer George Marino.

The plan was to remaster the 31 performances from the Zeppelin catalogue that had been missed off the first compilation, and once again Jimmy gave careful consideration to the sequencing so as to again offer as balanced a presentation

as possible. Although most of the more familiar Zeppelin classics found their way on to the first box, this second collection incorporates many lesser acclaimed but equally important stepping stones. From the gentle acoustic beauty of 'That's The Way' and 'Bron-Yr-Aur', through lengthy epics like 'How Many More Times' and 'Carouselambra', to off-the-wall nuggets like 'Walter's Walk' and 'Night Flight', the breadth of diversity is again quite startling, making *Boxed Set II* a hugely enjoyable companion to the earlier collection.

Boxed Set II contains just one previously unissued track - 'Baby Come On Home'...

 BABY COME ON HOME
Page, Plant
Studio: Olympic, London
This track stems from an old master reel marked 'Yardbirds, October 10, 1968,' a clear reference to its vintage as being the period when the name Led Zeppelin was still under consideration. The master tape went mysteriously missing for a number of years and allegedly turned up in a refuse bin outside Olympic Studios in 1991. Three takes from this source surfaced initially on the bootleg *Olympic Gold* in the early nineties.

On the original session, the engineer dubbed the track 'Tribute To Bert Berns', a reference to the renowned Sixties manager/producer/writer who wrote 'Twist And Shout' and 'Hang On Sloopy', and produced Van Morrison and Them, amongst others. The original master tape of this first album outtake was dusted down and mixed by Mike Fraser, the co-producer of the *Coverdale/Page* album. Appearing now under the title 'Baby Come On Home', it's a welcome bonus, a slow blues tune and possibly Robert's idea carried over from The Band Of Joy. It's very commercial, with backing vocals on the chorus, Jones on Hammond organ and Jimmy confined to some low key Leslied guitar runs.

It's not hard to see why it didn't fit into the more energetic feel of the rest of the first album, and perhaps it was under consideration as an early single as it would have sat nicely alongside the '68 blues boom period releases from Fleetwood Mac, Chicken Shack and the like.

Live performances: Never performed live.

THE COMPLETE STUDIO RECORDINGS

Atlantic: 7-82526-2; September 1993
Sales Figures approx. and counting:
US 200,000

With all officially available Led Zeppelin tracks now remastered, Atlantic issued a deluxe box set package containing all the original ten studio albums on CD. The version of the *Coda* album includes the bonus tracks to be found on the earlier boxed sets, specifically 'Baby Come On Home' (1968 outtake previously issued on *Boxed Set 2*), 'Travelling Riverside Blues'/'White Summer - Black Mountain Side' (BBC session recordings previously issued on the 1990 *Led Zeppelin* box set) and 'Hey Hey What Can I Do' (1970 outtake previously issued on the 1990 *Led Zeppelin* box set).

EARLY DAYS - THE BEST OF LED ZEPPELIN VOLUME ONE

Atlantic: 7567-83268-2; November 1999
UK Album Chart: No. 55

Good Times Bad Times/Babe I'm Gonna Leave You/Dazed And Confused/ Communication Breakdown/Whole Lotta Love/What Is And What Should Never Be/Immigrant Song/Since I've Been Loving You/Black Dog/Rock And Roll/The Battle Of Evermore/When The Levee Breaks/Stairway To Heaven

This was the first of a new two-volume 'Best Of' package. It includes an enhanced CD video version of 'Communication Breakdown' sourced from a mimed appearance the band made on a Swedish TV show in March 1969.

The sleeve design depicting the group members superimposed into Apollo space suits was sourced from a poster initially featured in the French *Rock And Folk* magazine in the early 70's.

LATTER DAYS - THE BEST OF LED ZEPPELIN VOLUME TWO

Atlantic: 7567-83278-2; April 2000
UK Album Chart: No 40

The Song Remains The Same/No Quarter/Houses Of The Holy/Trampled Underfoot/Kashmir/Ten Years Gone/ Achilles Last Stand/Nobody's Fault But Mine/All My Love/In The Evening

The second 'Best Of' volume, this time concentrating on the years 1973 to 1979. It includes an enhanced CD video version of 'Kashmir', featuring the studio version of the track synched to previously unseen footage of their 1975 Earls Court shows.

THE VERY BEST OF LED ZEPPELIN - EARLY DAYS AND LATTER DAYS

Atlantic: 75678-36195; February 2003
UK Album Charts: No 11

Good Times Bad Times/Babe I'm Gonna Leave You/Dazed And Confused/ Communication Breakdown/ Whole Lotta Love/What Is And What Should Never Be/Immigrant Song/Since I've Been Loving You/Black Dog/Rock And Roll/The Battle Of Evermore/When The Levee Breaks/Stairway To Heaven/The Song Remains The Same/No Quarter/ Houses Of The Holy/Trampled Underfoot/Kashmir/Ten Years Gone/Achilles Last Stand/Nobody's Fault But Mine/All My Love/In The Evening. (Includes Enhanced CD video of Communication Breakdown and Kashmir)

A straight repackage of the two volumes listed above in an outer slip case. Aided by a TV advertising campaign and interest spurred by the DVD and *How The West Was Won* live album, in 2003 this set took Zeppelin back into the top 20 UK album chart for the first time since 1990.

BBC SESSIONS

Atlantic: 7567-83061-2; November 1997
UK Album Charts: No 23
Sales figures approx. and counting:
UK 60,000; Silver US 2,000,000 - 2x
Platinum

You Shook Me/I Can't Quit You
Baby/Communication Breakdown/Dazed And
Confused/The Girl I Love She Got Long Black
Wavy Hair/What Is And What Should Never
Be/Communication Breakdown/Travelling
Riverside Blues/Whole Lotta Love/Somethin'
Else/Communication Breakdown/I Can't Quit
You Baby/You Shook Me/How Many More
Times/Immigrant Song/Heartbreaker/
Since I've Been Loving You/Black Dog/Dazed
And Confused/Stairway To Heaven/Going To
California/That's The Way/Whole Lotta Love
(Medley with Boogie Chillun'/Fixin' To
Die/That's Alright Mama/A Mess Of
Blues)/Thank You

Long since the source of countless Zeppelin
bootlegs, the group's 1969 and 1971 BBC
radio sessions were finally given an official
overhaul by Jimmy Page in 1997. Working
with mastering engineer Jon Astley (known
for his work on The Who catalogue), Page
edited the sessions into a cohesive double
CD set that serves to illustrate Zeppelin's
rapid musical development during their early
years together.

Jon Astley recalled: "Initially, I got a call from
Bill Curbishley to find out if I knew of a
studio which worked late hours. Jimmy was

about to undertake the mastering of the
BBC tapes and all the main studios were
booked. As it turned out, his specifications
could be accommodated by my own home
studio - so it was arranged that he would
link up with my place to commence on the
project. So rather than book a major studio
it was all done at The Pink Room at my
home in Twickenham. We did the whole
thing in under two weeks.

"Well initially, Jimmy turned up with a set of
DAT tapes - these were OK, but sounded a
little dull. I was much more keen to work
from the master tapes. Luckily, we managed
to get these out from the BBC archive. The
BBC are very reluctant to let anything out,
but we managed to arrange a 48-hour loan
of them. I was then able to transfer the
original 1/4 inch tapes onto the 96K desk
that I work from.

"The tapes were in surprisingly good shape.
These were the two track masters and they
had survived amazingly well. One of the
reasons we were able to complete the
project very quickly was that we were working
from very good source material. The 1969
tracks in particular sounded really bright."

Disc one draws on the four 1969 radios
sessions: studio recorded sets broadcasted
on March 23 and June 29 for John Peel's
Top Gear; a June 22 broadcast for Chris
Grant's *Tasty Pop Sundae;* and a live
broadcast from the Playhouse Theatre on
June 27, recorded as a pilot for what would
emerge as the long running Radio One *In
Concert* series (this live recording was
subsequently aired under the title *One Night
Stand* on August 10).

Throughout the disc, Page cleverly employs
differing versions of the same songs: three
versions of 'Communication Breakdown' and
two apiece of 'You Shook Me' and 'I Can't
Quit You Baby'. Each contains subtle
differences illustrating Zep's forte to
constantly expand and improvise their songs
in a live setting. The latter pair of Willie Dixon
numbers also illustrated how they took

traditional blues styles and turned them into something loud and primal. On the March 23 version of 'Dazed And Confused', their ability to build tension is evident on every wail of Page's wah-wah guitar.

The June 29 *Top Gear* broadcast features embryonic versions of 'Whole Lotta Love' and 'What Is And What Should Never Be' a clear four months before their appearance on *Led Zeppelin II*.

There are also two performances of songs that never graced a Zeppelin album, both drawn from the Chris Grant session. These are a rousing version of 'Something Else', the Eddie Cochran song, and 'The Girl I Love She Got Long Black Wavy Hair', a spontaneous rocker combining elements of the Sleepy John Estes song of the same name and a riff similar to the *Zep II* Bonham showcase 'Moby Dick'.

Disc two draws on the Radio One *In Concert* broadcast recorded at the Paris Cinema London on April 1, 1971, and aired originally on April 4. At the time, the band had just completed a 13-date 'back to the clubs' tour which had taken its toll on Plant's voice. This resulted in the postponement of the original *In Concert* date initially set for March 25. By Page's own admission, it was not a magic night but there is still much to enjoy. At that stage, the band were breaking in new material from their just recorded fourth album, which would eventually be released the following November.

This BBC show finds them running through a tentative, nervous first radio airing of the fabled 'Stairway To Heaven', a lovely 'Going To California' and a strident 'Black Dog', the later held back from the actual broadcast. The opening bombast of 'Immigrant Song' and 'Heartbreaker' recalled the intensity of their on stage prowess of the time. The near 14-minute edit of the 'Whole Lotta Love' medley includes delightful romps through 'Boogie Chillun', 'That's Alright' and 'A Mess Of Blues'. The final bonus is an emotive (and again previously untransmitted) encore of

'Thank You'. Despite the minimal chat between songs, the '71 show retained a strong live atmosphere and is an accurate portrayal of the band as they began to extend their sets ready for the mega stadium gigs to come.

Despite some misgivings from fans at the editing applied to the 1971 recording, overall the official sanctioning of these BBC Sessions provided much needed aural evidence of how the band were developing in those formative years. It stands as an important milestone in their catalogue.

In the UK, the album entered the charts at number 23 (its highest position). It remained on the chart for the next six weeks, clocking up nearly 100,000 sales adding another silver disk to the collection. The release was supported by a TV advert with a voice-over from Tommy Vance. In the US, the album entered the chart at number 12, racking up 100,000 sales in the first week. It is worth noting that Metallica's *Reload*, issued the same week, sold 400,000 in the same period, demonstrating the trends of young US rock buyers.

The press reaction was very favourable with Andrew Smith of the *Sunday Times* noting: "There are two categories of person for whom this record should be available free on the NHS. The first includes anyone who ever had the ghost of an affection for Led Zeppelin however faint - especially if they never saw them live. The second, anyone who has bought a record by The Seahorses, Ocean Colour Scene, Reef or any of the bands who take first wave British hard blues of the late sixties and seventies as their starting point.

In the US, the set was preceded by a two-track promo single distributed for radio purposes. This couples 'The Girl I Love She Got Long Black Wavy Hair' with a curious track titled 'Whole Lotta Led (Historical Medley)'. This six-minute montage features an extract (however brief) from every song from the band's studio catalogue. There are

also two limited sets made available to selected record chains in the US. The Best Buy chain exclusively sold a limited double collector's *BBC Sessions* set. This comes in a double case and aside from the standard double BBC set includes an extra 63 minute Interview disc. It includes the original 1969 BBC One Night Stand June 27 interview with Jimmy and Robert conducted by Alan Black, a rarely heard interview with Page conducted with Alan Freeman in late 1976 from the King Biscuit Flower Hour archive, plus the Remasters publicity interviews previously featured on the *Profiled* US promo CD.

HOW THE WEST WAS WON

Atlantic: 7567-8-3587-2 DVD-A version
Atlantic: 7567-8-3587-4, October 7,
2003; May 26, 2003
UK Album Chart: No. 5; US No. 1
Sales figures approx. and counting:
UK 100,000 - Platinum;
US 818,000 - Platinum

LA Drone/Immigrant Song/Heartbreaker/Black Dog/ Over The Hills And Far Away/Since I've Been Loving You/Stairway To Heaven/ Going To California/That's The Way/Bron-Yr-Aur Stomp/Dazed And Confused/What Is And What Should Never Be/Dancing Days/Moby Dick/Whole Lotta Love/Rock and Roll/The Ocean/Bring It On Home

"Led Zeppelin The Forgotten Giants?" was the headline that jumped out of *Melody Maker* in late June 1972. It contained Roy Hollingsworth's remarkable report from New York where Led Zeppelin had just performed two shows at the Nassau Coliseum. He witnessed a three-and-a-half hour marathon show that included four encores and heard firsthand the disappointment the group were feeling at being ignored in the press. In a moment of rare irritation John Paul Jones commented: "Here we are slaving away constantly getting incredible reactions and nobody back home cares."

Hollingsworth's description of the Nassau show remains one of the most evocative of their entire career: "The noise cajunked and beefed outwards, filling each corner of the

circular space aged Nassau Coliseum. 16,000 people didn't know whether they were coming or going. Led Zeppelin had been off stage four times and four times an unnatural din had brought them back for more. It was one of the most amazing concerts I'd seen from any band at any time. Nothing had gone missing. It had been the complete act. There had been power, climax after climax, beauty, funk, rock, boogie, totally freaked passages and such constant snarling energy that on this evening Led Zep could have provided enough human electricity to light half of America. Does anybody really know how big Led Zeppelin are?"

Who would have thought that 31 years on, this period would inspire a belated live album set that would top the US charts instantly? But that's exactly what happened following the release of *How The West Was Won* in the spring of 2003.

Before we get to that, it's worth reflecting on Zep's frame of mind at the time. As Plant told Hollingsworth: "Something has really clicked here. The spirit within the band is fantastic. They'd never believe how good it is here back home. They'd just never believe what happened tonight."

Zeppelin's US tour of that June took in a compact 17 dates. It was all but ignored in the press (bar that *Melody Maker* feature) and vastly overshadowed by the Rolling Stones' comeback US tour that kicked off at the same time. As Bonzo reflected a couple of months later to the *NME*'s Roy Carr: "It's the Stones this, the Stones that... it made us feel we were slogging our guts out and for all the notice we were getting we might as well been playing in Ceylon. Kids in England didn't even know we were playing the States."

The lack of press coverage would inspire Grant to hire a proper PR firm for the next US tour, and with Danny Goldberg on board it would be a very different story in 11 months time.

Despite the low key coverage, the tour found Zeppelin on fire musically. Fresh from the trip to Australia and a break back in England, and fuelled by the progress they made on their fifth album during the spring, the momentum within the band was at a new high.

Their eagerness to present the new material resulted in them premiering five songs from their fifth album, *Houses Of The Holy,* which would not be released for another nine months. With the acoustic set still intact, the shows consistently ran to three hours and over. This tour also allowed them to showcase material from their six-month-old watershed fourth album.

On June 19 they played a remarkable show at the Seattle Coliseum. One of their longest ever sets saw them preview 'The Ocean', 'Black Country Woman' (prepared for *Houses* but eventually issued on *Physical Graffiti*), 'Over The Hills And Far Away' plus 'Dancing Days' (the latter was actually performed twice - as they revived it as a final encore). A week later they were on their favoured west coast stomping ground for dates in San Bernardino, San Diego, the Los Angeles Forum and Long Beach Arena.

That summer found Zeppelin in absolute prime form. "1972 was a particularly great year for us. We were right on top of what we were up to," reflected Plant in the promotion for the new set.

Whilst researching the DVD project, Page delved deep into the Led Zeppelin tape archive. He discovered various soundboard recordings including their September 29 Festival Hall, Osaka Japan show in 1971 and a recording of their January 22, 1973 date at Southampton University. There were also the tapes of two complete shows recorded at the LA Forum on June 25 and Long Beach Arena on June 27 from their American tour of 1972. Both the latter dates were well known to ardent Zep collectors. The LA gig had been held in high esteem via an excellent audience recording released on a bootleg CD set titled *Burn Like A Candle*. Three soundboard extracts from the Long Beach gig - 'What Is And What Should Never

Be', 'Dancing Days' and 'Moby Dick' - had seeped out on bootleg, giving rise to rumours of the existence of the full tapes.

Eddie Kramer was the recording engineer on the shows as he recalled: "Alongside *The Song Remains The Same* I did two live recordings with them in 1972 at Long Beach and the Forum. That was always a challenge. You want to do a good job and recording any band live is a challenge because you want to get their shit down right. If their performance is right, if my mic's in the right place and I'm supposed to have done what I should do then it should work. It was a special time. I do remember that what became *How The West Was Won* was a set of stunning performances – as to why it didn't come out at the time, well Jimmy is in charge of the band's destiny and always was."

It was the America 1972 live recordings that Page decided to work on for an official release and, together with engineer Kevin Shirley, he edited the two shows to form a three CD set that finally captured the real deal of Zeppelin live. It's quite breathtaking to hear how far the band had developed barely a year on from the BBC 1971 *In Concert* show. They were simply on fire that summer of '72, brimming with confidence and a knowing arrogance that they had elevated to new heights of onstage telepathy. The set featured three previews from their forthcoming fifth album, *Houses Of The Holy*, which would eventually emerge nine months later. The assured deliveries of 'Over The Hills And Far Away', 'Dancing Days' and 'The Ocean' are typical of the wave of optimism they were rolling on. An experimental, marathon-length 'Dazed And Confused' includes spin-off improvisations on 'The Crunge', another *Houses* preview, plus the newly recorded backing track 'Walters Walk', which would not see the light of day until the posthumous *Coda* album. The version of 'Stairway To Heaven' featured an elongated Page solo and the three song acoustic segment - 'Going To California', 'That's The Way' and 'Bron-Yr-Aur Stomp' - offers further evidence of their growing acoustic maturity.

The third CD is an absolute tour de force with covers of 'Let's Have A Party', 'Hello Mary Lou' and 'Going Down Slow' within the 'Whole Lotta Love' medley, a storm through version of 'Rock And Roll', the full on riff power of 'The Ocean' and a rare (for the time) outing of 'Bring It On Home'.

The release of *How The West Was Won* on May 26, 2003 conclusively redressed the lack of a fully representative official live Zeppelin album. The fact that it entered the *Billboard* US chart at number one was a fitting testament to Zeppelin's longevity.

This is the official live album Zeppelin fans had craved. From the drone noise as they walked on stage through to a breathless 'Bring It On Home', here is a complete Zeppelin on stage experience. Individually, they are bursting with creativity. Plant's vocals would never again match the high register range he propels here, Page is off on a tangent at every turn of the way and Jones and Bonzo are locked together in familiar tight but loose fashion. The whole affair is superbly mixed with just the right amount of crunch and bluster. The last word goes to Jimmy Page, the creator of all this outpouring of material: "Playing the west coast was always fantastic. Each member of the band was playing at their best during those 1972 performances. And when the four of us were playing like that, we combined to make it a fifth element. That was the magic - the intangible."

THE LED ZEPPELIN DVD

DVD
Warner Music Vision 0349 701982;
May 26, 2003
UK Video Chart: No. 1

Disc 1: We're Gonna Groove/I Can't Quit You Baby/Dazed And Confused/White Summer/What Is And What Should Never Be/How Many More Times/Moby Dick/Whole Lotta Love/Communication Breakdown/C'mon Everybody/Something Else/Bring It On Home/Extras: Communication Breakdown promo/Danmarks Radio/Supershow/Tous En Scene.
Disc 2: Immigrant Song/Black Dog/Misty Mountain Hop/Since I've Been Loving You/The Ocean/Going To California/That's The Way/Bron-Y-Aur Stomp/In My Time Of Dying/Trampled Underfoot/Stairway To Heaven/Rock And Roll/Nobody's Fault But Mine/Sick Again/Achilles Last Stand/In The Evening/Kashmir/Whole Lotta Love/Extras: NYC Press Conference/Down Under/The Old Grey Whistle Test/Promos

The genesis of Page and the group's desire to be presented on film on their own terms stretches right back to the night of January 9, 1970, when Grant commissioned noted film director Peter Whitehead, whose previous credits included The Rolling Stones and Pink Floyd, to shoot the band's prestigious gig at London's Royal Albert Hall. The plan was to use the footage for an intended Zeppelin documentary to be sold to BBCTV and other worldwide networks. On the night, the gig was also professionally recorded on Pye Record's mobile unit. Further filming was planned on their next American tour. The gig was filmed on 16mm by two hand held cameras, but when the band looked at the original rushes they decided some of it was too darkly lit. Ultimately, the project was shelved and the film was left to languish in their archive.

In 1973 another attempt was made. Grant enlisted film director Joe Massot to shoot the final weeks of their hugely successful US tour, specifically three gigs at Madison Square Garden. This footage eventually made up the bulk of their feature film *The Song Remains The Same*, released three years later. In 1974, after a dispute with Massot, production duties for the film were handed over to Australian Peter Clifton. In order to assess his suitability for the job he was given access to the 1970 Albert Hall footage and asked to put together a showreel cut of 'Whole Lotta Love'.

As the demand to see Zeppelin increased, by 1975 they were playing huge arenas. When they played five sold out dates at the 17,000 capacity Earls Court in London, to ensure fans could benefit from the best possible presentation, they erected a giant eidophor screen above the stage - the first time this device was ever used. The Earls Court gigs were duly videotaped via three to four close cameras and beamed above the band as the action happened. The shows were also recorded professionally.

After the gigs, the masters were tucked away in their archive. The big screen presentation was used periodically on the 1977 US tour, notably at their Pontiac Silverdome and Seattle Kingdome shows, and again the tapes were retained by Page and Grant.

The huge scale of what would be their final two UK shows at Knebworth in August 1979 dictated the deployment of an impressively large back screen projection - a stunning visual effect that did much to enhance the grand scale of the shows.

The two gigs were filmed by a 16-strong multi-camera unit and professionally recorded. The fact that the band were asked to wear identical clothing for both gigs to aid continuity in any subsequent editing was a clear indication that the footage might be officially released.

The demise of the band following John Bonham's death in September 1980 put to rest any such plans. In 1990, Page did allow MTV access to some of the Seattle and Knebworth footage to promote the *Remasters* releases and the accompanying promo videos for the project. The Aubrey Powell directed 'Travelling Riverside Blues' and 'Over The Hills And Far Away' were also compiled using footage from these sources.

In January 1990, BBC2 screened one of the few surviving TV appearances of Zeppelin, the March 1969 half-hour showcase aired originally on the Danish TV network, the confusingly titled *Danmarks Radio*.

During the nineties, it became increasingly apparent that there was scope for a Zeppelin visual and audio history. Page had long harboured a plan to produce a chronological live album set from the tape sources they had logged, and tentative steps towards this were taken in 1976 when Jimmy had one of the first computerised mixing desks installed at his home studio in Plumpton. He revisited the idea in 1977 and again in 1981 when Atlantic asked for a posthumous album that would eventually emerge as the outtake set *Coda*. For whatever reason, he could not get the others to agree and nothing happened.

In the nineties, the idea was again mooted but Page's indignant comment in early 2000 seemed to put paid to such a project ever seeing the light of day. "I've always wanted to put out a chronological live album of Zeppelin stuff," he said. "There's some incredibly good stuff but I can't get the others to agree, so I've stopped trying."

Luckily for all concerned they finally reconciled their differences and all agreed something should be done with both their visual and audio archive.

A concerted effort to assess the extent of their visual archive was undertaken in 1997 when directors Nick Ryle and John Mayes employed a variety of clips including the aforementioned Albert Hall, Earls Court, Seattle and Knebworth sources for a promo video to support the release of 'Whole Lotta Love' as a UK single.

Significantly, in 1999 the band secured the rights and masters of the Royal Albert Hall from sources close to director Peter Whitehead. An initial screening of the footage in the presence of all three ex-members offered ample proof that the film had both historical and artistic merit.

It was also evident to Page that the development of the DVD format, with its enhanced sound capabilities, offered at last a real worthy medium to presenting the best possible sound and visual package. The initial idea was to present the Albert Hall show as a concert DVD in its own right, but this idea was quickly vetoed when they realised the full extent of their unreleased material.

In early 2002, Page enlisted the assistance of director Dick Carruthers to begin the long trawl to a proper official document. Carruthers' CV included work with The Rolling Stones, Oasis and The Who, with whom Page and Plant now shared manager Bill Curbishley. He had been impressed by Carruthers' direction of the DVD for The Who's Teenage Charity Royal Albert Hall gig in 2001 and suggested a meeting with Page, after which the task began.

The first job was to search out every master visual and audio in their archives. Various UK archive storage vaults were trawled and a full inventory compiled. They then began the painstaking task of matching visuals with the equivalent audio masters and digitally cleaning them up. Page brought in sound engineer Kevin Shirley, with whom he had previously worked on the *Live At The Greek/Black Crowes* album, to supervise the sound.

During the search Page came across the multi-tracks for 1972 performances at Long Beach and Los Angeles. It was these tapes that would eventually emerge as the accompanying live CD set *How The West Was Won*.

Part of the restoration process involved having the tapes baked at 55 degrees for three weeks to ensure they did not crumble when played back. There was also the problem of locating a video machine that would play back the old two inch masters.

They began with restoring the Albert Hall film. "The Albert Hall film was all mute so we had to match the relevant visuals with the audio," explained Carruthers. "All the film was cleaned up frame by frame as it had a lot of scratches on it. There was an added complication when we found some of the tracks had long gaps where the film reels had run out, so we had those to fill as well."

The bulk of the Royal Albert Hall performance filmed on January 9, 1970 takes up most of the first DVD. This is a vintage 102-minute portrayal of the band without the visual flash that would unfold in later years. Amid the denim, plimsolls and long hippie hair are some devastating performances and the 5.1 surround sound is awe-inspiring, with Bonham's straight from the wrist drumming sweeping across the speakers. Watching him clatter around the kit on the opener 'We're Gonna Groove' and it's immediately apparent how vital he was to the band and how irreplaceable he remains.

'Dazed And Confused' can be viewed at its most dark and dynamic with none of the hamming up of later years as Page reaches for the violin bow and attacks it straight off with *that* sequence that sends shivers every time. 'Whole Lotta Love' is offered in the relatively compact 45 rpm format that saw them ensconced in the top five of the American singles chart that very week back in 1970. Elsewhere, we see them as unpretentious good time rock 'n' rollers, romping through a remarkable back-to-back

Eddie Cochran tribute that takes in 'C'mon Everybody' and 'Something Else'. Page plays the rare Gibson 'Black Beauty' guitar that was stolen a few months later.

The second DVD opens with a ferocious 'Immigrant Song' sourced from the 1972 Long Beach gig as featured on the accompanying *How The West Was Won* CD cut to silent super-8 cine film of the band shot by a roadie on the side of the stage in the bright open air at their Sydney, Australia Showground gig on February 27 1972. It's the perfect linking track. Two years on from those auspicious Albert Hall beginnings Zeppelin were conquering the world.

A year later, American audiences were keener to see and hear Led Zeppelin than any other artist on the planet. They had elevated from being a mere rock group into a US institution and the following footage, taken from the filming that resulted in the *Song Remains* movie, is now ample proof.

"Jimmy was very keen to look at the outtakes from their Madison Square Garden footage used for the *Song Remains* movie," said Carruthers. "We received the Garden footage all spooled direct from the Warner's film archive in Burbank. It was all over the place. We had to rejoin the footage to identify it all. We knew what we were looking for - performances of 'Over The Hills And Far Away', 'Misty Mountain Hop', 'The Ocean' and 'Thank You'. 'Over The Hills' and 'Thank You' were just too incomplete, but we were pleased with 'Misty' and 'The Ocean'. Jimmy also wanted to recut 'Black Dog' and 'Since I've Been Loving You' as we had great audio of that. It took us over six weeks alone to do the four Madison Square performances."

The care and restoration that went into those clips paid massive dividends. The 1973 extracts are now vivid reminders of the way the band swept all competition aside as they blazed across the US that summer, with a cocksure arrogance and onstage showmanship evident in every shot. From Bonzo's hammerings in 'Black Dog' (which

appears here in a complete version unlike the edited cut in *Song Remains The Same* movie) through the jaunty version of 'Misty Mountain Hop', a familiar but no less impressive recut of 'Since I've Been Loving You' and a truly astounding delivery of 'The Ocean' that is one of the stand out moments of the whole package - happy, smiling, gelling and just chilling out on an encore groove. This is Zeppelin in all its unchained, unabashed, carnal glory.

The programme then cuts to Earls Court two years later via a striking image of a young Zep fan holding aloft a bootleg scarf with the words Led Zepplin (sic). In stark contrast to the exuberance of the Garden in 1973, we see Jones, Page and Plant relaxed and front of stage for the acoustic 'Going To California', all shot in crystal clear video. Subsequent intimate performances of 'That's The Way' and 'Bron-Y-Aur Stomp' are the absolute epitome of the light and shade that set them apart from their peers.

The Earls Court 1975 footage survived on two inch videotape. The challenge here was to overcome the limited camera angles - most of it was shot close up to the stage and there was no luxury of multi-camera tapes. What they found was the original footage as it was deployed on to the screens above the stage. The close proximity to the band only enhances the stark clarity of these images.

At Earls Court we see Zeppelin in all their celestial elegance. The thrill of seeing this, the most revered previously unseen footage of any band anywhere, is just electrifying. Marvel at the permanently out on the edge delivery of 'In My Time Of Dying', the chronically rampant 'Trampled Underfoot' and the emotion packed 'Stairway To Heaven'. The latter is a key highlight, bringing renewed dignity to the once much-maligned anthem, capturing Page in a thrillingly gratuitous flourish of twelve-string histrionics.

The two Knebworth gigs presented another challenge. This time they did have the luxury of multi-camera videotapes from the 16 cameras that were used - but Carruthers was keen not to oversimplify the spirit of the event with editing trickery. "There is a textual variation in how we presented the Knebworth sequence and made it look like film as opposed to video," he said. "It gave it a slightly refreshed look. I think it adds to the narrative structure we were aiming for. It's some of the most absorbing footage we had."

The Knebworth sequence is an absolute revelation - brilliantly edited and with subtle cine film juxtaposed within the main footage. By selecting the very best of the performances from the first date on August 4, Page and Carruthers have rewritten history. Far from looking like the tired old dinosaurs the press would label them, 'Achilles Last Stand', 'In The Evening' and 'Kashmir' offer vivid reminders of the band's still impressive majesty. They may have been a tad rusty from all the lay offs, but the spirit was more than willing. Further evidence is supplied by the stunning romp through of 'Rock And Roll' and the grand finale - the revamped arrangement of 'Whole Lotta Love' with its extending barrage of riffs repeatedly honed by Page, Jones and Bonham. "Thanks for eleven years," is Plant's final farewell. 'You'll Never Walk Alone' sung by the multitudes brought the journey to an end.

Watching Led Zeppelin leave the Knebworth stage evokes more than a tinge of regret, not least because the rapport and chemistry we'd see on that stage indicated that they still had new places to travel.

Alongside the main programme are a variety of additional extras and menus. On Disc 1 we see the band in its early incarnation. All black and white posing and thrashing blues rock on the mimed promo for 'Communication Breakdown' shot for a Swedish TV station. Similarly, we see the intense black and white live TV Byen Danish TV performance from the same era. The advent of colour brings new life to Page's psychedelically painted Telecaster and

Plant's hippie clothing for a compact delivery of 'Dazed And Confused', Zep's contribution to the *Supershow* feature film that showcased a variety of blues artists shot in a disused warehouse in Staines in March 1969. Finally, we are treated to the bizarre setting of Zep as the guests that spoilt the party on *Tous En Scene*, a French variety show that illustrates why Peter Grant was right to decide enough was enough when it came to Zeppelin on the small screen (but not before they had baffled the audience with another blitzkrieg that takes in a frantic 'Communication Breakdown' and part of 'Dazed And Confused').

On Disc 2 the extras include a 1970 New York press conference where a bearded Page and Plant hold court and answer questions surrounding their elevation to being 'bigger than The Beatles'. Black and white '72 Australian news footage shows a panoramic view of them blasting through 'Rock And Roll' and a period piece press reception where a young Germaine Greer eyes the young black country boys. It also includes Bonzo offering some articulate observations on their fourth album.

In an interview for the *Old Grey Whistle Test* in January 1975, we hear Robert Plant's comments to Bob Harris backstage in Brussels when asked about playing in England again: "What we want to do in England if we can find the right venue and I think we possibly can, is turn it into something of an event and go to town on it in true style" - a hint of the Earls Court glory to come. The 1990 promos for 'Travelling Riverside Blues' and 'Over The Hills And Far Away' with montage footage culled from Danish TV, Seattle '77, Knebworth '79, etc. can now be viewed as mouth-watering tasters for their archive - now finally served up to near full potential on this DVD. The menus are another treat. As Dick Carruthers told me: "The main features are the real focus - then you have all these extras that you may not notice until you've played the discs and menus a few times."

Click in the right place and there's the band arriving in Iceland in 1970 followed by an eerie segment featuring Page wielding the violin bow on stage in Reykjavik. We see fascinating cine film shot by the roadies in a car travelling to the Ulster Hall show in Belfast 1971 - culminating in the four of them crossing the road to go into the pub. There's atmospheric footage backstage at Madison Square Garden with Page looking every inch the quintessential English rock star.

Click the intro of the Knebworth menu to view some nostalgic cine film shot by *TBL* reader Andy Banks and first brought to Page's attention via the Knebworth feature in *TBL* 14. Then there's proof of Page's amnesty with the bootleggers in the epic version of 'The Song Remains The Same' from LA on June 21, 1977, direct from the *Listen To This Eddie* bootleg synced to some powerful 1977 tour cine film images (including a great side on shot view of them slaying across the stage in Birmingham Alabama). The audio prompt menu also has some atmospheric 1975 US tour cine film from Seattle matched to the version of 'The Crunge' segment during 'Whole Lotta Love' from Earls Court May 25, 1975.

There are a couple of notable omissions within the set – there's nothing from their Seattle Kingdome appearance in July 1977 (of which they have complete video tapes) but probably due to quality issues Page chose to pass on for this release. There is also strangely a complete lack of acknowledgement to Peter Grant. Aside from a couple of shots in the wings he is rarely seen - a menu of footage of the towering fifth Zep would have paid appropriate dues to the man who led them to so much worldwide success. From the main features, it would have been good to see Jones showcased fully on a version of 'No Quarter', but really this is mere nitpicking.

Five and a half hours of footage is an embarrassment of riches. It may have been a very long time coming, but as Zeppelin fans old and new soaked up this monumental outpouring, the massive sales and positive feedback was a clear indication that Page and Carruthers had exceeded all expectations. "I knew I had a huge responsibility in doing this," concludes Carruthers. "I had to do justice to the personalities and the canon of work, without ever losing the essence and integrity of the source material. Jimmy has applied, as only he can, his structural and sequencing knowledge of the band to present something lasting and special."

To support the release, all three ex-members attended the Leicester Square, London premiere on May 15. Prior to the screening, they took to the stage for a short introduction - the standing ovation they received was as deafening as Bonzo's opening snare shots on that introduction to 'We're Gonna Groove'. It was an emotional night for both the band and its guest audience. As John Paul Jones noted: "For me it was so great to see so much of Bonzo. It reminded me how much Led Zeppelin revolved around him. Sitting there watching him on the big screen at the premiere I really missed him. As people cheered at the end of his drum solo I joined in - it was like 'Play some more'. Everything on stage revolved around him. Whenever we started to improvise or change direction musically, you'd see everyone move towards the drums."

Plant was equally moved. He told Nick Coleman of the *Independent*: "Seeing Bonzo 40 foot high and across the screen doing his magnificent thing in front of all these people while sitting next to John's son Jason well... it was too much."

On May 27, Page, Plant and Jones attended the New York premiere at Loew's 34th Street Theater. They also made a joint appearance on the NBC *Today* talk show.

The extraordinary sales of both the DVD and accompanying *How The West Was Won* album was reminiscent of Zeppelin's chart domination in the seventies. The live album entered at number one on the *Billboard* chart, shifting 150,000 it its first week. In the UK it registered at number five. The DVD quickly became the biggest selling music DVD ever, topping the DVD charts in America, the UK, Australia, Canada, France, Norway and Sweden. In the US alone it shifted 120,000 copies.

During the many promotional interviews they undertook, the most-asked question was the inevitable: would all this renewed activity now lead to a full blown reunion? Page was slightly optimistic in his reply: "None of us have actually discussed reforming. If we got back in a room and played a Zeppelin number and there were smiles behind our eyes then maybe it could be possible. Until that happens, it's hypothetical. I wouldn't discount it. I just don't know."

John Paul Jones had this to say: "One quarter of Led Zeppelin is gone. It wasn't just a drummer. It couldn't ever be the same."

Robert Plant, always the most reticent when such talk emerges, perhaps summed it all up by stating: "I don't know if it could work in this century. You're talking about a lot of years later. I'm sure it would be evocative for people in the crowd, but I don't know if we could do it properly. If anything the DVD really opens and closes the issue because it's so explicit of what it was all about. It's the epitaph of Led Zeppelin - stunning, a lot of energy, a rollercoaster ride, four guys melding in this great fusion of music... and it's gone."

Gone but not forgotten. Now, at the flick of the DVD scanner, we can relive so many magic moments from their history. And every time he comes into view or supplies that integral percussive groove to it all, John Bonham's presence is a constant reminder of why it can never really ever be the same. The DVD is a reunion in itself - and it confirms without question that they are, were and always will be the best.

MOTHERSHIP

Swan Song/Atlantic: 8122 7961 5;
Released November 12, 2007
UK Album Chart: No. 4; US: No. 7
Sales figures approx. and counting:
UK 300,000 - Platinum;
US 1,000,000 - Platinum

Good Times Bad Times/ Communication Breakdown/ Dazed And Confused/ Babe I'm Gonna Leave You/ Whole Lotta Love/ Ramble On/ Heartbreaker/ Immigrant Song/ Since I've Been Loving You/ Rock And Roll/ Black Dog/ When The Levee Breaks/ Stairway To Heaven/ The Song Remains The Same/ Over The Hills And Far Away/ D'yer Ma'ker/ No Quarter/ Trampled Underfoot/ Houses Of The Holy/ Kashmir/ Nobody's Fault But Mine/Achilles Last Stand/ In the Evening/All My Love

Deluxe version bonus DVD:
"We're Gonna Groove" (Royal Albert Hall - January 9, 1970)
"I Can't Quit You Baby" (Royal Albert Hall - January 9, 1970)
"Dazed and Confused" (Royal Albert Hall - January 9, 1970)
"White Summer" (Royal Albert Hall - January 9, 1970)
"What Is and What Should Never Be" (Royal Albert Hall - January 9, 1970)
"Moby Dick" (Royal Albert Hall - January 9, 1970)
"Whole Lotta Love" (Royal Albert Hall - January 9, 1970)

"Communication Breakdown" (Royal Albert Hall - January 9, 1970)

"Bring It On Home" (Royal Albert Hall - January 9, 1970)

"Immigrant Song" (Video: Sydney - February 27, 1972; Dubbed Audio: Long Beach June 27, 1972)

"Black Dog" (Madison Square Garden - July 28, 1973)

"Misty Mountain Hop" (Madison Square Garden - July 27, & 28, 1973)

"The Ocean" (Madison Square Garden - July 27, 28, & 29, 1973)

"Going to California" (Earls Court - May 25, 1975)

"In My Time of Dying" (Earls Court - May 24, 1975)

"Stairway to Heaven" (Earls Court – May 25, 1975)

"Rock and Roll" (Knebworth - August 4, 1979)

"Nobody's Fault but Mine" (Knebworth - August 4, 1979)

"Kashmir" (Knebworth - August 4, 1979)

"Whole Lotta Love" (Knebworth - August 4, 1979)

In 2007, with Led Zeppelin readying a one-off comeback in honour of the late Ahmet Ertegun, Atlantic took the opportunity to reconfigure a new greatest hits package through their Rhino catalogue imprint. The release was also timed to coincide with the launch of the Zeppelin catalogue on iTunes.

In a press statement at the time, Jimmy Page said: "We are pleased that the complete Led Zeppelin catalogue will now be available digitally. The addition of the digital option will better enable fans to obtain our music in whichever manner that they prefer."

Edgar Bronfman, chairman and chief executive of Warner Music Group, added: "In their 12 years together, Zeppelin created one of the most powerful, influential, and timeless bodies of work in the history of modern music. They not only enjoyed enormous commercial success, but their groundbreaking musical innovation transformed the cultural landscape. We have

been planning for this landmark day for a long time, and we look forward to expanding Led Zeppelin's presence across a full array of digital platforms."

In the selection of 24 tracks, this new 'best of' had minor differences from the 26 *Remasters* package – losing 'Misty Mountain Hop', 'The Battle Of Evermore' and 'The Rain Song', but adding 'When The Levee Breaks'. Packaged in a distinctive sleeve designed by Shepard Fairey (best known for his iconic Barack Obama 'Hope' poster), the appropriately titled *Mothership* came packaged in a variety of configurations: a standard two CD package containing 24 tracks; a deluxe edition containing the two CD set plus a DVD that features an 80-minute edit of the Led Zeppelin 2003 DVD – a cut used for the premiere screenings of the DVD project in 2003; and a four-LP vinyl edition pressed on high-end audiophile quality vinyl.

Predictably, this compilation sold very well and has gone on to become the standard Zep greatest hits primer in attracting new generations of fans, racking up worldwide sales of over 3 million.

THE SOUNDTRACK FROM THE FILM THE SONG REMAINS THE SAME

Swan Song: 8122 79961 1; November 20, 2007
UK Album Chart: No. 73; US: No. 23

Rock And Roll/ Celebration Day/ Black Dog (incl. Bring It On Home intro)/
Over The Hills And Far Away/ Misty Mountain Hop/ Since I've Been Loving You/
No Quarter/ The Song Remains the Same/ The Rain Song / The Ocean/
No Quarter/ Dazed And Confused/ Stairway To Heaven/ Moby Dick/ Heartbreaker/Whole Lotta Love

At the same time as compiling the *Mothership* 'best of' set, Jimmy Page took the opportunity to revisit the much-maligned *The Song Remains The Same* feature film and accompanying soundtrack. Working again with noted engineer/producer Kevin Shirley, he overhauled the soundtrack to include 16 songs that were performed during their three-night stand in July 1973 at New York's Madison Square Garden.

"We have revisited *The Song Remains The Same*," commented Page at the time, "and can now offer the complete set as performed at Madison Square Garden. This differs substantially from the original soundtrack released in 1976 and highlights the technical prowess of Kevin Shirley who worked with us on *How The West Was Won*. When it comes to *The Song Remains The*

Same, the expansion of the DVD and the soundtrack are as good as it gets on the Led Zeppelin wish list."

The jury was out on that claim. Though the addition of six previously unreleased performances – 'Black Dog', 'Over The Hills And Far Away', 'Misty Mountain Hop', 'Since I've Been Loving You', 'The Ocean' and 'Heartbreaker' was much welcomed, on its release there was criticism among fans that Page had meddled with the original set too much. Most notable differences from the original 1976 release were: the insertion of a completely different guitar solo in 'Celebration Day' (from the second night, while the original was from the third night); the removal of a long, brilliant section of Page's solo in 'No Quarter'; and a brutal, uneven edit in 'Whole Lotta Love'. Several of Robert Plant's familiar ad-libs were also removed throughout the soundtrack, especially during 'Celebration Day', 'The Song Remains The Same', and 'Stairway to Heaven'. After listening to the original soundtrack for 30-plus years, it's strange not to hear all of them in this newly expanded edition. There were also missed opportunities to present the full version of 'Black Dog' (as it had appeared in full for the only time on the 2003 Led Zeppelin DVD release) and 'Thank You', the only song performed during their Madison Square Garden run (on the third night), but not included on the CD set.

All that said, this new package did at last present a more complete version of the celebrated 1973 Madison Square Garden recordings in a mix that wholly benefited from modern day studio techniques.

The new soundtrack was also made available as a four-LP box set – of which only 100 were pressed on white vinyl. This was distributed by the band's official website, with the 100 winners being chosen at random from pre-orders.

THE SOUNDTRACK FROM THE FILM THE SONG REMAINS THE SAME DVD REVAMPED EDITION

Warner Home Video November 2007

This new package of their 1976 film came in a DTS Dolby digital 5.1 surround sound version on DVD, HD and Blu-ray formats. There was also a limited collector's edition that included a vintage T-shirt plus reproductions of premiere ticket invites, lobby cards and cuttings.

Although copyright reasons prevented Page from altering the original film footage in any way, he did take the opportunity to add several extras. From the Madison Square Garden shows he added 'Celebration Day' and 'Over the Hills And Far Away' for the very first time on DVD. Also added were 'Misty Mountain Hop' and 'The Ocean', which had also been included on the 2003 Led Zeppelin DVD. Unfortunately, the incomplete version of 'Black Dog' from the original film had to be used, instead of the complete version with two additional minutes that had been used for the 2003 DVD release. On the plus side, the jarring edit in the original DVD version of 'The Rain Song' was smoothed over.

Page also included the following bonus material: newsreel footage of the robbery that occurred at the time from their hotel safe deposit box at New York's Drake Hotel; the Robert Plant and Peter Grant *Old Grey Whistle Test* interview concerning the film

from 1976; the original film trailer plus a news story on their record breaking Tampa Stadium show in 1973 (this would later be used on as an intro film before they took to the stage at their 02 reunion concert in 2007); and a 1976 radio profile by Cameron Crowe. The menu features also presented short audio edits of the 'Whole Lotta Love' theremin extract, 'No Quarter' and 'The Song Remains The Same' taken from the three Madison Square Garden 1973 recordings.

THE DEFINITIVE COLLECTION

WEA Japanese SHM CD set
B001BWTVP6 September 2008
Rhino Entertainment/Atlantic/Swan Song
US 513820 November 2008

In 2008, the Japanese Warner stable produced a new Led Zeppelin box set in an SHM CD format 12-CD box set limited to 5,000. This presented the 10 original albums packaged in miniature replica sleeves. Paying minute attention to detail on all the sleeves, it features the *Led Zeppelin I* sleeve in the rare turquoise edition available briefly in the UK in 1969, plus the reproduction of all six of the alternate sleeves originally produced for *In Through The Out Door*. The soundtrack to *The Song Remains The Same* is the revamped version. The set was subsequently issued by Rhino Entertainment as a standard CD set.

YOUR TIME IS GONNA COME: THE ROOTS OF LED ZEPPELIN 1964-1969

(Castle CMQCD 1550 - 2008)

John Paul Jones – *Baja, A Foggy Day In Vietnam*; Carter-Lewis & The Southerners - *Skinny Minnie*; The Kinks - *I'm A Lover Not A Fighter*; The First Gear - *Leave My Kitten Alone*; The Primitives - *How Do You Feel*; Heinz & The Wild Boys - *Diggin' My Potatoes*; The Fifth Avenue - *Just Like Anyone Would Do*; Nico - *The Last Mile*; Fleur De Lys - *Wait For Me*; Glyn Johns - *Like Grains Of Yellow Sand*; Twice As Much - *Sittin' On A Fence*; Jeff Beck - *Beck's Bolero*; Marc Bolan - *Jasper C. Debussy*; The Yardbirds - *Little Games*; Chris Farlowe - *Moanin'*; Billy Nicholls - *Portobello Road;* Donovan - *Hurdy Gurdy Man*; P.J. Proby - *Merry Hopkins Never Had Days Like These*; P.J. Proby – *Medley: It's So Hard To Be A Nigger/ Jim's Blues/ George Wallace Is Rollin' In This Morning;* Alexis Korner & Robert Plant – *Operator, Steal Away*; Screaming Lord Sutch & Heavy Friends - *Wailing Sounds, Flashing Lights, Baby Come Back*

In 2008, the Castle label tackled the complex licensing issues of the pre-Zep catalogue to come up with *Your Time Is Gonna Come* – a fascinating overview of the offshoot projects Jimmy, Robert, JPJ and Bonzo were involved with covering the years 1964 to 1969. By their own admission, the compilers know it's not the complete picture. They acknowledge the failure to secure rights to Jimmy's 1965 solo single, 'She Just Satisfies'/'Keep Moving', and I would imagine contractual issues prevented any of the Plant CBS singles/Band Of Joy acetate being included (some of which ended up on the Robert Plant best of compilation, *Sixty Six To Timbuktu*); however, it's great to have all 25 selections together in one convenient package, as opposed to the time and expense associated with tracking down all of these items in their original form.

Take the first two tracks for instance - both sides of John Paul Jones's only UK solo single 'Baja'/'A Foggy Day in Vietnam' cut for Andrew Loog Oldham. The original on the Pye label goes for at least £200!

Elsewhere, the set focuses on Jimmy's early to mid-sixties session work, combining the more familiar First Gear's 'Leave My Kitten Alone', The Primitives 'How Do You Feel', and Fifth Avenue's 'Just Like Anyone Would Do', along with lesser known obscurities such as Glyn Johns 'Like Grains Of Yellow Sand' and Heinz & The Wild Boys 'Digging My Potatoes'. There's also a sample of his work as a producer/writer on Andrew Loog Oldham's Immediate label including Nico's 'The Last Mile'. The Beck and Yardbirds era is represented by the always thrilling 'Beck's Bolero' (the session with Keith Moon and John Paul Jones where the name 'Led Zeppelin' was first touted) and the quirky Yardbirds 1967 single 'Little Games' with the then session man John Paul Jones's cello arrangement merging with Page's guitar.

Robert Plant's pre-Zep work is represented by the two sides cut with Alexis Korner in 1968 - his rasping blues vocal ripe for the mass exposure it would soon attain. There are two notable, rare 'Zep as session men' excursions. The first is PJ Proby's album *Three Week Hero* - a leftover session JPJ was arranging as Zep were forming. It marked the debut of all four of them together on record. Then there are the three tracks Jimmy and Bonzo worked on with Lord Sutch for his much maligned *Lord Sutch & Heavy Friends* album. Recorded in May 1969 at Mystic

Studios in Hollywood where parts of the second Zeppelin album were being recorded at the time, the track 'Wailing Sounds', in particular, has a cut and thrust from the Zep pair well in keeping with the spirit of 'The Lemon Song'/'Heartbreaker', etc.

The CD comes complete with an engrossing foldout inlay sleeve notes which has some enlightening contributions from Obs-Tweedle (the band Page and Grant saw Plant singing with) member Bill Bonham and early Plant agent Roger Bolton.

For newcomers to the Zep legacy via *Mothership,* this compilation is a great method of discovering the lengthy and obscure apprenticeship served by the band, while for more seasoned collectors it's a most convenient way of finding an abundance of rare Zep related pre-fame material on one CD.

KESHA

PART III
THE
BOOTLEGS
AND
OUTTAKES

"Led Zeppelin Hammer Bootlegs!" proclaimed the headline on the front page of the *Melody Maker's* October 3, 1970 issue. The story went on to reveal that certain London record shops were stocking Led Zeppelin bootleg albums – much to the disgust of Zep manager Peter Grant.

In one of the few naive statements of his career, Grant was quoted in the *Melody Maker* as saying. "As far as I know there can be no Led Zeppelin tapes available. After hearing some time ago that there was going to be an attempt to bootleg some tapes of the band, I flew to America. We've managed to retrieve all the tapes and we know nothing in existence that can be issued."

When Grant heard that Zeppelin bootlegs were being sold from a shop in Chancery Lane in London, Grant and Richard Cole, along with RAK management partner Mickie Most, paid the proprietor a visit and with a little 'not so gentle' persuasion made sure that said albums were quickly withdrawn.

Bootlegs, however, were here to stay and though the market would quickly go underground and exist mainly on mail order, there was soon a whole alternate catalogue of Zep titles on bootleg vinyl LPs.

Despite the long shadow of Peter Grant (he also once destroyed the equipment of a noise pollution expert, thinking it was bootleg recording gear at a 1971 Zep show in Vancouver), their expanding reputation as a live act ensured a steady stream of vinyl issued during the seventies with titles such as *Mudslide, Going To California, BBC Broadcasts, Earls Court* and many more on labels such as TMQ, The Swingin' Pig, Amazing Kornyphone, and Smilin' Ear.

After the band's demise, a steady stream of vinyl releases appeared on labels such as Toasted/Condor and Rock Solid in a variety of coloured vinyl issues and extensive multi disc packages such as the box set *Strange Tales From The Road* and the rare 70 disc vinyl set *The Final Option*.

The real explosion, however, occurred with the advent of the CD format. The extended playing time of the CD format with its eighty minute playing capacity perfectly accommodated the marathon length of their shows, and throughout the nineties multi-disc Zep sets appeared at a rapid rate. Japanese specialist labels such as Tarantura, Empress Valley and many others ensured a plethora of titles hitting the underground market.

This would ultimately lead to Led Zeppelin being recognised as the most bootlegged act of all time, outstripping strong competition from The Beatles, Dylan, Springsteen and The Rolling Stones. For example, their final seven shows in the UK alone (five at Earls Court and two at Knebworth) account for over 200 distinct releases between them.

The bulk of original surviving amateur cassette recordings made by fans of the band's live gigs have made it on to CD, alongside various soundboard tapes and radio & TV broadcasts. Whatever legal and moral arguments exist, the fact remains that many of these recordings offer key insight and perspective into Led Zeppelin's onstage development throughout their career.

In recent years, the advent of online downloading and file sharing has curtailed the demand for physical bootleg product – though there are still plenty of packaged titles appearing out of Japan. Mostly though, these are just rehashed and repackaged versions of earlier tapes, some with minor improvements in quality. There have been some exceptions, notably the appearance of a series of 1975 and 1977 soundboard tapes and the emergence of a full rehearsal from Shepperton Studios recorded five days before their 2007 reunion show at the 02.

What follows is a guide to 30 of the best live bootleg recordings drawn from all stages of their career. For simplicity's sake, I have listed just one CD version of each – many of these shows have been issued countless times on various labels under various titles. Suffice it to say, the following list acts as an important alternate discography and demonstrates Led Zeppelin's improvisational onstage brilliance.

Led Zeppelin Live Bootleg Recordings

30 Key Titles:

Fresh Garbage (Scorpio)
Five-CD set of audience recordings from their January 9, 10, & 12, 1969 shows and a partial soundboard recording of their January 11, 1969 show. All shows were recorded at the Fillmore West in San Francisco.

Go West Young Man! (Scorpio)
Three-CD set of a soundboard recording (with an audience recording used to fill gaps) from their April 27, 1969 Fillmore West show in San Francisco plus the 60 minute soundboard from the April 24, 1969 Fillmore West show.

Only Way To Fly (Empress Valley)
Two-CD set of soundboard and audience recordings from their August 31st, 1969 Texas International Pop Festival appearance.

The Complete BBC Recording Sessions (Empress Valley)
Four-CD set of their March 1969, June 1969, and April 1971 BBC radio sessions. Also includes Jimmy Page's appearance on the Julie Felix TV show in April 1970.

One Night Stand (The Chronicles Of Led Zeppelin)
Two-CD set of the FM *Musicorama Europe 1* broadcast from their October 10th, 1969 show at the Olympia in Paris. Originally broadcast on November 2, 1969, re-broadcast on *Europe 2* December 7, 2007.

Royal Albert Hall The Initial Tapes (The Godfatherecords)
Two-CD set of a soundboard recording from their Royal Albert Hall January 9, 1970 show, drawn from tapes deployed for their 2003 official DVD.

I Left My Heart In Montreux 1970 (Wendy Records)
Two-CD set of the March 7, 1970 Montreux casino show – mainly the audience recording with some gaps filled with the soundboard source.

Live On Blueberry Hill (Sanctuary)
Two-CD set of audience recordings from their September 4, 1970 show at The Forum in Inglewood, California. One of the early bootleg vinyl releases.

Previews And Novelties (Equinox)
Two-CD set of an audience recording from their KB Hallen, Copenhagen May 3, 1971 show. Notable for rare live performances of 'Gallows Pole' and 'Four Sticks'.

Going To California (Shout To The Top)
Two-CD set of an audience recording from their September 14, 1971 Community Theatre show in Berkeley, California. Another early vinyl bootleg favourite.

Flying Rock Carnival 1971 Complete (No Label Name ~ Silver CDs)
Three-CD set of audience recordings from their September 23, 1971 Budokan Japan show. Notable for a medley of 'Whole Lotta Love' that includes the rarely played 'Good Times Bad Times'.

Geisha, Smoke Gets In Your Eyes (Tarantura)
Two-CD set of audience recordings from their September 29, 1971 Festival Hall, Osaka show. A remarkable set, it includes the rarely played Friends from *Led Zeppelin III,* a cover of Smoke Gets In Your Eyes and a medley of Whole Lotta Love that includes Good Times Bad Times and a version of Twist And Shout.

Feelin' Groovy Definitive Edition (Empress Valley)
Two-CD set of audience recordings from their November 16, 1971 St Matthews Baths, Ipswich show – notable for rare versions of Gallows Pole and Eddie Cochrans' Weekend.

No Longer Down Under (Graf Zeppelin)
Two-CD set of audience recordings from their February 25, 1972 Western Springs Stadium, Auckland, New Zealand show.

Dancing Again (Empress Valley)
Three-CD set of an audience recording from their June 19, 1972 Seattle Center Coliseum show. Though not of the highest quality, this tape is notable for previews of the yet to appear on record Over The Hills And Far Away, Black Country Woman and Dancing Days (the latter performed twice!).

Welcome Back: How The West Was Won Tapes Revisited (The Godfatherecords)
Eight-CD set of audience recordings from their June 22, 1972 Swing Auditorium, San Bernardino, June 25 The Forum, Inglewood, and June 27 Long Beach Arena shows. The Inglewood and Long Beach shows are audience recording alternatives to the official *How The West Was Won* set.

Live In Southampton The Working Tapes (Empress Valley)
Two-CD set of a soundboard recording from their January 22, 1973 Old Refectory show at the University of Southampton, drawn from tapes considered for their 2003 live album project.

Vienna 1973 (The Diagrams of Led Zeppelin)
Two-CD set of audience recordings from their March 16, 1973 Stadhalle, Vienna show.

A Celebration For Being Who You Are (The Godfatherecords)
Three-CD set of audience and soundboard recordings from their June 2, 1973 Kezar Stadium, San Francisco show.

St. Valentine's Day Massacre (Empress Valley)
Three-CD set of a soundboard recording from their February 14, 1975 Nassau Coliseum, Uniondale, New York show.

Having A Fit (Tarantura)
Three-CD set of audience recordings from their March 21, 1975 Seattle Center Coliseum show. Notable for one of the longest ever performances of Dazed And Confused.

To Be A Rock And Not To Roll (Watch Tower)
Four-CD set of soundboard and audience recordings from their May 24, 1975 Earls Court Arena, London show.

When We Were Kings (Empress Valley)
Four-CD set of soundboard and audience recordings from their May 25, 1975 Earls Court Arena, London show. Notable for the additional encores of 'Heartbreaker' and 'Communcation Breakdown'.

The Destroyers (Tarantura)
Six-CD set of soundboard and audience recordings from their April 27 and April 28, 1977 shows at the Coliseum in Richfield, Ohio.

Listen To This Eddie (Empress Valley)
Three-CD set of an audience recording from their June 21, 1977 show at The Forum in Inglewood, California. Arguably their most popular bootleg title.

Blind Date (Empress Valley)
Six-CD set of soundboard recordings from their August 4 and August 11, 1979 Knebworth Festival, Stevenage shows.

Tour Over Europe 1980: A Good Hot One (The Diagrams Of Led Zeppelin)
Two-CD set of a soundboard recording from their June 29, 1980 Hallenstadion, Zurich, Switzerland show.

Eternal Magic (Empress Valley)
Four-CD set of soundboard and audience recordings from their final show with John Bonham at the Eissporthalle in Berlin, Germany on July 7, 1980.

The Show Of The Century Rehearsals (The Godfatherecords)
Two-CD set of a soundboard recording from their December 5, 2007 Shepperton Studios rehearsals for their Ahmet Ertegun tribute reunion show at the 02 Arena on December 10, 2007.

Legendary Reunion (Wendy Records)
Two-CD set of audience recordings from their Ahmet Ertegun tribute reunion show at the 02 Arena on December 10, 2007.

The Outtakes/Rehearsals

Alongside the emergence of the many live recordings of the band, a substantial catalogue of studio outtakes and rehearsals has surfaced over the last three decades.

Unsurprisingly, such material has provided the basis of many more bootleg releases. The fact that a significant proportion of these recordings were lifted from Page's own archive has been a source of some frustration to the guitarist, and perhaps one of the key reasons why the band has shied away from releasing such material officially. Whilst the ethic of how they came to be heard can be questioned, these alternate recordings offer key insight into the development of their songs from rehearsal to studio delivery.

The following is a summary of the various rehearsal tapes and outtakes that have surfaced on CD bootlegs over the years. Much of it can be found by searching on You Tube.

Led Zeppelin 1 era:
The main *Zep 1* era outtakes revolve around a couple of sessions from Olympic Studios during the making of the first album in the autumn of 1968. A master tape allegedly recovered from a rubbish bin in the early nineties soon found its way into the hands of the bootleggers. It contained embryonic version takes of 'Babe I'm Gonna Leave You' (takes 8 and 9), 'You Shook Me' (take 1) and three takes of 'Tribute To Bert Burns' (which would be officially released as 'Baby Come On Home' on the 1993 *Boxed Set 2* compilation). This tape first appeared on the boot title, *Olympic Gold* (Scorpio), and has been reissued many times over on other bootleg titles, including *Meet Led Zeppelin* (Akashic).

Led Zeppelin II era:
The first 'outtake' from this era is actually an unreleased track performed for Alexis Korner's *Rhythm And Blues* BBC radio program called 'Sunshine Woman'. The session was recorded on March 19, 1969 and aired on April 13, 1969.

The majority of *Zep II* outtakes were recorded in May & June 1969. Snippets of in progress recordings of outtakes and monitor mixes of *Zep II* tracks such as 'Whole Lotta Love', 'The Lemon Song', 'Moby Dick', 'Heartbreaker' and 'Ramble On' had surfaced on several bootlegs over the years. In 2012, 'Whole Lotta Love', 'What Is And What Should Never Be', 'Heartbreaker', and 'Ramble On' multi-track isolated recordings emerged on the internet and subsequent CD bootlegs such as *The Making Of Led Zeppelin II* (Empress Valley).

Also of note from this era is 'Sugar Mama', cut at Morgan Studios in June of 1969 but never officially released. Three other 'non-LP' cover tracks from June 1969 BBC radio sessions had previously found their way onto the official 1997 *BBC Sessions'* release – 'The Girl I Love She Got Long Black Wavy Hair', 'Somethin' Else', and 'Travelling Riverside Blues'.

Most of these outtakes and rehearsals can be found on comprehensive bootleg CD releases such as *Sessions* (Antrabata – 11 CDs) and *Studio Sessions Ultimate* (Scorpio – 12 CDs). Selected tracks can also be found on bootleg CDs such as *Meet Led Zeppelin* (Akashic), *Sunshine Woman* (Flagge), *Lost Sessions Vol. 8* (Empress Valley) and *Complete BBC Sessions* (Empress Valley).

Led Zeppelin III era:
From the beginning of the third album sessions in late 1969, an outtake known as 'Jennings Farm Blues' (named after Robert Plant's farmhouse) emerged in the early nineties in multiple takes. This was basically a backing track dubbed 'Bar III' by Page that would later be used as the tune for the acoustic 'Bron–Y-Aur Stomp'.
Instrumental backing tracks for 'Celebration Day', 'Out On The Tiles' and the *Zep III* side cut 'Hey Hey What Can I Do' exist along with alternate mixes of 'Since I've Been Loving You' and 'That's The Way'. A full outtake known as 'Blues Medley' cut at the recording of 'Hat's Off To Roy Harper' has also surfaced. It contains snippets of 'That's Alright Mama' and 'Fixin' To Die'.

Rehearsal tapes from Headley Grange also present acoustic run downs of 'Down By The Seaside' (later to appear on *Physical Graffiti*), 'That's The Way', 'Hey Hey What Can I Do' and 'Poor Tom' (later to appear on *Coda*). Also included is the never completed 'I Wanna Be Your Man' and early rehearsal run-throughs of 'Immigrant Song' and 'Out On The Tiles'. These recordings can be found on bootleg CDs such as *Lost Sessions Vol. 6* (Empress Valley), *Scorpio Rising* (Akashic), *Led Zeppelin III* (Tarantura), *Another Way To Wales* (Black Swan), *Tribute To Johnny Kidd And The Pirates* (Scorpio), *The Smithereens 1 – The Court of Demons* (Akashic), *and Lost Sessions Vol. 3* (Empress Valley).

Led Zeppelin IV era:

Rehearsal tapes from Headley Grange with work in progress attempts at 'Black Dog', 'No Quarter' (later to appear on *Houses Of The Holy*) and 'Stairway To Heaven' have long since been in circulation. There are also pristine studio quality outtakes of 'Black Dog', 'Four Sticks' (both vocal and backing track takes) and two alternate mixes of 'When The Levee Breaks'. A version of 'The Battle Of Evermore' minus Sandy Denny's vocal contribution has also surfaced. These recordings can be found on bootleg CDs such as *Stairway Sessions* (Silver Rarities), *All That Glitters is Gold* (Celebration), *Sessions* (TDOLZ), and *Lost Sessions Vol. 9* (Empress Valley).

Bombay 1972:

On the way back from their 1972 Australian tour, Page and Plant recorded experimental versions of Friends from *Led Zeppelin III* and Four Sticks from *Led Zeppelin IV* with members of the Bombay Symphony orchestra. Though yet to be issue officially, they have been much bootlegged and can be found on CD bootlegs such as *All That Glitters is Gold* (Celebration), *Complete 1972 Bombay Sessions* (Tecumseh), *The Smithereens 1 – The Court of Demons* (Akashic), and *Lost Sessions Vol. 2* (Empress Valley).

Southampton Soundcheck 1973:

A soundcheck extract recorded before their Old Refectory show at Southampton University on January 22, 1973 has surfaced. It contains drum and mellotron tune ups plus Elvis covers 'Love Me', 'Frankfurt Special' and 'Kid Creole'. This can be heard on the CD *Elvis Presley Has Left The Building* (no label).

Houses Of The Holy era:

A work in progress compositional demo of 'The Rain Song' can be found on CD bootlegs such as *All That Glitters Is Gold* (Celebration) and *The Smithereens 3 – Mobile Of The Holy* (Akashic). Various outtakes of 'No Quarter' can be found on the *Studio Daze* CD (Scorpio). An instrumental take of 'Walters Walk' recorded at Stargroves in May 1972 surfaced on *Coda Advanced Tapes* (Boogie Mama). This track did not make the *Houses Of The Holy* album, but appeared on *Coda* with additional vocals and guitar overdubs recorded at the Sol Studio in 1982.

Another song title, St. Tristan's Sword, is said to come from this era though nothing has surfaced on bootleg.

1973 Soundcheck:

A soundcheck recording surfaced in the early nineties of the band running through several off-the-cuff rock 'n' roll standards, including 'Nadine', 'Round And Round' and 'School Days', plus early initial attempts at 'Night Flight' and 'The Wanton Song' (at the time yet to appear on record – they would surface on *Physical Graffiti*). Also included were playful renditions of Cliff Richard's 'Move It' and 'Please Don't Tease', and Johnny Kidd's 'Shakin' All Over' and 'I'll Never Get Over You'. The actual recording date has never been confirmed, with possible locations being cited as LA Forum 1972, Atlanta 1973, Chicago 1973 (the most common attribution), or Minneapolis 1975. Much bootlegged, this essential recording can be found on bootleg CDs such as *Johnny Kidd And The Pirates* (Scorpio), *The Lost Sessions Vol. 5* (Empress Valley) and *The Smithereens 2 – Songs of Innocence* (Akashic).

Physical Graffiti era

There are rehearsal tapes from Headley Grange that offer work in progress takes of 'In The Light' (known as 'Take Me Home' and 'In the Morning'), plus run-throughs of 'The Wanton Song', 'Sick Again', 'Trampled Underfoot', 'Kashmir' and 'In My Time Of Dying'. Also included are some Page 'at home' composing demos of 'Ten Years Gone'. In 1987, a remarkable 33-minute tape of alternate takes of 'Custard Pie', 'Trampled Underfoot', 'The Wanton Song' and 'In The Light' surfaced (affectionately known as the "Oh My God' outtakes). This also contained the Page instrumental composition 'Swan Song', which was never officially released but would later emerge as the structure to the Page/Rodgers song 'Midnight Moonlight' (issued on The Firm's debut album in 1985). These recordings can be found on bootleg CDs such as *Brutal Artistry I & II* (Midas Touch), *Alternative Graffiti* (Celebration), *Totally Tangible* (Blimp), *Swansongs* (Tarantura), and *The Lost Sessions Vol. 10* (Empress Valley).

There is said to exist a completed reel of a warm-up rehearsal from Headley Grange dated October 17, 1973 with Ron Nevison engineering on 16-track. It contains the following tracks: 'Baby I Don't Care' (takes 1 and 2)/'Jailhouse Rock' (takes 1 and 2)/'One Night'/'Don't Be Cruel' (takes 1 and 2)/'The Girl Of My Best Friend'/'Jailhouse Rock' (takes 1, 2 and 3)/'Money Honey' (takes 1 and 2)/ 'Summertime Blues'. Whether this reel was logged for their own reference or was intended to be released in some format is unknown. This has never surfaced on bootleg.

Presence era:

A tape extract recorded during rehearsals for the Presence album at SIR Studios in Hollywood has surfaced – this includes a run though of the riff of 'Royal Orleans', a blues skit on 'Don't Stop Me Talking'/'Minnie The Moocher' and a run down of 'Tea For One'. These recordings can be found on bootleg CDs such as *Midnight Rehearsals* (Gejm), *Rehearsing Clearwell Castle* (CG), and *Brutal Artistry II* (Midas Touch).

In Through the Out Door era

A rehearsal from Clearwell Castle in May 1978 has two early run-throughs of 'Carouselambra', plus a number titled 'Fire' (aka 'Say You Gonna Love Me') that was never completed.

From Stockholm's Polar Studios in November/December 1978 there are takes of 'In The Evening', 'South Bound Saurez', 'Fool In The Rain',' Hot Dog' and 'All My Love'. The latter is an extended version with full ending and one of the most essential outtakes. There are also fascinating, isolated drum monitor mix takes of 'Carouselambra' 'Fool In The Rain', 'Ozone Baby', 'All My Love' and 'Wearing And Tearing'. These recordings can be found on bootleg CDs such as *In Through The Out Door Sessions* (Boogie Mama), *Lost Sessions Vol. 4* (Empress Valley) and *Coda Advanced Tapes* (Boogie Mama).

Coda era:

Initial mixes from the *Coda* album including 'Poor Tom' and a backing track of 'Walter's Walk' (recorded for *Houses Of The Holy*) have surfaced alongside outtakes of the Polar Studio *In Through The Out Door* outtakes 'Ozone Baby', 'Darlene' and 'Wearing And Tearing'. These recordings can be found on bootleg CDs such as *Coda Advanced Tapes* (Boogie Mama) and *Lost Sessions Vol. 8* (Empress Valley).

1980 Rehearsal:

A 40-minute tape of the band rehearsing for their 1980 Over Europe tour from the rehearsals at the Rainbow Theatre in London in April/May 1980 has surfaced – it can be found on bootleg CDs such as *1980 Rehearsal* (Empress Valley) and *The Last Rehearsal Remastered* (Missing Link).

Note: As mentioned earlier, the *Studio Sessions Ultimate* – 12 CD box set (Scorpio) and *Sessions* – 11 CD box set (Antrabata) contain the bulk of most available rehearsals and outtakes.

PART IV
THE AHMET
REUNION C
O2 ARENA
DECEMBER

In November 2006, during an acceptance speech for Led Zeppelin's induction to the UK Hall Of Fame, Jimmy Page dedicated the award to the legendary Atlantic Records co-founder Ahmet Ertegun, and noted that Ahmet had been taken ill following a fall backstage at a recent Rolling Stones concert. Sadly, he never recovered and passed away on December 14th.

In early 2007, plans were made for a special tribute show for Ahmet Ertegun. In April, the three ex-members of Led Zeppelin attended a memorial show in New York for Ahmet. Following discussions with Ahmet's wife Mica, a plan was hatched to stage a tribute show in the UK for which Led Zeppelin would reform for a one off appearance. Initially, the idea was for a two night concert with Cream, but very quickly it was decided that Zeppelin would perform a full show.

Bringing in Jason Bonham to man his dad's old seat, they began rehearsals at Black Island Studios in Acton, London on June 10. The Ahmet Ertegun tribute concert was duly announced by promoter Harvey Goldsmith at a press conference at the 02 Arena on September 12. He revealed that the 17,000 tickets for the show at the 02 Arena in London on November 26 would be made available via a special online ballot.

The response staggered the music world. Within hours of the ticket ballot opening, a reported 20 million clicked on the site to try and obtain tickets. Talking about the forthcoming show in the official launch press statement, Robert Plant commented: "During the Zeppelin years, Ahmet Ertegun was a major foundation of solidarity and accord. For us he WAS Atlantic Records and remained a close friend and conspirator. This performance stands alone as our tribute to the work and the life of our longstanding friend."

Unlike previous ad hoc reunions at Live Aid in 1985 and the Atlantic Records 40th anniversary show in 1988, the band undertook extensive rehearsals at

Shepperton Studios prior to the show to prepare a two hour plus set.

Jason Bonham told *Drummer* magazine at the time: "I joke about it in rehearsal, but I think after the first couple of songs Robert should ask the audience to close their mouths. That's how confident I feel, and not just for me but them too. I'm telling you, if we play half as good as day one in rehearsal, people will be speechless."

With the tension mounting, three weeks before the intended show on November 26, Jimmy Page sustained a broken finger and the original date was rescheduled to December 10.

Any self-doubt amongst themselves in their ability to deliver evaporated at the final rehearsal held on December 5. "The passion and intensity is still there" said John Paul Jones. "We sounded great in rehearsals. It would really take your breath away. I was very happily surprised. I can't believe how well [Jason] fits into the scheme of things. He's a great drummer, he hits really hard. He's got certain musical mannerisms of his dad, but he doesn't really play like his dad, although it's uncanny because he sounds like his dad when he speaks."

Page's final words backed up that confidence: "All I know is that the vitality that we'd have in the rehearsal period that we've had up until now, and the passion for the music, I mean, it's urgent, it's still scary, and that's all there is for me ... That's what it would have to have, and it's a synergy. It's a synchronized energy between the musicians, and the more that we've been playing together, the more that it's gelled."

The band staged an open rehearsal for competition winners on the afternoon before of the show, running through 'Ramble On', 'In My Time Of Dying' and 'No Quarter'.

The expectancy as the 17,000 converged on the 02 Arena on the night of Monday, December 10 was tangible. The lucky ballot winners were drawn from 50 countries from around the world. Fellow musicians and celebrities in attendance included Paul McCartney, Mick Jagger, Dave Grohl, Jeff Beck, Brian May, David Gilmour, Peter Gabriel, Marilyn Manson, Jerry Hall, Priscilla Presley, Lulu and Noel Gallagher.

Following appearances by Atlantic artists past and present such as Keith Emerson, Paulo Nutini, Paul Rodgers, Maggie Bell and Foreigner, Led Zeppelin took to the stage and roared into 'Good Times Bad Times' – an appropriate set opener, having been the first track on their debut album but rarely played live in the Zep era.

Over the next two hours, they preceded to exceed all expectations with a simply stunning performance. The set list (with nine of the songs played in a slightly lower key to aid Plant's vocal) ran as follows: 'Good Times Bad Times', 'Ramble On', 'Black Dog', 'In My Time Of Dying', 'For Your Life', 'Trampled Under Foot', 'Nobody's Fault But Mine', 'No Quarter', 'Since I've Been Loving You', 'Dazed and Confused', 'Stairway To Heaven', 'The Song Remains the Same', 'Misty Mountain Hop', 'Kashmir', plus encores of 'Whole Lotta Love' and 'Rock And Roll'.

The stage presentation benefitted from striking tech visuals displayed on a giant backdrop, and the show was filmed under the direction of Dick Carruthers, employing 17 cameras. (At the time of writing, nearly five years on, this footage has yet to be officially released and it remains eagerly anticipated by every Zep fan.)

Once they had overcome the sheer shock of being back on stage and some minor sound problems, the four of them relaxed and recreated their glory days with ease. 'In My Time Of Dying' saw Page perform a scintillating bottleneck solo. 'For You Life' from the *Presence* album was performed live for the very first time and 'Dazed And Confused' was played in a compact arrangement featuring Page's trademark violin bow. 'Stairway To Heaven' appeared

mid set with little fanfare, but much stately reverence – after which Plant poignantly commented "Ahmet we did it."

The real crowning glory, though, was the performance of 'Kashmir' that engulfed the entire dome and prompted the 'watching in awe' Noel Gallagher to comment afterwards that it was "fookin' awesome!" Encores of 'Whole Lotta Love' and 'Rock And Roll' sealed a truly remarkable comeback.

The band reaction was one of pure elation. "That is what was so thrilling - to come together after all this time and find that there was so much chemistry and so much electricity involved in these four characters. We'd all agreed to take it very, very seriously and have a really good time at the same time. We worked out the songs we were going to play, and it was exhilarating, it was fantastic" - Jimmy Page speaking at a press conference in Japan.

"It was gripping. We had a lot to lose if it had all gone wrong. It would have been the end of the real deal about what we had in the first place. Musically and emotionally we matched it and it put a lot of things to bed. For Ahmet, it was great to get up one more time - it was a fitting thing because he meant so much to us and far beyond just getting our records out. Then for Jason well, he's now the complete man... he's dealt with his demons. I think he wanted to prove something to himself. It was important for his family too - I mean I've known his Mum since we were 15. There was so much anticipation and we matched it. It was marvellous and at the end we all shook hands and said 'Wow that was amazing'" - Robert Plant talking to Steve Jones on Indie 103.1 FM radio Los Angeles.

"Jason was fantastic. A lot of his fills were not what his dad did at all. He did an amazing job when you consider he had to answer to every drummer in the world after the show. With that sort of pressure, to bring that off was astonishing. Kashmir was absolutely wonderful, the way he led in an out of the chorus and bridges. The excitement was there on stage at the O2 as it was in the old days. It could be fun to do more stuff." - John Paul Jones talking to David Fricke in *Rolling Stone.*

"I wanted to take in every moment which is why at the end I had to bow to them. As I grew older, I became a fan as well as a part of the family. It wasn't until after my Dad's death that I could really appreciate his music. The day after (the O2 reunion), I took the sticks that I used and put them on the grave and said "We did it Dad, you handed me these, I'll hand them back." - Jason Bonham talking to Tamara Conniff.

The press reaction was unanimously thumbs up. "It's difficult to believe this is a band who have barely played together for the best part of three decades," commented Alex Petridis in *The Guardian*. He also added: "They sounded awesomely tight, bizarre, beguiling and better than ever." While *Q's* Paul Rees weighed in: "It's quite shocking to find men of advanced years wielding such power. If there is an entirely unique Zeppelin moment, 'Kashmir' is it, and they nail it here - a great set's greatest moment. If indeed this is to be their final stand, then Zeppelin will have bowed out with a proper command performance. One is left to wonder though how they can now possibly leave all this behind again."

Following the success of the O2 show, there was massive speculation that they would play further shows around the world; however, Robert Plant was already committed to a tour with Alison Krauss off the back of his Grammy award winning *Raising Sand* album.

Undeterred, Page, Jones and Bonham booked rehearsal time in London during the summer of 2008 to work on some ideas. It was hoped that Plant would eventually join them, but the singer issued a statement in September effectively ruling out further performances: "It's both frustrating and ridiculous for this story to continue to rear its head when all the musicians that surround the story are keen to get on with their individual projects and move forward. I wish Jimmy Page, John Paul Jones and Jason Bonham nothing but success with any future projects."

In a further twist, during the rehearsals they enlisted the assistance of some guest vocalists, namely Myles Kennedy from Alter Bridge and Aerosmith's Steven Tyler. Asked about this during a question and answer session when he appeared at the Manson Guitar Weekend in Exeter, John Paul Jones said: "As you probably know, Jimmy, Jason and I are actually rehearsing and we've had the odd singer come in and have a bash. We are trying out a couple of singers. We want to do it. It's sounding great and we want to get on and get out there."

In a report on *Rolling Stone.com,* a comment from an insider within the Page camp gave indication that Page, Jones and Jason planned to work together as a new band. The source was quoted as saying "Whatever this is, it is not Led Zeppelin – not without the involvement of Robert Plant."

However, no sooner was that news being touted, when further reports appeared revealing that all plans had been abandoned. Jimmy Page's manager of the time, Peter Mensch stating emphatically: "Led Zeppelin are over. If you didn't see them in 2007 [when they played a one-off reunion at London's O2 Arena], you missed them. It's done. I can't be any clearer than that."

Robert Plant has stated that fear of disappointment was the main stumbling block in his reasoning for not agreeing to undertake a reunion tour. Speaking to *Absolute Radio's* Ben Jones, Robert said it would have been "delicate" to "visit old ground" again with the group. "The disappointment that could be there once you commit to that and the comparisons to something that was basically fired by youth and a different kind of exuberance to now, its very hard to go back and meet that head on and do it justice," he said. "The reason that it stopped was because we were incomplete, and we've been incomplete now for 28 years."

In the wake of the aftermath of all the 'will they or wont they' speculation, Page told *Mojo:* "One of the key things to the point of the three of us playing together was that at least we knew where we were and hopefully where we could go musically within it, and that seemed enticing for me. The whole aspect of bringing in a singer or vocalists beyond the point of having a jam, or whatever it would be, was this juggernaut of politics that would accompany them, and I certainly wasn't ready for that. I wasn't keen on bringing singers in at that point. I was keen on getting more of the material that we were writing together... I was really keen on the instrumental side of what we were doing getting heard, mainly because the three of us had been working together, albeit playing Led Zeppelin numbers, but we had a different take on it. I certainly don't think I would have felt comfortable if we'd

proceeded the way we were going. I would have felt pushed into something and compromised. I don't know that John Paul Jones or Jason Bonham would have felt the same thing. But when it came to playing music, what we were doing was certainly happening; there's no doubt about that. People who saw us at the O2 would have known that. It's just a shame that they didn't get to see any more."

As it stands, despite the efforts of Page in particular to keep the show rolling, the O2 Arena show may well have been the final sighting of Led Zeppelin on stage. If that is the case, it will be remembered as a magnificent swan song and a night when they proved exactly why they will always be regarded in such high esteem by fans and fellow musicians alike.

AUTHOR'S NOTES

Recommended Led Zeppelin website references:
www.uuweb.led-zeppelin.us/index.htm
www.ledzeppelin.com
www.royal-orleans.com
www.ledzeppelin-reference.com
www.argenteumastrum.com/studio_vaults.htm
www.ledzepconcerts.com
www.rambleonzep.com

Dave Lewis first heard the music of Led Zeppelin in 1969 at the age of 13. The effect has been a lasting one. He is acknowledged and respected throughout the world as a leading chronicler of the group. Dave founded the Led Zeppelin magazine *Tight But Loose* in 1978 and is also the author of a number of books including *Led Zeppelin: Led Zeppelin The Final Acclaim, Led Zeppelin A Celebration, Led Zeppelin Celebration 2: The Tight But Loose Files, Led Zeppelin The Concert File. Led Zeppelin then As It Was – At Knebworth 1979, Led Zeppelin Feather In The Wind – Over Europe 1980*. His work has also appeared in *Record Collector, Q, Mojo* and *Classic Rock*. He has also been featured on various TV and radio stations including BBC Radio 2, Planet Rock and Get The Led Out and has acted as consultant on several Zeppelin related projects including the Robert Plant box set *Nine Lives* and the BBC2 documentary *Robert Plant By Myself*.

In his role as editor, publisher and freelance journalist, Dave continues to chronicle the work of Led Zeppelin and the solo projects of the ex members via the *Tight But Loose* website (www.tightbutloose.co.uk) and magazine. He lives in Bedford with his wife Janet, and has a daughter Samantha and son Adam.

*For details of the *Tight But Loose* magazine visit www.tightbutloose.co.uk Contact Dave at davelewis.tbl1@ntlworld.com